Sport and the American Occupation of the Philippines

Sport and the American Occupation of the Philippines

Bats, Balls, and Bayonets

Gerald R. Gems

LEXINGTON BOOKS
Lanham • Boulder • New York • London

Published by Lexington Books
An imprint of The Rowman & Littlefield Publishing Group, Inc.
4501 Forbes Boulevard, Suite 200, Lanham, Maryland 20706
www.rowman.com

Unit A, Whitacre Mews, 26-34 Stannary Street, London SE11 4AB

Copyright © 2016 by Lexington Books

All rights reserved. No part of this book may be reproduced in any form or by any electronic or mechanical means, including information storage and retrieval systems, without written permission from the publisher, except by a reviewer who may quote passages in a review.

British Library Cataloguing in Publication Information Available

Library of Congress Cataloging-in-Publication Data

Names: Gems, Gerald R., author
Title: Sport and the American occupation of the Philippines : bats, balls, and bayonets / Gerald R. Gems.
Description: Lanham : Lexington Books, an imprint of The Rowman & Littlefield Publishing Group, Inc., [2016] | Includes bibliographical references and index.
Identifiers: LCCN 2016022424 (print) | LCCN 2016030778 (ebook) | ISBN 9781498536653 (cloth : alk. paper) | ISBN 9781498536660 (Electronic)
Subjects: LCSH: Sports--Phillippines--History--20th century. | Philippines--Civilization--American influences. | Philippines--History--1898-1946.
Classification: LCC GV663.P45 G45 2016 (print) | LCC GV663.P45 (ebook) | DDC 796.09599--dc23
LC record available at https://lccn.loc.gov/2016022424

∞™ The paper used in this publication meets the minimum requirements of American National Standard for Information Sciences Permanence of Paper for Printed Library Materials, ANSI/NISO Z39.48-1992.

Printed in the United States of America

Contents

1	Introduction	1
2	Social Darwinism	19
3	Military	41
4	Politics	63
5	Religion	85
6	American Capitalism in the Philippines	105
7	Education	127
8	Sport	145
9	The Legacy of the American Occupation	167

Bibliography 183
Index 195
About the Author 203

ONE
Introduction

The American occupation of the Philippines, a result of the brief Spanish-American War of 1898, lasted nearly a half-century, and continues to have political, military, economic, and religious ramifications today. In the increasingly globalized world of the twenty-first century with its myriad conflicts of cultures and beliefs it is imperative to learn from the past. How might past mistakes be rectified? How might better solutions to continuing issues be addressed in the future? This case study intends to shed some light on the United States' ascendance to a position of world dominance in the twentieth century and the lessons both learned and apparently unlearned in the process. It invokes an interdisciplinary framework of inquiry drawing upon historical, sociological, and anthropological study to address the numerous factors relative to the US occupation. While much has been written on the subject, this examination will pay particular attention to a topic relatively unscrutinized by scholars in its analysis of the role of sport in the policies and programs delivered to the Filipinos. Sport also influenced the lives of many of the major figures who formulated those policies and programs in a transitional era relative to gender roles and racial politics. The Philippines provided not only a new geographical frontier, but a social and psychological one that allowed for experimentation in addressing the issues of democracy, equality, and freedom.

While the book is designed as a coherent whole, each chapter may stand alone to augment teaching purposes. In each chapter sport serves as a unifying thread as demonstrated by its uses for and by the military, for political purposes and religious proselytism, its economic and educational values, and the lasting legacy left upon the Philippines.

THE SCIENCE OF RACE

The Enlightenment, also known as the Age of Reason, emerged in Europe in the late seventeenth century and continued beyond 1800, promoting a greater reliance on science and secularism in the quest for truth and understanding of the natural world. The scientific method, based on trial and error, produced a number of strategies and practices that proved faulty, among them the belief in phrenology.

Franz Joseph Gall (1758–1828), born in Germany in 1758, is credited as the progenitor of phrenology. As an anatomist, Gall specialized in the study of the cranium and he believed that the brain possessed a number of regions specific to particular abilities and that personal characteristics might even be discerned by the protuberances of the skull. Gall's lectures spread his teachings in Europe, and by the 1830s such beliefs traveled to North America as well. By the mid-nineteenth century phrenologists claimed to be able to predict not only intelligence, but proclivities such as criminality. Practitioners believed that such personal characteristics could be transmitted to succeeding generations as part of the genetic transfer of biological components.[1]

Ethnology, or the comparative study of different groups, focused on the demographics of societies and their cultural beliefs and practices. It developed theories about the evolution of mankind based upon levels of civilization, and assumed that there were three stages in the process, which correlated to savage groups, barbarians, and eventually civilized societies. Differences in skin color and physical features led to categorization of humans into racial groups. Some scholars also debated whether or not humans derived from a singular source (monogenesis) or constituted different species of mankind (polygenesis). Scholars also believed that acquired knowledge might be lost and that more primitive groups had degenerated in their levels of technology, religious practices, and political systems, possibly due to environmental or climatic conditions. The American Ethnological Society, established in 1842, elected Albert Gallatin (1761–1849), a monogeneticist, as its first president, and polygeneticists lost favor by the advent of the American Civil War.[2]

By the latter nineteenth century phrenology too had been largely discredited, although elements of its features remained in popular stereotypes of racial groups and in the eugenics movement that proposed the genetic elimination of undesirable traits through sterilization. Ethnology was gradually incorporated as a component of the burgeoning discipline of cultural anthropology. Among the early anthropologists, Lewis Henry Morgan (1818–1881), a New York lawyer by profession, embarked on a study of the Iroquois nation of American Indian tribes, which eventually culminated in support for the theory of evolutionary stages. Morgan's practice of participatory observation contributed to the early methodology of the discipline, and he was elected president of the American Association for the Advancement of Science in 1879.[3]

Charles Darwin's (1809–1882) *On the Origin of the Species*, published in 1859 as a culmination of his five-year voyage around the world two decades earlier, proved to be one of the most provocative books of all time. His prognostications on the natural selection of flora and fauna provided a scientific explanation for adaptation and survival in species that countered the Biblical theory of divine evolution. Herbert Spenser (1820–1903), a British philosopher and contemporary of Darwin, applied the theory to human beings, coining the phrase "the survival of the fittest" to explain the dominance of some individuals over others in the battle for survival. By the late nineteenth century economists and capitalists rationalized their ascendance to the top of the business and financial world in similar terms. Likewise, nation-states accumulated global empires by subjugating presumably weaker peoples by the power of their intelligence, technology, force of arms, organization, and superior breeding. European nations had embarked on a systematic conquest of territories in the Americas, Africa, and Asia as early as the sixteenth century. The "science" of the nineteenth century enabled them to rationalize their success by virtue of racial superiority. Competitive sports provided one means to directly test such assumptions. Such science generally emanated from groups claiming white, Anglo-Saxon, and Protestant heritage (WASPs); although the Catholic Spanish and French also clung to an imperial past.[4]

Religion played a prominent part in such ventures and assuaged any guilt as part of "the white man's burden" of saving the subjugated masses from themselves by educating them in the ways of whiteness on the path toward civilization, which included Christianizing them—by force if necessary—to gain entry to heaven. Josiah Strong (1847–1916), a Congregationalist minister, exhorted the United States to assume its proper role in such ventures in an 1885 book entitled *Our Country*. "Does it not look as if God were not only preparing in our Anglo-Saxon civilization the die with which to stamp the peoples of the earth, but as if he [sic] were massing behind that die the mighty power with which to press it?"[5] Strong opined that the Anglo-Saxon was "divinely commissioned to be . . . his brother's keeper . . . [and was possessed of the] purest Christianity and the highest civilization."[6] Missionaries perceived themselves as "Christ's warriors storming the ramparts of Satan for worldwide, evangelical victory."[7] Among those missionaries, the Young Men's Christian Association (YMCA) implemented a comprehensive sports program to achieve such goals in the Philippines.

Theodore Roosevelt (1858–1919), an ardent proponent and later an instigator of American intervention, rationalized conquest on racial grounds in his 1893 history, *The Winning of the West*. "The most ultimately righteous of all wars is a war with savages. . . . [It establishes] the foundations for the future greatness of a mighty people . . . it is of incalculable importance that America, Australia, and Siberia should pass out of the hands of their red, black, and yellow aboriginal owners, and become the heritage of the dominant world races."[8]

The United States soon embarked on its imperial mission in the Spanish-American War of 1898 despite the warnings of British writer, Rudyard Kipling (1865–1936), whose poem "The White Man's Burden" appeared in the popular *McClure's* magazine. The opening stanza both encouraged and remonstrated.

> Take up the white man's burden-
> Send forth the best ye breed-
> Go bind your sons to exile
> To serve your captives' need;
> To wait in heavy harness,
> On fluttering folk and wild-
> Your new caught sullen peoples
> Half devil and half child.

MANIFEST DESTINY

Americans considered themselves to be uniquely qualified to undertake such a mission. The early Puritan colonists had founded their settlements as beacons upon a hill to enlighten all others as to the righteousness of their ways. As early as 1839 a journalist labeled American expansionism to be part of its "manifest destiny," as it spread westward. A decade later the United States wrested much of its western territory from its southern neighbor in the Mexican-American War; then spent the remainder of the century consolidating the lands it took from the Native American Indians. Theodore Roosevelt explained that "the conquest and settlement by the whites of the Indian lands was necessary to the greatness of the race and to the well-being of civilized mankind."[9]

That same year (1893) Professor Frederick Jackson Turner (1861–1932) delivered an address entitled "The Significance of the Frontier in American History" at the World's Fair in Chicago in which he lamented the closing of the frontier and its free land, which fostered the particular American characteristics of democracy, individualism, opportunity, self-reliance, and energy. Such qualities suggested an American exceptionalism, different from the old cultures of Europe, and if the frontier had reached its boundaries according to the census of 1890, where then might future generations learn to become Americans?[10]

Education

Education was intended to be one of the primary means of assimilation and acculturation. As early as 1879 the US government initiated such a program by establishing a residential school for Native American Indian children at Carlisle, Pennsylvania. There the children learned to speak the English language, adopt western clothing and lifestyles, garner skills for employment in the industrial workforce, and gain a greater sense of what scholars have termed "whiteness." Eventually thirty-nine such schools (some of them still in existence) intended to assimilate the Indians into the white, mainstream culture. For Native Americans who did not speak English, sports became an effective method of instruction.[11]

G. Stanley Hall (1844–1924), the first American to obtain a PhD in psychology, had a distinct influence on child development and education. He established the *American Journal of Psychology* in 1887 and became the president of Clark University two years later. In 1892 Hall was elected the first president of the American Psychological Association. As a proponent of Ernst Haeckel's (1834–1919) recapitulation theory, Hall taught that children passed through evolutionary stages, beginning in a savage state. They might and should be taught the characteristics of civilized society through play. While physical activities such as tag and chase games were indicative of the primitive stage of hunters and gatherers, more sophisticated team sports that required cooperation and cognitive strategies pertinent to more civilized groups could be gleaned through education. Moreover, all sports taught competition, the basis for the capitalist economy, as well as the elements of democracy in providing leadership opportunities and cooperation for the good of the whole, and respect for authority in the person of umpires or referees for sporting competitions.[12] In 1917, Professor Frederic Paxson (1877–1948), a former student of Frederick Jackson Turner, declared sport to be the new frontier as a means to teach American cultural values.[13]

THE PROGRESSIVE ERA

Hall's directives comprised only one aspect of a much larger social movement in the United States between 1880 and 1920. During that period social reformers, largely WASP middle-class activists, attempted to enact numerous changes to create a better and more efficient American society. The widespread reforms included women's rights (especially suffrage), temperance, addressing political corruption and economic monopolies, poverty, labor issues (particularly child labor), social inequality (which resulted in enactment of the income tax in 1913), and the assimilation of immigrant groups.[14]

Like the Native American Indian children, the offspring of immigrants would be required to attend public schools, where they could be assimilated and learn to become good Americans as defined by the racial, religious, and social class perspectives of the Progressive reformers. This proved a daunting task as more than twenty million immigrants comprising a multitude of racial, ethnic, and religious groups traveled to the United States during the era. The American occupation of the Philippines proved to be a laboratory for social experimentation with a particular emphasis on sport as a vehicle for education.[15] US Army soldiers acted as the initial instructors of Filipino youth before the arrival of American teachers in 1901. Among their first lessons were baseball and boxing. Baseball taught American values inherent in the national game, such as teamwork on defense, individualism on offense, and the efficiency, order, and discipline imposed by an umpire. Boxing offered the practical application of Social Darwinian beliefs in the survival of the fittest and demonstrations of physical superiority.[16]

Militarism

Alfred Thayer Mahan (1840–1914), the son of a professor and dean at the US military academy at West Point, for a career in the navy. An avid reader as a boy, Mahan would become one of the most influential historians of his time. Described as "vain, self-assured, arrogant, contentious, humorless, and without close, personal friends," Mahan found some solace in writing. He served in the Civil War as a young man in the Union navy and acquired a great sense of patriotism, but did not experience combat in his forty years in the military service. The navy seemed an odd choice for one actually troubled by a fear of the sea, and who easily became seasick. Nevertheless, Mahan would rise to the position of head of the Naval War College, and the 1890 publication of *The Influence of Sea Power upon History, 1660–1783*, gained international renown. In it, Mahan claimed that strong navies were a necessity for national strength and secure commerce.[17]

International markets required the occupation or at least the control of foreign territories to protect and expand the capitalist system, and Mahan argued that the Unites States trailed the European imperial powers in respect to naval power. The French constructed steel battleships by 1872, and the British followed four years later. After the Prussian victory over France in 1871 and the consequent unification of Germany, it too quickly built a military machine capable of its imperial ambitions.[18] In Asia, Japan quickly modernized in the latter half of the nineteenth century and began to assume its own hegemony in Asia, a development Mahan, a Social Darwinist, considered an affront to the "world of civilized Christianity." He predicted an eventual war with Japan, and by 1898 the United States had heeded his warnings to build a powerful navy, trailing only those of Great Britain and Germany.[19] Mahan also registered disgust for the crumbling Spanish empire that had once made Spain a dominant power in Europe. He considered the Spanish to be "a broken race," whose bullfights were "brutal, savage, and disgusting," evidence of the degeneration theory that marked cultural decline.[20]

Theodore Roosevelt, an admirer and ardent supporter of Mahan and his theories, had waged his own battles. A sickly, frail, and near-sighted child, as a young man, he adopted the "strenuous life" of a cowboy, outdoorsmen, and athlete to build his body and his masculine image. His wealth, political connections, ambition, and personal drive enabled him to assume the roles of New York City police commissioner, assistant secretary of the Navy, governor of New York, vice president of the United States, and eventually president upon the assassination of William McKinley in 1901. Both before and during his presidency Roosevelt espoused sport as integral to the development of a martial spirit necessary to achieve his vision of world leadership.[21]

In his role as assistant secretary of the Navy he largely engineered the war plan of 1898, and then quickly resigned his post in order to lead a regiment of volunteers known as the Rough Riders, to test his own courage in Cuba. Like many men of his time, Roosevelt saw war as the ultimate test of masculinity, stating that "the timid man who cannot fight, and the selfish, short-sighted, or foolish man who will not take the steps that will enable him to fight, stand on almost the same plane." As president, he propelled the United States into the top ranks of world powers.[22]

Spain had accrued its global empire as early as the sixteenth century, but by 1896 it had experienced numerous revolts throughout its colonies. In that year both Cuban and Filipino rebels were in armed insurrection against their Spanish overlords. The Philippines posed a logistical problem for any occupier with more than 7,100 islands in the archipelago, inhabited by disparate tribes speaking more than 100 languages and dialects, and practicing pagan or Muslim beliefs. Despite such handicaps, the Spanish missionaries, led by the Augustinian, Dominican, and Franciscan orders of priests managed to convert the vast majority (excepting the Muslims of the southern islands) to Catholicism. In the process the friars managed to enrich the Church and themselves by conscripting much of the land and administrative offices. Unlike the colonies of Cuba and Puerto Rico, the Filipinos were not accorded any political representation in the Spanish Cortes.[23]

In 1892 Andres Bonifacio (1863–1897) founded the Katipunan organization in opposition to the Spanish authorities and in 1896 the oppressed proletariat engaged in an armed rebellion. Internecine quarrels within the group resulted in Bonifacio's execution and the ascension of Emilio Aguinaldo (1869–1964) to leadership. Aguinaldo's revolutionary army succeeded in surrounding the Spanish garrison in the capital of Manila in 1898.[24]

Unfortunately for Aguinaldo, before he could secure the Spanish surrender, the Spanish-American War erupted after the USS Maine battleship mysteriously blew up in the harbor of Havana, Cuba, on February 15, 1898, with the loss of 262 members of its 350-man crew. American media clamored for war and the government acquiesced in a formal declaration on April 25. Although Americans focused on the ensuing battle to take place in Cuba, Admiral George Dewey's (1837–1917) Pacific squadron was already en route to the Spanish colony due to the prescient war plan devised by Theodore Roosevelt. Dewey arrived in Manila Bay on April 30 and engaged the feeble Spanish fleet, completely destroying it the next day. Dewey and American emissaries consequently stalled Aguinaldo until the arrival of the American army and a negotiated surrender with the Spanish allowed the United States to claim the victory.[25]

The failure of the American government to recognize Aguinaldo as president and his representative assembly as a legitimate democracy, despite it being patterned after the American Constitution, resulted in animosity and eventual warfare. John Barrett, and American writer who reported on the revolutionary government, stated that "These men, whose sessions I repeatedly attended, conducted themselves with great decorum and showed knowledge of debate and parliamentary law. . . . The executive portion of the government was made up of a ministry of bright men who seemed to understand their respective positions."[26] While some allowed that Aguinaldo was "clever, sincere, and ambitious," the American media characterized him as evil, with Frank Millet of *Harper's Weekly* racializing his description as Aguinaldo having "the keen cunning of the Chinaman, and the personal vanity and light mental caliber of the Filipino." The *New York Times* further denounced Aguinaldo's masculinity and credibility as a "vain popinjay, a wicked liar, and a perfectly incapable leader" leading "dupes, a foolish incredulous mob."[27] Filipino males in general were feminized until they could prove their claims to masculinity through physical prowess in sporting competitions.

The confrontation of competing armies encircling Manila resulted in bloodshed on the night of February 4, 1899 and erupted into a full-scale war thereafter.[28] By 1900 the United States counted 70,000 soldiers in the Philippines, 75 percent of its total force engaged in a guerrilla war with Aguinaldo's followers. Aguinaldo was captured in 1901 through a spectacular ruse enacted by Frederick Funston (1865–1917), but fighting continued on the main island of Luzon until 1911 and until 1916 in Mindanao.[29] In the initial stages of the war President William McKinley (1843–1901), beset by conflicting opinions about the carnage and the mission, reminded himself in a note about the commercial ramifications. "While we are conducting war and until its conclusion, we must keep what we can get. When the war is over, we must keep what we want."[30]

Economy

The US economy had made great strides in the latter half of the nineteenth century. Between 1860 and 1897, despite the depressions of 1873, 1884, and 1893, exports had tripled. By the mid-1880s the United States had become the world leader in the production of timber, steel, meat-packing, and the mining of coal, iron ore, gold, and silver. It consumed more energy than any other country by 1890. By 1893 only Great Britain surpassed it in world trade, and by the turn of the century the United States produced more coal and steel than Great Britain and Germany combined.[31]

The 1890s revealed a growing culture of consumption in the United States, as marketers advertised new products and produced by new technologies to be consumed by new customers who sought credit from banks. The depression of 1893, which lasted for about four years, slowed such growth and indicated the need for external markets for the overproduction of American goods. American farmers suffered as well, as the excess production of crops drove prices down and many lost their land and hundreds of banks failed. Workers and farmers protested and rebelled as 1,394 industrial strikes occurred in 1894. The Pullman Company strike in Chicago that year shut down much of the national rail network. The severity of the economic downturn forced the Treasury Department to solicit the aid of financier J. P. Morgan (1837–1913) and British bankers to bail out the depleted gold reserves of the country.[32]

As an emerging world power the United States competed with the Old World powers of Great Britain, France, and Germany, as well as the new Asian rival in Japan. All sought the massive Asian markets for their goods. In 1895 the United States confronted Great Britain over the boundary of British Guiana in South America relative to land where gold had been discovered, which was also claimed by Venezuela. In addition, the United States, Great Britain, France, and Japan all sought the Hawaiian Islands as a vital Pacific crossroads and refueling station. The latter supplied many of the workers on Hawaiian plantations. American settlers had already usurped the monarchy in an 1893 coup, but President Grover Cleveland (1837–1908) refused to recognize a request for annexation. Under the Republican administration of McKinley and the outbreak of the Spanish-American War, Hawaii was formally annexed by the United States on July 7, 1898.[33] The *Baltimore American* claimed that "It is the same old law of the survival of the fittest. The weak must bend to the strong and today the American race is the sturdiest, the noblest on earth."[34]

The US economy had rebounded by 1900 as its food imports amounted to $226 million and it had surpassed Great Britain in all major industrial measures.[35] Later that year, Senator Henry Cabot Lodge (1850–1924) wrote to William Howard Taft (1857–1930), who then headed the Second Philippines Commission as the legislative body in the islands. "It has been my firm belief that the Philippines would not only become an important market for us for our finished goods but what is still more important would furnish a large opportunity for the investment of surplus capital" and offer a better return than in the United States. American officials in the Philippines came to the same conclusions in the succeeding years, much to the chagrin of the local populace.[36]

THE IMPERIALISM DEBATE

Americans divided over the propriety of the occupation of the Philippines. Even those who supported the war had misgivings on the issue of imperialism. Although the United States had begun to take a more active role in global politics and asserted itself as a burgeoning world power by the latter nineteenth century, it had arrived too late at the imperialists' table relative to the European acquisitions. Spain, France, the Netherlands, Portugal, and Great Britain had been accumulating territories for centuries. At the Berlin conference of 1884–1885 the British, French, Germans, Portuguese, and Belgians divided Africa up into their own spheres of influence, providing both markets for their goods and natural resources for their industries.[37]

It is no coincidence that during the latter volatile decades of the nineteenth century the violent and warlike game of football exploded in popularity across college campuses. The game invoked military strategies to gain an opponents' territory and produced mounting casualty lists and even deaths. While some educational leaders and clergy deemed it unworthy and harmful, others, such as Teddy Roosevelt, extolled its aggressive nature and martial qualities as a necessity for global competition.

In 1889 the Unites States and Germany risked a war over control of the Samoan islands in the South Pacific as each sought refueling stations for their ships. When a civil war broke out each country backed rival factions and sent ships (and in Germany's case, troops) to assist their favorites. War was averted when a typhoon destroyed the vessels of both countries, with the loss of one hundred German and fifty-three American lives. The two potential belligerents later divided the islands between them at an 1899 conference, and American Samoa remains a United States' possession today.[38]

As Germany rushed to accumulate its own global empire, Japan and Russia cast eyes on the vast Chinese market. Japan's rapid rise to international significance became quite evident after its quick defeat of China in the Sino-Japanese War of 1894–1895 over the control of Korea. Great Britain, France, Germany, and Russia all used the hostilities as an excuse to seize parcels of Chinese land. Ten years later Japan defeated Russia in another war over similar issues, firmly establishing itself as a modern power.[39]

During and after the culmination of the hostilities with Spain, Americans debated what to do with the spoils of war. Capitalists saw the Philippines as a stepping stone to the lucrative Chinese markets. Admiral Dewey favored the islands as potential sites for military bases, while others argued that the United States' Constitution made no legal provision for colonies; therefore the Philippines would have to be granted statehood. Still others opposed acquisition on moral grounds. Henry Van Dyke (1852–1933), a Presbyterian minister, wrote that such a move would set the nation on a new path inconsistent with its democratic ideals, quoting the Declaration of Independence in that "government derives its just powers from the consent of the governed" and that there should be "no taxation without representation."[40] Even Great Britain and Japan weighed in, advising the United States to keep the islands rather than subject them to takeover by Germany or Russia.[41] In any case it was clear that the United States had embarked on a new frontier.[42]

Henry Cabot Lodge, elected to the Senate in 1892, proved to be among the most vociferous of the imperialists. Described by historians variously as small, bookish, aristocratic, and dependent on his mother's money, but energetic and aggressive to the point of being combative and conspiratorial, Lodge could also be vane, insolent, stubborn, chilly and austere. The Republican senator admired robust men, such as athletes, particularly prizefighters, and hunters. He reveled in his youthful memories of football, baseball, and hockey games, and snowball fights against working class boys. He viewed the Philippines venture as an opportunity to display such martial spirit.[43] Acquisition might also prove beneficial politically. "The senator wanted the East Asian markets opened for the benefit of the nation, his party, and his Massachusetts constituents—industrialists, merchants, missionaries, and the state's working classes—and favored taking the entire chain, temporarily." They might later be sold to Great Britain or traded for Caribbean islands closer to American shores.[44]

Lodge extolled his expansionist desires in 1895, even before the opportunities afforded by the war with Spain.

> From the Rio Grande to the Arctic Ocean there should be but one flag and one country.... For the sake of our commercial supremacy in the Pacific we should control the Hawaiian Islands and maintain our influence in Samoa. England has studded the West Indies with strong places which are a standing menace to our Atlantic seaboard. We should have among those islands at least one strong naval station, and when the Nicaragua canal is built, the island of Cuba, still sparsely settled and of almost unbounded fertility, will become to us a necessity.[45]

Although opposed to slavery and a supporter of black rights, Lodge maintained a firm belief in Social Darwinism and impeded the immigration of southern and eastern Europeans to the United States. He feared a dilution of white racial superiority if merged with darker races.[46]

Lodge found a kindred spirit in Theodore Roosevelt. Both were noted historians who shared a Social Darwinian attitude, an imperialist vision, and an adherence to sport as a component of masculinity and a progenitor of the martial spirit that would be necessary to propel the United States to its destiny as a world power. Lodge lobbied hard for the appointment of Roosevelt to the Department of the Navy, and Roosevelt did not disappoint in that capacity.[47] Roosevelt firmly established the United States as a global political force upon assuming the presidency in the wake of the McKinley assassination. He rationalized his belligerent approach as one of moral rectitude by stating "our history has been one of expansion [which] is not a matter of regret, but of pride. . . . We were right in wresting from barbarism and adding to civilization the territory out of which we have made these beautiful states. Barbarism . . . has no place in a civilized world. It is our duty toward the people living in barbarism to see that they are freed from their chains, and we can free them only by destroying barbarism itself."[48]

In 1899 Albert Beveridge (1862–1927) joined Lodge in the US Senate as a Republican from Indiana and soon asserted himself as one of the most effective proponents of imperialism. Like Roosevelt and Lodge, Beveridge portrayed the mission in the Philippines as a moral duty. "And of all our race He [God] has marked the American people as His chosen nation to finally lead in the regeneration of the world. This is the divine mission of America. . . . We are trustees of the world's progress, guardians of its righteous peace."[49] He, too, coveted the commercial possibilities and railed against his Congressional opponents. "Our largest trade henceforth must be with Asia. The Pacific is our ocean. . . . China is our natural customer. . . . That statesman commits a crime against American trade—against the American grower of cotton and wheat and tobacco, the American manufacturer of machinery and clothing—who fails to put America where she may command that trade."[50]

Before assuming his seat in the Senate, Beveridge actually traveled to the Philippines, then citing his first hand accounts as proof of his assertions. He maintained his stance on the acquisition of the archipelago, but in other matters he favored the Progressives' initiatives during his years in the Senate. He followed Theodore Roosevelt into the Progressive Party in 1912.[51]

Religious denominations, with the exception of the Quakers and Unitarians, ardently favored the occupation of the Philippines and the opportunities for conversion. As early as May of 1898 the *Baptist Union* clamored that "the conquest by force of arms must be followed by conquest for Christ." The *Methodist Review* stated that "by the direction of divine Providence [the policy of foreign colonization should be] the foreign policy of the U.S. is foreign missions." Presbyterians called for

Christian education as a duty, disregarding the fact that the Filipinos had been already Christianized by the Catholic Spaniards. Congregationalists declared that "Morally and religiously, we should not shun an opportunity to lift up a barbarous people." On July 13, 1898, at an interdenominational conference in New York, the Baptists, Methodists, and Presbyterians divided up the Philippines for their missionary objectives.[52]

Both President McKinley and his wife professed themselves to be ardent Methodists. He revealed to a group of Methodist ministers that he had invited to the White House that his final decision to colonize the Philippines had come from a divine inspiration. He portrayed the American invasions of the Spanish lands as humanitarian missions, as the benevolent assimilation of wayward children who required discipline.[53]

Arrayed against the expansionists were a host of prominent luminaries, many of whom joined the Anti-Imperialist League (AIL). The organization, established in Boston on June 15, 1898, spread throughout the urban areas of the country, enlisting members until its demise in 1920. They included Grover Cleveland, twice president of the United States; William Jennings Bryan (1860–1925), three times a candidate for that same office; and Carl Schurz (1829–1906), who had migrated from Germany after participating in a failed revolution in 1848, but honed his leadership abilities in the United States. Schurz served as a general of German troops in the Civil War, and won election to the US Senate and also served as a statesman and journalist. Among the numerous scholars enrolled were Charles W. Eliot (1834–1926), president of Harvard University; David Starr Jordan (1851–1931), president of Stanford University; G. Stanley Hall, president of Clark University; Charles F. Adams, Jr. (1835–1915), the offspring of American presidents and himself the president of the American Historical Association; William James (1842–1910), one of the foremost philosophers and psychologists in the nation; John Dewey (1859–1952), his counterpart as a founder of the pragmatic philosophy and also an influential educator; Charles Eliot Norton (1827–1908), art professor at Harvard and a president of the Archaeological Institute of America; and William Graham Sumner (1840–1910), a prominent sociologist at Yale. A bevy of influential writers also joined the ranks, including Henry James (1843–1916), E. L. Godkin (1831–1902), Mark Twain (Samuel Clemens, 1835–1910), William Dean Howells (1837–1920), and Finley Peter Dunne (1867–1936). Seemingly opponents in the labor movement, industrialist, steel tycoon, and philanthropist Andrew Carnegie (1835–1919), and Samuel Gompers (1850–1924), founder of the American Federation of Labor in 1886, joined forces in the AIL. Jane Addams (1860–1935), who established the field of social work in the United States and later won the Nobel Peace Prize, added a feminine perspective to the mix.[54]

Their motives were as varied as their backgrounds. Schurz called the Filipinos "A large mass of more or less barbarous Asiatics . . . far less good-natured, tractable, and orderly than the negro [sic] is," and he correctly predicted that the Filipinos would fight before accepting subjugation. He maintained that acquired territories would have to become states and favored a US protectorate over an independent Philippines.[55] Godkin also opposed annexation on racial grounds, fearing a dilution of the white, Anglo stock.[56] Gompers' objections rested upon racial and labor issues, as he intended on "saving American labor from the evil influence of close and open competition of millions of semi-barbaric laborers." Nor would American labor in the islands prove beneficial, as he considered the climate to be inhospitable for whites.[57] Carnegie feared embroilment with other imperial powers and even offered McKinley $20,000,000 (the purchase price in the Treaty of Paris) to grant independence rather than annex the islands.[58]

Others voiced more humanitarian concerns. Thomas Wentworth Higginson (1823–1911), a Unitarian minister, an early abolitionist, leader of an African American regiment in the Civil War, and a proponent of civil rights for the oppressed, continued that campaign throughout his life.[59] Issues of morality and legality would persist throughout the American occupation and beyond as the United States maintained a military presence in the islands over the next century.

Aftermath

The Spanish-American War and the resultant carnage and occupation in the Philippines held lasting repercussions for the United States. The policies, procedures, and military and political strategies evident throughout the American interventions in the Caribbean, Central and South America, Vietnam, and the Mideast were/are reminiscent of those conducted in the Philippines. The limited occupation of foreign territories and the creation of local constabularies to enforce American dictates, the establishment of military bases on a global scale, the co-optation of wealthy families to insure political influence across future generations, and the education programs sponsored by American agencies all initiated in the Philippines. Today there is an increasing use of "soft" power in the guise of popular culture, such as entertainment, sport, music, movies, and social media to entice foreign youth to adopt the American value system and its inherent ideologies. Superior technology and the attraction of sport powered similar motives more than a century ago, and still remain viable means of promoting cultural imperialism.

NOTES

1. Robert E. Bieder, *Science Encounters the Indian, 1820–1880: The Early Years of American Ethnology* (Norman: University of Oklahoma Press), 1986, 8–10, 68–70.
2. Ibid., 10–12, 43–4.
3. Ibid., 194–5, 244–5; Elisabeth Tooker, "Lewis Henry Morgan: The Myth and the Man," *University of Rochester Library Bulletin*, 37 (1984), n.p.
4. Paul. A. Kramer, "Empires, Exceptions, and Anglo-Saxons: Race and Rule between the British and United States Empires, 1880–1910," *Journal of American History*, 88:4 (March 2002), 1315–53.
5. Strong cited in Stuart Creighton Miller, *"Benevolent Assimilation": The American Conquest of the Philippines, 1899–1903* (New Haven, CT: Yale University Press, 1982), 6.
6. Strong cited in Julius W. Pratt, *Expansionists of 1898: Acquisition of Hawaii and the Spanish Islands* (Gloucester, MA: Peter Smith, 1959), 5.
7. Kramer, "Empires, Exceptions, and Anglo-Saxons", 7.
8. Roosevelt cited in David Haward Bain, *Sitting in Darkness: Americans in the Philippines* (Boston: Houghton Mifflin, 1984), 66.
9. *The Winning of the West*, 174–5, cited in Warren Zimmerman, *The First Great Triumph: How Five Americans Made Their Country a World Power* (New York: Farrar, Straus and Giroux, 2002), 218–19.
10. nationalhumanitiescenter.org/pds/gilded/empire/text1/turner.pdf (May 26, 2015); Allan G. Bogue, *Frederick Jackson Turner: Strange Roads Going Down* (Norman: University of Oklahoma Press, 1998).
11. On the concept of whiteness, see Peter Kolchin, "Whiteness Studies: The New History of Race in America," *Journal of American History*, 89:1 (June 2002), 154–73; and the special issue of *International Labor and Working Class History*, 60 (Fall 2001). On the Indian schools, see David Wallace Adams, *Education for Extinction: American Indians and the Boarding School Experience, 1875–1928* (Lawrence: University Press of Kansas, 1995); Frederick E. Hoxie, *A Final Promise: The Campaign to Assimilate the Indians, 1880–1920* (New York: Cambridge University Press, 1989); Jack Newcombe, *The Best of the Athletic Boys: The White Man's Impact on Jim Thorpe* (Garden City, NJ: Doubleday, 1975); John Bloom, *To Show What an Indian Can Do: Sports at Native American Boarding Schools* (Minneapolis: University of Minnesota Press, 2000).
12. Benjamin G. Rader, *American Sports: From the Age of Folk Games to the Age of Televised Sports* (Englewood Cliffs, NJ: Prentice Hall, 1990), 219–20; Gerald R. Gems, Linda J. Borish, and Gertrud Pfister, *Sports in American History: From Colonization to Globalization* (Champaign, IL: Human Kinetics, 2008), 175–226.
13. Frederic L. Paxson, "The Rise of Sport," *Mississippi Valley Historical Review*, 4 (1917), 143–68.
14. Among the voluminous scholarship on the Progressive Era, see Jane Addams, *Twenty Years at Hull House* (New York: Macmillan, 1930); Allen F. Davis, *Spearheads for Reform: The Social Settlements and the Progressive Era, 1890–1914* (New York: Oxford University Press, 1967); Robert M. Crunden, *Ministers of Reform: The Progressive Achievement in American Civilization, 1889–1920* (New York: Basic Books, 1982); William J. Reese, *Power and the Promise of School Reform: Grassroots Movement During the Progressive Era* (Boston: Routledge & Kegan Paul, 1986); and Gerald R. Gems, *Windy City Wars: Labor, Leisure, and Sport in the Making of Chicago* (Lanham, MD: Scarecrow Press, 1997).
15. See Gerald R. Gems, *Sport and the Shaping of Italian American Culture* (Syracuse, NY: Syracuse University Press, 2013) for an analysis of the process among one ethnic group.
16. Gerald R. Gems, *The Athletic Crusade: Sport and American Cultural Imperialism* (Lincoln: University of Nebraska Press, 2006), 48–64.
17. H. Paul Jeffers, *Colonel Roosevelt: Theodore Roosevelt Goes to War, 1897–1898* (New York: John Wiley & Sons, 1996), 2, 67–9, 68 (quote); Zimmerman, *First Great Triumph*, 94–122; Walter Millis, *The Martial Spirit* (Chicago: Ivan R. Dee, 1989), 293.
18. Jeffers, *Colonel Roosevelt*, 42; Zimmerman, *First Great Triumph*, 94–101.

19. Zimmerman, *First Great Triumph*, 120, 235 (quote); Jeffers, *Colonel Roosevelt*, 68–9.
20. Zimmerman, *First Great Triumph*, 238.
21. Fred Anderson and Andrew Cayton, *The Dominion of War: Empire and Liberty in North America, 1500–2000* (New York: Viking, 2005); Millis, *The Martial Spirit*, 290, 295, 322–24, 333–34.
22. Jeffers, *Colonel Roosevelt*, 1, 50–1, 138–49; Zimmerman, *First Great Triumph*, 239 (quote), 403–15.
23. Amado Guerrero, *Philippine Society and Revolution* (Hong Kong: Ta Kung Pao Press, 1971), 4–19; Gems, *The Athletic Crusade*, 82–98; Paul A. Kramer, *The Blood of Government: Race, Empire, the United States & the Philippines* (Chapel Hill: University of North Carolina Press, 2006), 36–42, 50–81; Bain, *Sitting in Darkness*, 159–73; Leon Wolff, *Little Brown Brother: How the United States Purchased and Pacified the Philippine Islands at the Century's Turn* (New York: Bookspan, 2006 [1960]), 17–18.
24. Guerrero, *Philippine Society and Revolution*, 26–8.
25. Bain, *Sitting In Darkness*, 60. More recent investigations of the USS Maine tragedy have discredited any claims of Spanish sabotage in favor of a faulty design that placed the storage of fueling coal next to a powder magazine, resulting in a spontaneous combustion.
26. Wolff, *Little Brown Brother*, 147.
27. Bain, *Sitting In Darkness*, 12. See Kristin L. Hoganson, *Fighting for American Manhood: How Gender Politics Provoked the Spanish-American War and Philippine-American Wars* (New Haven, CT: Yale University Press, 1998); Christina S. Jarvis, *The Male Body at War: American Masculinity during World War II* (DeKalb: Northern Illinois University Press, 2004), and Mary Louise Roberts, *What Soldiers Do: Sex and the American GI in World War II* (Chicago: University of Chicago Press, 2013) on the correlation between masculinity and the military.
28. Anderson and Cayton, *The Dominion of War*, 332.
29. Zimmerman, *First Great Triumph*, 386; John M. Gates, *Schoolbooks and Krags: The United States Army in the Philippines, 1898–1902* (Westport, CT: Greenwood Press, 1973), 156–78; Stanley Karnow, *In Our Image: America's Empire in the Philippines* (New York: Random House, 1989), 12, 146; Guerrero, *Philippine Society and Revolution*, 35.
30. Jeffers, *Colonel Roosevelt*, 143.
31. Zimmerman, *First Great Triumph*, 25; Thomas McCormick, "From Old Empire to New: The Changing Dynamics and Tactics of American Empire," in Alfred W. McCoy and Francisco Scarano, eds., *Colonial Crucible: Empire in the Making of the Modern American State* (Madison: University of Wisconsin Press, 2009), 63–79.
32. H. W. Brands, *The Reckless Decade: America in the 1890s* (New York: St. Martin's Press, 1995), 3, 37–41, 75–9; Bain, *Sitting in Darkness*, 38–40.
33. Gems, *The Athletic Crusade*, 67–81; Jeffers, *Colonel Roosevelt*, 331; Pratt, *Expansionists of 1898*, 260–61.
34. *Baltimore American*, June 11, 1898, n.p. cited in Miller, "*Benevolent Assimilation*," 15.
35. Kristin Hoganson, "Buying into Empire: American Consumption at the Turn of the Twentieth Century," and McCormick, "From Old Empire to New," both in McCoy and Scarano, eds., *Colonial Crucible*, 248–59, and 63–79 respectively.
36. Lodge to Taft, November 22, 1900, in Peter W. Stanley, *A Nation in the Making: The Philippines and the United States, 1899–1921* (Cambridge, MA: Harvard University Press, 1974), 106.
37. Thomas Pakenham, *The Scramble for Africa: The White Man's Conquest of the Dark Continent from 1876 to 1912* (New York: Random House, 1991).
38. J. A. C. Gray, *Amerika Samoa: A History of American Samoa and Its United States Naval Administration* (Annapolis, MD: United States Naval Institute, 1960), 99–107; Zimmerman, *First Great Triumph*, 7, 444; Richard E. Welch, Jr., *Imperialists vs. Anti-Imperialists: The Debate Over Expansionism in the 1890s* (Itasca, IL: F. E. Peacock, 1972), 32–33; militaryhistorynow.com/2012/10/08/samoan-showdown-america-risks-war-with-germany-in-1880s/ (May 30, 2015).

39. James Bradley, *The Imperial Crusade: A Secret History of Empire and War* (New York: Little, Brown & Co., 2009), 186–99; Zimmerman, *First Great Triumph*, 446–47.

40. Van Dyke, "The American Birthright and the Philippine Pottage," *The Independent*, L (December 1, 1898), 1579–1585, cited in Welch, *Imperialists vs. Anti-Imperialists*, 72–81.

41. Anderson and Cayton, *The Dominion of War*, 167–68.

42. The concept of a new frontier is espoused by historian Donald E. Pease, "New Perspectives on U.S. Culture and Imperialism," in Amy Kaplan and Donald E. Pease, eds., *Cultures of United States Imperialism* (Durham, NC: Duke University Press, 1993), 22–37.

43. Hoganson, *Fighting for American Manhood*, 147–49.

44. Eric T. Love, *Race Over Empire: Racism and U.S. Imperialism, 1865–1900* (Chapel Hill: University of North Carolina Press, 2004), 159–60; Zimmerman, *First Great Triumph*, 149.

45. Lodge, "The Business World vs. the Politicians," 1895, cited in Walter Millis, *The Martial Spirit* (Chicago: Ivan R. Dee, 1989), 27.

46. Zimmerman, *First Great Triumph*, 184–87, 459.

47. Ibid., 175.

48. Bradley, *The Imperial Crusade*, 203.

49. Zimmerman, *First Great Triumph*, 348.

50. Brands, *The Reckless Decade*, 334.

51. Miller, *"Benevolent Assimilation,"* 131.

52. Pratt, *Expansionists of 1898*, 288–301, *Baptist Union*, VIII: 338 (May 14, 1898), cited on pp. 291–92; *Methodist Review*, 80 (July 1898), 513–23, and (September–October 1898), 824, cited on p. 295; Congregationalist *Advance* (May 18, 1898), p. 658, cited on p. 301.

53. Wolff, *Little Brown Brother*, 84; General James Rusling, "Interview with President William McKinley," *The Christian Advocate* 22 January 1903, 17, reprinted in Daniel Schirmer and Stephen Rosskamm Shalom, eds., *The Philippines Reader* (Boston: South End Press, 1987), 22–23; Bradley, *The Imperial Crusade*, 73, 79–80, 99; Vicente L. Rafael, "'White Love': Surveillance and Nationalist Resistance in the Colonization of the Philippines," in Kaplan and Pease, eds., *Cultures of United States Imperialism*, 185–218.

54. Zimmerman, *First Great Triumph*, passim; Miller, "Benevolent Assimilation," 114, 122.

55. Zimmerman, *First Great Triumph*, 337 (quote), 335–36, 339; Brands, *The Reckless Decade*, 331.

56. Zimmerman, *First Great Triumph*, 334–35.

57. Love, *Race Over Empire*, 184.

58. Brands, *The Reckless Decade*, 331; Zimmerman, *First Great Triumph*, 334.

59. Miller, *"Benevolent Assimilation,"* 122.

TWO

Social Darwinism

THE SCIENCE OF RACIALIZATION

As stated in the introduction, Social Darwinism is an ideology that organizes societies and humankind in a hierarchical fashion based upon the social construction of races and their perceived abilities that conferred a level of power. The visual configuration of such categorization is often depicted in a pyramid with dark-skinned people at the base of the pyramid and whites—more specifically white, Anglo-Saxon Protestants—at the apex. Whiteness conferred social and psychological advantages, as stated by Edward Said (1935–2003), in his influential tome entitled *Orientalism*. Westerners (whites) were perceived as "rational, progressive, manly, and morally and racially superior—and the non-Western other, typically represented as heathen, primitive, treacherous, and de-masculinized." Race, however, proved to be a fluid construct, and individuals or groups might win greater rank and social acceptance over time. Such was the hope for Filipinos, whom the Americans intended to instruct and tutor in the ways of whiteness until they reached a civilized stage capable of self-government.[1]

Concurrently the United States was engaged in the same process of Americanization of the millions of European immigrants who had begun flooding its shores in 1880 and continued to seek a better life in America over the next four decades. With historical hindsight it is easy to criticize American policies and practices in the assimilation process as racist and immoral, but knowledge is built upon previous knowledge, and in that respect the beliefs, assumptions, opinions, and practices of that era rested upon faulty knowledge. For example, southern Italians, one of the largest groups of migrants to the United States, were labeled with deficiencies even before their arrival due to the practice of phrenology. Cesare Lambroso (1835–1909), an Italian scientist, believed that such physical features as high cheek bones, large jaws, dark skin, low brows, small heads, and a childlike mentality were hereditary signs of criminality. Sociologist Enrico Ferri (1856–1929) seemingly corroborated such assertions by measuring the size and shape of his subjects' skulls. In the United States at least two thousand Native American skulls were sent to a government museum in Washington, DC, for such study, and immigrants passing through inspection at Ellis Island might be rejected based on the circumference of their head, weak eyes, or even a facial expression that presumed intellectual deficiencies. While the "science" of phrenology was discredited by the late nineteenth century, such stereotypes of criminality continue to afflict Italian Americans today.[2]

Well before the American occupation of the Philippines, white Europeans and Americans had accepted and fully endorsed their belief in their own racial superiority. University professors taught the doctrine in their classes, and political leaders, such as Teddy Roosevelt, justified and rationalized the violent conquest of savages as inevitable and necessary. Journalists continually supported the belief that "the tropics are peopled with millions of low social efficiency; and it seems to be the fate of the black and yellow races to have their countries parceled out and administered by efficient races from the Temperate Zone," while another determined that "the rule of the survival of the fittest applies to nations as well as the animal kingdom. It is a cruel, relentless principle being exercised in a cruel, relentless competition of mighty forces."[3] The *Baltimore American* agreed that "it is the same old law of the survival of the fittest. The weak must bend to the strong and today the American race is the sturdiest, the noblest on earth."[4]

Even some of the anti-imperialists based their arguments on race. Southern senators feared that Filipinos might travel to the United States, dilute the gene pool, and destroy American culture. Senator John Tyler Morgan of Alabama, however, favored annexation and even devised a plan to export African Americans to the Philippines. Other anti-imperialists feared the participation of the Filipinos in the political affairs of the nation. One writer for the popular *Nation* claimed that "our government was made for peaceable, industrious, homogeneous, Protestant men."[5]

Even David Starr Jordan, erudite president of Stanford University, declared that "Civilization is . . . suffocated in the tropics," and the Philippines "lie in the heart of the torrid zone, Nature's asylum for degenerates."[6] Historian David Brody determined that "the atmosphere of the late nineteenth century was so thoroughly permeated with racist thought (reinforced by Darwinism) that few men managed to escape it. The idea that certain cultures and races were naturally inferior to others was almost universally held by educated, middle class, respectable Americans—in other words, by the dominant majority."[7]

Among those one might expect to assume a more benevolent perspective were the missionaries, but many of them only reinforced the popular belief in Filipino inferiority in their books and reports. While some occasionally admired the physical prowess and admirable qualities of those they characterized as *noble savages*, others decried the Filipinos as physically, intellectually, and morally lacking. They graded *mestizos* as intellectually superior due to their Spanish blood, but none favored intermarriage with the natives. Methodist bishop James Thoburn (1836–1922) who spent only three weeks in the islands nevertheless reported to a US Senate committee in 1902 that the Filipinos ranked above American Indians, but below the Chinese and far below Anglo-Saxons.[8] A Presbyterian minister deplored the lack of a Filipino work ethic, claiming it to be a serious problem in the Philippines. He "found a disgusted contractor who could not induce men to load a *lorcha* (sailboat) at any price because they had won enough for their immediate necessities at the Sunday cockfight, and they would not work until the money was spent."[9]

American teachers, some of them missionaries, espoused similar sentiments. Harry Cole wrote about teaching "monkeys" to speak English. "How can we expect a colored race, with the baser natures and the natural tendencies to evil, to attain without years and years, or even generations of training, even to a crude imitation of a good form of government." After two more years of service he determined that "when I get home, I want to forget about this country and people as soon as possible. I shall probably hate the sight of anything but a white man the rest of my life."[10]

President William McKinley established the First Philippines Commission in 1899, charged with investigating American operations in the archipelago and making recommendations. Chaired, reluctantly, by Jacob Gould Schurman (1854–1942), the president of Cornell University, the real voice of the group rested with Dean Worcester (1866–1924), a zoologist at the University of Michigan. Worcester had first traveled to the Philippines as part of an expedition led by his professor, Joseph Beal Steere (1842–1940) in 1887. Worcester returned on a second expedition in 1890 and spent two years gathering specimens. He had already published a book on the Philippines and its people when James Angell (1829–1916), president of the University of Michigan arranged a meeting with President McKinley that resulted in his selection to the commission. Worcester would be reappointed to the Second Commission, chaired by William Howard Taft (1857–1930), and became the most powerful and most hated of the American administrators in his long tenure as Secretary of the Interior. During his 1887 sojourn Worcester had beaten a Filipino servant accused of stealing with a hickory stick, and his opinion of the indigenous people hardly improved over time. In the report of the First Philippines Commission Worcester adhered to Social Darwinian categorizations, listing "three sharply distinct races, the Negrito, the Indonesian, and the Malayan, along with an estimated eighty-four tribes. He ranked the Negritos "near the bottom of the human series." Worcester trained as an entomologist, not an anthropologist, and Sixto Lopez (1863–1947), a nationalist politician, challenged his findings as "entirely incorrect"; yet such preliminary findings were published as fact.[11]

Taft's initial impressions were delivered in a letter to Elihu Root (1845–1937), Secretary of War in 1900.

> The population of the Islands [sic] is made up of a vast mass of ignorant, superstitious, well intentioned, temperate, somewhat domesticated, fond of their families, and deeply wedded to the Catholic church.... They are generally lacking in moral character; are, with some notable exceptions, prone to yield to any pecuniary consideration; and difficult persons out of whom to make an honest government. We shall have to do the best we can with them.[12]

The American administration enacted the first census in the Philippines in 1903, with Christian tribes categorized as "civilized," and non-Christian tribes deemed "wild." Intellectually the Filipinos were judged to be mimics incapable of original thought.[13] Such early perceptions colored American opinions of the indigenous population throughout the colonial era.

The less educated members of the American military forces proved even more racist in their contact with the indigenous peoples. An American major complained that "soldiers and also many officers refer to the natives in their presence as 'niggers' and natives are beginning to understand what the word 'nigger' means."[14] Once hostilities escalated into actual warfare, American soldiers often killed Filipinos indiscriminately, a situation rationalized by an American journalist in the *New York Evening Post*.

> There is no question that our men do "shoot niggers" somewhat in the sporting spirit, but that is because war and their environment have rubbed off the thin veneer of civilization.... Undoubtedly, they do not regard the shooting of Filipinos just as they would the shooting of white troops. This is partly because they are "only niggers," and partly because they despise them for their treacherous servility.... The soldiers feel that they are fighting with savages, not with soldiers.[15]

One such soldier explained that "No cruelty is too severe for these brainless monkeys, who can appreciate no sense of honor, kindness or justice," and another remarked that "I am in my glory when I can sight some dark skin and pull the trigger."[16] Such indoctrination of white supremacy had been long underway.

World's Fairs as Hegemonic Symbols

Western nations began showcasing their supposedly superior intelligence, technology, and culture in a series of world's fairs beginning in London in 1851. The American Centennial Exposition in Philadelphia introduced the telephone, the typewriter, the refrigerated railcar, the sewing machine, and the mighty Corliss steam engine, which generated 1,400 horsepower. The World's Columbian Exposition in Chicago in 1893 proclaimed itself the "White City," a magnificent exhibition of classic Anglo architecture and learning, illuminated by electric lights, and offering a cultural contrast to the less civilized attractions of other countries and peoples on the Midway annex to the main display. Among the spectacles, Buffalo Bill Cody's Wild West Show reenacted whites' conquest of the "primitive" Native Americans, a performance that he also presented to European audiences.[17]

Designed by architect Daniel Burnham (1846–1912), who would also be engaged in the Philippines, the 1893 fair exemplified the Progressive reformers' belief in their abilities to refashion society in their own image of order, efficiency, and morality. A religious congress lasted for seventeen days, and white women gained a measure of leadership and public recognition, but African Americans were almost entirely excluded from participation. Frederick Douglass (1818–1895), a national leader for black rights, stated that "America was posing before the world as a highly liberal and civilized nation, and has brought a greater variety of mankind here than ever before. But as if to shame the Negro, the Dahomians (an African tribe exhibited on the Midway) are also here to exhibit the Negro as a repulsive savage."[18]

A games exhibit organized by Stewart Culin (1858–1929) also suggested an increasingly significant element of the popular culture, as the play theory espoused by G. Stanley Hall and the importance of sport in producing the desired qualities for citizenship became prominent in American schools and in the Philippines.[19]

The Exposition of 1901 in Buffalo, New York included the first Philippines exhibit, a collection of artifacts, handicrafts, and assorted products, but lacking any Filipinos as live specimens.[20] The St. Louis World's Fair of 1904 (also known as the Louisiana Purchase Exposition) provided such attractions and more in a most controversial manner. Americans were interested in what its government had accomplished in its new territory. The anthropology department constructed native villages within the fairgrounds to depict a wide variety of "primitive" peoples in various stages of evolution. W J McGee (1853–1912), first president of the American Anthropological Association and president of the National Geographic Society, served as chairman of the anthropology department and he proposed "to trace the course of human progress and classify human individuals and peoples in terms of that progress, and thus to learn as much as may be possible of the origin and destiny of Man."[21] The official photo album of the festival duly complied. A photo of the Sioux Indians labeled them as "takers of scalps. . . . Under government tutelage they are becoming useful citizens, but it is not easy for them to relinquish the individualism of the tribesmen and accept the communism [sic] of organized, conventional society."[22]

The book stated that there were five different classes of Filipinos at the fair:

> These range in the scale of civilization and intelligence from the Negritos, who are so primitive that they have no fixed habitation, to the Visayans whose culture is equal to that of the finest classes of Americans. . . . The Visayans are Christians. . . . The Moros, who rank next to them in intelligence, are Mohammedans and are truly piratical in instinct. . . . They are fearless fighters, and many of them are religious fanatics.[23]

The book included photos of the various tribes and their domiciles, including the tree houses of the Mindanao Moros, claiming that "cannibalism is practiced among them."[24] The photo of the Samal (district) Moros indicated that they "play their own music on curious, crude instruments," but admitted that the "little brown men" of the Philippine Constabulary Band "are natural musicians and capable of the highest training."[25] The album noted that less than one-seventh of the population were considered to be savages, but that wild Filipinos attracted more attention than conventional ones. To that effect the daily dance of the Igorots from the northern island of Luzon proved the most popular. "In the Igorotte village at the Exposition, there are more than a hundred spirit-worshipping barbarians. . . . Tattooing is common with these people, the men employing it to show their record of lives taken, the women to enhance their charms. . . . The strong, lithe, graceful savages move in a circular path. . . . With any more attire (in loin cloths) than they employ, the beauty of their supple limbs and of their transparent copper-brown skins would be hidden."[26] Viewers were especially taken by the eroticized vision of Chief Bolon of the Bagobo tribe. The *St. Louis Post-Dispatch* described him as

> the peacockiest, proudest, handsomest biped that ever strode the earth . . . [compared to the paintings in the Fine Arts Palace] Bolon stood in a class of his own. . . . Thousands of people went to the Bagobo village for the express purpose of seeing the Adonic savage. . . . He dressed in a way that was at once simple and gorgeous. . . . Bolon's demeanor . . . was something akin to that of a pretty woman primping before a mirror. . . . Though a savage he impressed me quite as much for his intelligent dignity as he did for his physical perfection. . . . He was beautiful beyond compare. His long hair was as black as a raven's back and as soft as an ostrich plume. His bronze skin had a rich autumnal tint.[27]

Large crowds flocked to the scene daily and at least one of the young American women took to dancing with a joyous Filipino partner.

THE ANTHROPOLOGY DAYS AND RACIAL COMPARISON

W J McGee, however, had more serious business in mind. He "organized the Ethnology Section as an implicit comparison to the industrial and technological displays—electricity, mechanical engineering—that proclaimed America as the most technologically and intellectually advanced culture in the world."[28] McGee teamed up with James E. Sullivan (1862–1914), head of the Physical Culture Department at the fair, and at Sullivan's suggestion, decided to conduct an athletic experiment to test the capabilities of "primitive peoples" in comparison to whites. It was assumed by many that such savages lived closer to animals and possessed natural physical abilities in excess of whites. Sullivan—as one of the founders of the Amateur Athletic Union in 1888, chairman of the athletic records committee, publisher of the *Athletic Almanac*, delegate to the 1900 Olympic Games, and director of athletics at the 1901 Buffalo Expo—was the dominant figure in American sport at the turn of the century. Described as "ambitious, powerful, arrogant, influential, self-promoter, and a meticulous organizer," he brooked little opposition. Under Sullivan's guidance the fair would include the 1904 Olympic Games, which proved to be less than successful. Most countries declined to send competitors to such a remote destination; as a result, 525 of the 687 competitors were Americans, largely contesting among each other.[29]

Sullivan's joint venture with McGee, known as the Anthropology Days, proved even more controversial. Diverse members of the ethnic and national groups assembled in the "human zoo" were conscripted to participate in numerous athletic events, whose marks could then be compared across racial groups to judge physical prowess among the peoples of the world. McGee convinced some to participate by paying them in the initial trials, but Sullivan refused to pay the winners to return for the final events. His firm adherence to "amateurism" resulted in numerous dropouts from the competition. Swimming competition had to be cancelled when only the seafaring Samal Moros of the Philippines volunteered for the event. Eventually nine Native American Indian tribes, the Ainus of Japan, three African tribes (including the Mbuti pygmies), three Filipino groups (Moros, Negritos, and Igorots), Syrians, and Patagonians joined in the eighteen events, which included running, jumping, throwing, weight lifting, archery, a tug-of-war, and a pole-climbing contest. The competitors were forbidden to practice, but could watch the Olympic athletes perform. The organizers provided no rules or explanations until those delivered in English (which few understood) by the referee, Luther Gulick (1865–1918).[30]

Gulick, the foremost physical educator of his time, was the scion of missionaries in Hawaii. After earning his medical degree, Gulick headed the physical education department at the YMCA training school in Springfield, Massachusetts. There in the winter of 1891 he assigned James Naismith (1861–1939), an instructor at the school, to devise a winter game that would hold the attraction of young men between football and baseball seasons. Thus did basketball enter the American pantheon of sports. Gulick moved on to the New York public schools after the turn of the century, where he devised the interscholastic athletic league and then became a cofounder of the Playground Association of America. Elected president of the American Physical Education Association, he and his wife then formed the Camp Fire Girls organization. Both Gulick and Sullivan adhered to G. Stanley Hall's belief in sport as not only a means to acquire physical skills, but a vehicle for moral development as well. The conduct of the Anthropology Days games however, resulted in neither for the participants.[31]

The eighteen events ensued over two days, August 11–12, with unforeseen problems that ensued from linguistic and cultural differences. Sprinters unfamiliar with a finish line ducked under it, while others who ran fast waited for friends to catch up. The relay races proved disappointing as the runners did not know what to do with the baton. The field events were conducted in succession, leaving contestants tired and unwilling to continue. The finalists were allowed one recorded performance with no repeats. Few competitors agreed to the 56 lb. weight throw, and when some dropped it without much effort, their marks of 3' were scored as official tallies. Some of the American Indians appeared at the tug-of-war in full feathered headdress, hardly intending to sully themselves in the event. The Mbuti pygmies disdained almost any competition—instead cavorting with the photographers, mimicking the other contestants and referees, and being generally mischievous and disruptive—although they earnestly enjoyed the pole climb and the culminating mud fight. The 50' pole climb was won by Basilio, an Igorot tribesman, in the time of 20 seconds, 10 seconds better than the American record holder. Sullivan failed to acknowledge the latter feat and considered the pygmies "childlike" and the contestants in general intellectually incapable of team sports. He concluded that "the savage has been a very much overrated man from an athletic point of view."[32]

McGee admitted the faulty nature of the research experiment. It assumed that the participants were average members of their race and he realized that their confusion and lack of training greatly affected the results. At least eleven of the eighteen events were won by Native American Indians, those most familiar with the American sports and games and the nature of competition due to their residence in Indian boarding schools. William (Lone Star) Dietz (1884–1964), winner of the shot put competition, played football at Carlisle Indian School and then coached numerous collegiate squads before becoming head coach of the professional Boston Braves (now Washington Redskins) in the National Football League.[33]

Despite the disapproval of Sullivan, McGee conducted a second round of competitions in September after a period of training. This time the contestants were paid to participate and won cash awards of 50¢ to $2 based on their performance to assure their best efforts, which achieved better results, and an estimated thirty thousand spectators viewed the performances. Unfortunately, no surviving records of the results have yet been uncovered. Despite the improvement, McGee still concluded that "making every allowance for the lack of training on the part of the primitives, the tests nevertheless established in quantitative measure the inferiority of primitive peoples.[34]

Except for an honorary contingent the upper classes in the Philippines refused to participate in the World's Fair and complained about the portrayal of their country. Provincial governor Vicente Nepomuceno complained that "In furtherance of this determination to hold our reins of government they have gone into the remotest corners of the islands, gathered together the lowest types of the inhabitants and brought them to this country to exhibit them in an attempt to justify their paternal grip on the islands." Even Colonel Clarence Edwards (1859-1931) of the Bureau of Insular Affairs admitted that "the Igorrotes were no more representative of the Philippines than the most savage Indians are representative of Americans."[35]

Media Reinforcement of WASP Hegemony

When George Dorsey (1868–1931), an anthropologist at the Field Museum in Chicago, arrived in the Philippines in 1912 his description matched his preconceived notions of its people. He described the dock workers as pirates, who

> at first sight might look familiar, like undersized, underfed mulattoe.... On closer investigation you decide that they are a new breed of men ... a little like the Japanese, a little like Malays ... and ... blood will tell, a little like negroes [sic]. These are the Filipinos, our Little Brown Brothers. But when a white man addresses them they degenerate instantly. They become just scrubby stevedores, clad in shirts that may have been whole once, trousers that merely answer the purpose, and hats, no two alike, all fished out of ash barrels.[36]

Filipinos were judged not only by their physical stature, but by their apparel as well. Adoption of western clothing assumed a greater level of civilization and a measure of social capital.

Humiliating racial comparisons purporting to show Filipino deficiencies continued throughout the American occupation. The National Geographic Society, established in 1888, contributed greatly to such perceptions in its presentation of the Philippines and its many peoples. By 1912 its membership had swelled to more than 100,000 as the Spanish-American War and its aftermath raised Americans' geographical and cultural interests. Between 1898 and 1908 the society's magazine published thirty articles alone on the Philippines "that justified or reinforced expansionist ideologies . . . for new overseas markets . . . and a moral responsibility to bring progress, self-government, and material prosperity to the so-called weaker races of the earth."[37] Among its early contributors was W J McGee, then one of the society's vice presidents, who espoused American superiority "as the strongest stock the world has seen. . . . Fit representatives of humanity, invincible in war yet generous to fallen foes, subjugators of lower nature, and conquerors of the powers of primal darkness. . . . who seeks ever to lift to his own plane the world's weaklings, whether white or yellow, red or black."[38]

Dean Worcester was another early and frequent contributor who expounded upon the natural resources of the islands, but found the indigenous people to be "as a rule extremely ignorant . . . harmless and simple children of nature" in an 1898 article.[39] Worcester would continue to publish denigratory articles on Filipinos throughout his long tenure in the country. A long article in the November 1913 issue of the *National Geographic* portrayed the Filipinos as savages and slaveholders, whose men were effeminate and whose women were masculine. He characterized them as primitive and bloodthirsty, wild headhunters, who were exceedingly filthy, superstitious spirit worshippers, who not only practiced human sacrifice, but ate the victims. Worcester claimed that the Negritos are "probably the lowest type of human beings known and . . . not far above the anthropoid apes . . . absolutely incapable of civilization."[40] He further stated that the Ilongots were "so primitive that they are unable to count beyond ten," and the Moros were "unexcelled pirates and slave traders, treacherous and unreliable to the last degree."[41] Worcester, however, found redeeming virtues in the power of sport. A photo of Igorot boys engaged in a baseball game stated that "baseball is one of the really important things which the Bureau of Education has taught the boys. . . . These games serve to bring the people together and results in endless good."[42] In his trips to the United States Worcester earned considerable sums by lecturing and offering slide shows that presented the Filipinos as primitive, exotic, and erotic beings.

Robert Bennett Bean (1874–1944), an anthropology professor at the University of Michigan, accepted a similar post at the Philippine Medical School. In 1910 he published a book entitled *The Racial Anatomy of the Philippine Islanders*, using Worcester's photos and his own research in Manila, in which he classified human beings based on "ear form, cephalic index, nasal index and other factors, that such types may be studied in families through several generations to establish their hereditary characteristics."[43] Not far removed from previous studies in phrenology, Bean measured the ears, noses, and heads of students and corpses and made subjective assessment of intelligence based on students' grades in their classes. He judged the Benguet Igorot girls as pretty, while men of the same tribe as ugly, and suspected Indian ancestry in one town near Manila because of residents of "tall stature, almost black skin, long nose and open-eyed expression as of surprise, a characteristic East Indian countenance."[44] He further determined that "by the ear alone the susceptibility to tuberculosis may be indicated," and that ears provided a better indicator of race than skin color. His ultimate objective was racial classification for the purpose of selective breeding, a key component of the eugenics movement popular during the late nineteenth and early twentieth centuries.[45]

American officials in the Philippines placed their faith in sport as a means to develop a bigger, stronger, and healthier stock among the varied tribes in the archipelago. By 1913 the *New York Times* reported the physical and moral transformation achieved through baseball. "Actual measurements show that the young Filipinos are becoming more healthy and robust, and increasing in stature over their fathers. The game takes most of the youths away from cockfighting and gambling, to which their fathers and uncles are still devoted, and it is contributing much to make the coming generation of Filipinos a sane and healthy people."[46]

Eugenicists favored sterilization of those that they deemed physically, intellectually, and morally inferior. Other Americans, including David Barrows (1873–1954), who served as superintendent of the Manila school system, wrote a history of the Philippines and a 1910 article in *Popular Science Monthly* that claimed the persistence of headhunting and the murder of an American researcher who had lived among the Ilongots for a year before his death. He described the males as "short, with long bodies and short legs, weak, with effeminate faces, and occasionally bearded." Americans often belittled the masculinity of Filipino men, and Barrows asserted that the taking of heads offered proof of masculinity within the tribe and was a requirement for marriage. Such descriptions continued to fuel white Americans' perceptions of their own superiority.[47]

Social Segregation

Whites believed that despite their superior qualities their morality could be compromised by the climate in the tropics and their bodies were susceptible to its parasites. Benjamin Kidd (1858–1916), synthesized his Social Darwinian beliefs with the Social Gospel movement in his influential book, *Social Evolution*, in 1894. He followed that with *The Control of the Tropics* in 1898, in which he stated that "in climactic conditions which are a burden to him; in the midst of races in a different and lower stages of development; divorced from the influences which have produced him, from the moral and political environment from which he sprang, the white man . . . tends himself to sink slowly to the level around him."[48] By 1904, Episcopalian bishop Charles Brent (1862–1929) asserted that "the Orient is no fit place for persons, especially young men, who have not moral stamina. The Philippines are almost the sure undoing of the weak." He buttressed his argument by claiming that church attendance in Manila had declined considerably.[49] As early as 1901 the colonial government established laboratories to study such effects. The following year cholera ravaged Manila and smallpox afflicted other areas. Worcester, as Secretary of the Interior, put hundreds of Filipino homes to the torch, but cholera epidemics continued to take heavy tolls in later years, and whites feared contagion by contact with Filipino bodies. A journalist remarked that "in the American and European life of Manila . . . there is scarcely any social communication between the two races."[50]

If an American married a Filipino during the colonial period he would be banished from the American community. One female member of the Anglo community explained that "as to marrying a Filipino, no woman one could speak to would even dream of such a horrible fate."[51]

In 1904, the US government called upon Daniel Burnham (1846–1912), architect for the 1893 World's Fair, to reconstruct the Philippines to American standards. Burnham's selection was aided by his close friendship with W. Cameron Forbes (1870–1959), a colonial administrator who later became governor general. Forbes and Burnham recommended each other to President Teddy Roosevelt for the Philippines posts. In Manila, Burnham located a complex of government buildings near the bay on elevated sites with the Hall of Justice at the highest point. Symbolically Filipinos would have to look up to such edifices. He placed streets diagonally, radiating from the city center "because every section of the Capital City should look with deference toward the symbol of the Nation's power [sic]."[52] A magnificent park known as the Luneta was constructed upon landfill dredged from the harbor and a lengthy boulevard named for the American hero, Admiral George Dewey (1837–1917), skirted the bay. The private Army and Navy Club adjoined the Luneta along the oceanfront, and the opulent Manila Hotel rested on prime property near the bay. The American-owned *Manila Times* newspaper praised the structure "as a striking introduction to Manila for all incoming tourists."[53] Burnham ecstatically described the area as "magnificent. . . . This site will be finer than anything in any capital in the world . . . [the] most prominent spot in Manila." Americans obtained a ninety-nine-year lease on the property, and the best land was reserved for American ownership. Manila streets would assume the names of American heroes to honor the colonial rulers and inspire the deference of the indigenous residents.[54]

Burnham's vision included concepts derived from his European sojourns. He believed that Manila might develop its waterways like the canals of Venice, a winding river as in Paris, and a bay such as in Naples.

"Manila has before it an opportunity unique in the history of modern times, the opportunity to create a unified city equal to the greatest of the Western World [sic] with the unparalleled and priceless addition of a tropical setting." The plan, however, rested upon western, and particularly American ideals of aesthetics and social order as defined by the City Beautiful movement, where monumental structures located upon conspicuous sites both established and objectified American dominance.[55]

Burnham was also charged with the design of Baguio, the summer capital located in the mountains of northern Luzon in order to protect Americans from the dreaded tropical heat in Manila. There too, Burnham placed the government buildings at an elevation on the hillsides with a plaza in front of the government complex, whose setting provided it with "preeminence over all other buildings of the city." The governor general warranted his own mansion. The commercial district lay on a meadow and a peaceful artificial lake offered repose. A trade journal, the *Inland Architect*, acclaimed the design as one which would "develop civilizing influences side by side with commercial advancement."[56] Baguio served as an elite enclave with lots and residences priced for Americans and the wealthy Filipinos who became collaborators in the colonial government.[57]

CHALLENGES TO WHITENESS

White hegemony, however, was under assault. The US failure to recognize Emilio Aguinaldo's (1869–1964) nationalist movement resulted in years of warfare and even under the American occupation the Filipino Nationalist Party campaigned for independence. As early as 1903, W. E. B. Du Bois (1868–1963), a black intellectual, identified "the problem of the twentieth century is the problem of the color-line."[58] It was not an issue confined to the United States, as indigenous peoples began to challenge their colonial masters on a global scale.[59]

Throughout the latter half of the nineteenth century Japan absorbed western knowledge and technology to assume a position of global importance by the end of the period. It assumed the Pacific region to be its own domain and in 1894 it declared war on China over the control of Korea. The quick Japanese victory and occupation of the peninsula signaled its rising status in the region.[60]

In 1900, Chinese insurgents rebelled against foreign domination, killing European officials and Christian missionaries, until the western powers and Japan sent military forces to restore their domination. In 1904 the Russian-Japanese War erupted over Russian incursions in Korea and conflicting interests in Manchuria. The Battle of Mukden in that region resulted in nearly 200,000 casualties, but a Japanese victory over a white nation. President Theodore Roosevelt brokered the peace agreement for which he was awarded the Nobel Peace Prize.[61] Growing Japanese ascendance in the Pacific, however, would eventually result in confrontation with the United States in the nearby Philippines.

Less bloody, but equally visible assaults on Social Darwinian beliefs occurred in the public confrontations occasioned by sporting events. In the United States white ballplayers began driving black players from the highest echelons of the national game in the 1880s. At the racetracks, however, black jockeys continued to demonstrate their mastery. Isaac Murphy (1861–1896) captured the Kentucky Derby in 1884, 1890, and 1891, before jealous whites chased him from the sport. Willie Sims (1870–1927) then defeated his white opponents in the same race in 1896 and 1898, earning $300,000 by 1901. His successor, Jimmy Winkfield (1882–1974) then won consecutive Kentucky Derbies in 1901 and 1902, before whites' retaliatory measures forced him to seek his fortune in Europe. On the popular cycling tracks Marshall "Major" Taylor (1878–1932) established seven world records between 1898 and 1900, capturing the world championship in the latter year despite the tactics of white opponents who tried to force him off the track. In 1901 he too opted for competition in Europe and Australia, where he garnered as much as $10,000 annually.[62]

Football evolved from the British games of soccer and rugby to become the favorite of the upper classes at American colleges in the late nineteenth century. At a time when many males feared the growing feminization of the culture, football symbolized a rugged masculinity. G. Stanley Hall, the eminent psychologist, feared that "too much association with girls diverts the youth from developing his full manhood."[63] Theodore Roosevelt particularly favored the game. In an 1893 article he stated that athletics create "the virtues which go to make up a race of statesmen and soldiers, of pioneers and explorers . . . of bridge-builders and road makers, of commonwealth builders . . . [they] minimize dissipation . . . and fight against debauchery. . . . Of all these sports there is no better sport than football."[64]

W. Cameron Forbes, who greatly promoted sports as governor-general of the Philippines, had previously been a football coach at Harvard. As a youth he considered football coaches "the greatest men on earth." He had played with a broken nose and expected his players to exhibit the same stoicism and tenacity. He did not allow his players to take time-outs and denied them the services of doctors or masseuses to heal their injuries. Even medicines were forbidden.[65]

Roosevelt thoroughly agreed, often extolling the opportunities to practice self-sacrifice, courage, leadership, and morality, while instilling a martial spirit necessary for the global role that he envisioned for the United States. In an address at the Harvard Union he stated

I emphatically disbelieve in seeing Harvard or any other college turn out molly coddles instead of vigorous men. . . . I do not in the least object to sport because it is rough. . . . We cannot afford to turn out college men who shrink from physical effort or from a little physical pain. In any republic, courage is a prime necessity for the average citizen if he is to be a good citizen; and he needs physical courage no less than moral courage, the courage that endures, the courage that will fight valiantly against the foe of the soul and the foes of the body. Athletics are good, especially in their rougher forms, because they tend to develop such courage. They are good also because they encourage a true democratic spirit, for in the athletic field, the man must be judged not with reference to outside and accidental attributes but by a combination of bodily vigor and moral quality which go to make up prowess.[66]

While football enabled WASP elites to demonstrate their physical prowess and masculinity in public spectacles, it also enabled people of color to challenge the precepts of racial superiority. Carlisle Indian School, established in 1879, required the Native American students to cut their hair, adopt Anglo clothing, speak English, learn vocational skills for the industrial workforce, and assimilate into the mainstream white culture. Sports became a primary means of teaching the American value system, and by the last decade of the twentieth century the Carlisle football team confronted the eastern powers, defeating Penn in 1899 and both Harvard and the Army team of West Point Military Academy thereafter. The competitions with Army were particularly significant for the Indians as a form of surrogate warfare in which they might exact symbolic retribution for the violence perpetrated upon their ancestors. Despite the Indians' success as one of the top teams in the country, the white media continually portrayed them as savages, similar to the depictions of the Filipinos. The 1912 Carlisle team, featuring Jim Thorpe (1887–1953), led the entire nation in scoring and Thorpe was proclaimed the world's greatest athlete after winning both the pentathlon and decathlon at the 1912 Olympic Games and defeating a host of white competitors in the process.[67] In addition to Thorpe the 1912 Olympic team included his Carlisle teammate, Louis Tewanima (1888–1969), Hawaiian Duke Kahanamoku (1890–1968), Howard Drew (1890–1957), an African American, and Gaston Strobino (1891–1961), an Italian American (not yet considered to be white), a clear refutation of the supposed debility of people of color.

The ultimate assault on the doctrine of white racial supremacy, however, came in the sport of boxing, as individuals publicly displayed their courage, skills, stamina, and toughness in gruesome altercations that might last for hours. It was believed at the time that the boxing ring was the only place in which a black man could hit a white man without going to jail, and interracial fights were crowd favorites. While some black boxers in the lower weight classes gained recognition as world champions, opportunities for black heavyweights proved limited. In 1891 Peter Jackson (1860–1901), the best of the black heavyweights, fought a 61 round draw with James J. Corbett (1866–1933). When Corbett wrested the heavyweight crown from the seemingly invincible John L. Sullivan (1858–1918) the next year, he invoked the color ban instituted by Sullivan, refusing to fight any man of color and possibly relinquishing the symbolic crown as the toughest man in the world. Whites thus maintained their monopoly until 1908.[68]

When Jim Jeffries (1875–1953) retired as the undefeated champion in 1905, the title eventually fell to Tommy Burns (1881–1955), who traveled to Australia to maximize the value of his new title. Jack Johnson (1878–1946), considered to be the black champion of America, followed, and managed to secure a title bout, which he won decisively, deriding his white opponent in the process. Johnson, bold, brash, proud, and highly skilled continued to decimate white challengers, known as the "great white hopes," over the next two years, until Jim Jeffries finally agreed to come out of retirement and restore the crown to its rightful place among the white race. They met in Reno, Nevada, on July 4, 1910, in front of a raucous crowd of twenty thousand who traveled to the desert to witness Johnson's undoing, but they were miserably disappointed, as Johnson easily destroyed Jeffries, breaking his nose, and knocking his blood spattered body through the ropes (Jeffries had never been knocked down). In the aftermath race riots ensued throughout the country as blacks rejoiced and whites retaliated. Johnson further enraged white society by cohabiting and marrying a series of white women as he continually challenged white societal norms and values. Unable to defeat him in the ring, white officials charged him with crimes that forced him to flee the country. He relinquished his title in a controversial fight in Cuba in 1915, later spent a year in prison, and was never again accorded a chance to fight for the championship.[69]

Such racial statements were not lost on Filipinos, who anxiously awaited the film of the Johnson-Jeffries bout in Manila. They waited in vain as the municipal board banned its showing.[70] Despite the introduction of automobiles, like Jack Johnson, some surly drivers of the horse-drawn coaches on Manila streets refused to yield to their supposedly social superiors.[71] Filipino athletes also began to test the assumption of white prowess in the Americans' own sport forms. Soon Filipino boxers adopted and adapted the American sport to their own culture, not only challenging the Americans in the islands, but on the American mainland.

Americans had taught their national game of baseball to the Filipinos, and by 1911 Luis Santiago, the principal of an intermediate school in San Mateo, assumed the role of pitcher on his school team that proved so successful that it defeated an American army team in a series of games. Two years later Filipino employees defeated their American bosses in a volleyball game, a sport invented by the American YMCA. The Filipinos cleverly maneuvered the ball by repeated hits, while the less inventive Americans returned each hit on the first volley. When the Filipino strategy proved victorious, the Americans changed the rules to limit the Filipinos to only three hits, while they were permitted unlimited touches.[72]

INSTILLING RACIAL FEARS

Despite such evidence to the contrary racialists continued to promote the belief in white superiority. Edward Alsworth Ross (1866–1951) obtained his PhD in political economics, but worked mainly as a controversial sociologist at several universities. A prolific author who favored eugenics, Ross was elected president of the American Sociological Association in 1914. In that year he published *The Old World In the New: The Significance of Past and Present Immigration to the American People*, in which he once again categorized people into subordinate racial groups, with people of color ranking below those of lighter skin. He feared that the immigration of those he deemed inferior would dilute the intelligence, the morality, and the beauty of the Anglo-American stock.[73] His stature as a respected intellectual gave credence to such assertions.

Such beliefs were reinforced with the publication of Madison Grant's (1865–1937) *The Passing of the Great Race or the Racial Basis of European History* in 1916. Similar to the work of Robert Bennett Bean and the earlier phrenologists, Grant, a lawyer by profession, claimed that skull shapes and sizes could determine criminality. He attributed the best of culture and civilization to the Nordic, and only pure race. He further declared that "moral, intellectual, and spiritual attributes are as persistent as physical characters, and are transmitted unchanged from generation to generation." He advocated sterilization for those he deemed defective. The book became a best seller, buttressing Ross' assertions and Grant's political contacts carried legislative weight.[74]

In 1920 another eugenicist, Lothrop Stoddard (1883–1950), published *The Rising Tide of Color*, which adhered to Grant's racial classifications and predicted a rising nationalism and retaliation by the nonwhite peoples of the world. Several other authors fueled white fears with similar books and articles, and calls for immigration restrictions in the United States. The US Congress passed the Johnson-Reed Act of 1924, which excluded nonwhite immigrants from the country and established annual quotas for European groups. The previous year more than two thousand Filipinos had journeyed to California. A decade later they would be classified as aliens by the Tydings-McDuffie Act and limited to fifty migrants per year.[75]

ENDURING RACISM

One of the migrants, Carlos Bulosan (1911?–1956), followed his two older brothers to the United States in 1930 in search of a better life and the equality promised by his American education in the Philippines. While in the Philippines he had resorted to posing naked for the American tourists in Baguio in order to make some money, and found employment as a houseboy. With the onset of the Depression he found neither a better life nor equality in America. Scarce jobs forced him into menial work for little pay. While living in Los Angeles' Little Manila neighborhood, he found only a demeaning existence. "There was no other district where we were allowed to reside, and even when we tried to escape from it, we were always driven back to this narrow island of despair."[76] "We are not admitted to any American recreations except theaters and some tennis courts."[77]

Bulosan found solace at the public library and in writing as both a poet and a novelist. He found work in the fields picking crops, which only further alienated him and radicalized him. In Oregon his money was taken and he was beaten by police, simply for being a Filipino. He became a labor organizer, which resulted in being blacklisted during the McCarthyism purge of the 1950s. Although he had published many of his works, including a 1944 best seller, Bulosan died in poverty and was buried in a pauper's grave. He had suffered a dehumanizing existence in the nation he had expected to fulfill his dreams. He wrote that "I know deep down in my heart that I am an exile in America. I feel like a criminal running away from a crime I didn't commit. And this crime is that I am a Filipino in America."[78] Despite his literary success, he never achieved whiteness and the social capital attached to it. Filipinos in his homeland also absorbed the American values, technologies, and value systems, but racial attitudes persisted even a half century after the Americans' promise of deliverance, and remained so, especially among the military.

NOTES

1. Edward Said quoted in Walter L. Hixson, *American Settler Colonialism: A History* (New York: Palgrave Macmillan, 2013), 3; www.odec.umd.edu/CD/RACE/CRT.PDF (July 7, 2015). Whiteness studies and their debates can be followed in Reginald Horsman, *Race and Manifest Destiny: The Origins of American Racial Anglo-Saxonism* (Cambridge, MA: Harvard University Press, 1981); David R. Roediger, *The Wages of Whiteness: Race and the Making of the American Working Class* (London: Verso, 1999 [1991]); Theodore W. Allen, *The Invention of the White Race: Racial Oppression and Social Control* (London: Verso, 1998); Lee D. Baker, *From Savage to Negro: Anthropology and the Construction of Race, 1896–1954* (Berkeley: University of California Press, 1998); Matthew Frye Jacobson, *Whiteness of a Different Color: European Immigrants and the Alchemy of Race* (Cambridge, MA: Harvard University Press, 1998); Matthew Frye Jacobson, *Barbarian Virtues: The United States Encounters Foreign Peoples at Home and Abroad, 1876–1917* (New York: Hill & Wang, 2000); David R. Roediger, *Working Toward White-*

ness: How America's Immigrants Became White, The Strange Journey from Ellis Island to the Suburbs (New York: Basic Books, 2005); Eric Arnesen, "Whiteness and the Historians' Imagination," *International Labor and Working Class History*, 60 (Fall 2001), 3–32; Peter Kolchin, Whiteness Studies: The New History of Race in America," *Journal of American History*, 89:1 (2002), 154–73; and C. Richard King, "Cautionary Notes on Whiteness and Sport Studies," *Sociology of Sport Journal*, 22:3 (2005), 397–408.

2. Yehudi O. Webster, *The Racialization of America* (New York: St. Martin's, 1992), 33–63; Stephen Jay Gould, *The Mismeasure of Man* (New York: W. W. Norton, 1996 [1981]); William H. Tucker, *The Science and Politics of Racial Research* (Urbana: University of Illinois Press, 1994), 9–36; "*The Modoc War*," PBS, WYCC, Chicago (July 9, 2015); "*Forgotten Ellis Island*," PBS, WYCC, Chicago (July 11, 1915). See Miroslava Chavez-Garcia, "Youth of Color and California's Carceral State: The Fred C. Nelles Youth Correctional Facility," *Journal of American History*, 102:1 (June 2015), 47–60, on intelligence testing and authorities' reluctance to believe the superior intelligence of a black inmate.

3. Zimmerman, *First Great Triumph*, 35–6; Richard Slotkin, "Buffalo Bill's Wild West and the Mythologization of the American Empire" in Kaplan and Pease, eds., *Cultures of United States Imperialism*, 164–81; John R. Procter, "Isolationism or Imperialism, *Forum*, XXVI (September 1898), 14–26, and John Barrett, "The Problem of the Philippines," *North American Review*, CLXVII (September 1898), 259–67, both quoted in Welch, *Imperialists vs. Anti-Imperialists*, 25, 66, respectively.

4. Miller, *"Benevolent Assimilation,"* 15.

5. Joseph O. Baylen and Jack Hammond Moore, "Senator John Tyler Morgan and Negro Colonization in the Philippines, 1901 to 1902," *Phylon*, 29:1 (1968), 65–75. Samuel McCall, cited in Christopher Lasch, The Anti-Imperialists, the Philippines, and the Inequality of Man," *The Journal of Southern History*, 24:3 (August 1958), 319–31 (quote, 328).

6. Ibid., 328.

7. Ibid., 330.

8. Kenton J. Clymer, *Protestant Missionaries in the Philippines, 1898–1916: An Inquiry into the Colonial Mentality* (Urbana: University of Illinois Press, 1986), 72–74.

9. Arthur Judson Brown, quoted in Janet M. Davis, "Cockfight Nationalism: Blood Sport and the Moral Politics of American Empire and Nation Building," *American Quarterly*, 65:3 (September 2013), 549–74 (quote, 558).

10. Kimberley Alidio, "'When I Get Home I Want to Forget': Memory and Amnesia in the Occupied Philippines, 1901–1904," *Social Text*, 59 (Summer 1999), 105–22 (quotes, 117, 118, respectively).

11. Paul A. Kramer, *The Blood of Government: Race, Empire, the United States and the Philippines* (Chapel Hill: University of North Carolina Press, 2006), 112, 122–24 (123, quote), 179–81.

12. Anne Paulet, "To Change the World: The Use of American Indian Education in the Philippines," *History of Education Quarterly*, 47:2 (May 2007), 177–202 (quote, 176).

13. Census of Philippine Islands, 1903–1905, in Kaplan and Pease, eds., *Cultures of United States Imperialism*, 187–207.

14. Bain, *Sitting in Darkness*, 76.

15. Richard E. Welch, Jr., "American Atrocities in the Philippines: The Indictment and the Response," *Pacific Historical Review*, 43:2 (May 1974), 233–53 (quote, 241).

16. Karnow, *In Our Image*, 154.

17. Joy S. Kasson, *Buffalo Bill's Wild West: Celebrity, Memory, and Popular History* (New York: Hill & Wang, 2000), 83–88, 90–121.

18. R. Reid Badger, *The Great American Fair: The World's Columbian Exposition and American Culture* (Chicago: Nelson Hall, 1979), 17, 91–106 (quote, 106); David Brody, "Building Empire: Architecture and American Imperialism in the Philippines," *Journal of Asian American Studies*, 4:2 (June 2001), 123–45.

19. Niko Besnier and Susan Brownell, "Sport, Modernity, and the Body," *Annual Review of Anthropology*, 41 (2012), 443–59. Culin was a cofounder of the American Anthropological Association in 1902.

20. Kramer, *The Blood of Government*, 233–37.

21. William John McGee preferred to use only his initials without periods in his identification. Nancy J. Parezo, "A 'Special Olympics': Testing Racial Strength and Endurance at the 1904 Louisiana Purchase Exposition" in Susan Brownell, ed., *The 1904 Anthropology Days and Olympic Games: Sport, Race, and American Imperialism* (Lincoln: University of Nebraska Press, 2008), 59–126 (quote, 64).

22. *The Greatest of Expositions: Completely Illustrated*, official publication (St. Louis, MO: Samuel F. Myerson, 1904), 192.

23. Ibid., 230.

24. Ibid., 237–38.

25. Ibid., 232 and 226–27 respectively.

26. Ibid., 233.

27. Clark M'Adams, "Cheer Up, Mere Man! You Are The Real–Real Beauty," *St. Louis Post-Dispatch*, October 23, 1904, Section 3:1.

28. Parezo, "A 'Special Olympics,'" 65.

29. Ibid., 74–77 (quote, 75); Mark Dyreson, "The Physical Value of Races and Nations: Anthropology and Athletics at the Louisiana Purchase Exposition," in Brownell, ed., *The 1904 Anthropology Days and Olympic Games*, 127–55.

30. Parezo, "A 'Special Olympics,'" 87–93.

31. Gerald R. Gems, "Anthropology Days, the Construction of Whiteness, and American Imperialism in the Philippines," in Brownell, *The 1904 Anthropology Days and Olympic Games*, 189–216.

32. Ibid., 92–97, 104 (quote); Henning Eichberg, "Forward Race and the Laughter of Pygmies: On Olympic Sport," in Mikulas Teich and Roy Porter, eds., *Fin de Siecle and Its Legacy* (Cambridge, UK: Cambridge University Press, 1990), 115–131.

33. Gerald R. Gems, *For Pride, Profit, and Patriarchy: Football and the Incorporation of American Cultural Values* (Lanham, MD: Scarecrow Press, 2000), 122. Dietz's Native American ancestry is contested, but he did attend two Indian schools and self-identified as a Native American.

34. Parezo, "A 'Special Olympics,'" 103–10, quote, 105.

35. Kramer, *The Blood of Government*, 229 and 264–65, respectively.

36. *Chicago Sunday Tribune*, July 7, 1912, 8.

37. Julie A. Tuason, "The Ideology of Empire in National Geographic Magazine's Coverage of the Philippines, 1898–1908," *Geographical Review*, 89:1 (January 1999), 34–53 (quote, 35).

38. Ibid., 38.

39. Ibid., 40.

40. Dean C. Worcester, "The Non-Christian Peoples of the Philippine Islands: With an Account of What Has Been Done for Them under American Rule," *National Geographic*, 24:11 (November 1913), 1157–256 (quote, 1180, 1251).

41. Ibid., 1182, 1189, respectively.

42. Ibid., 1252.

43. Robert Bennett Bean, *The Racial Anatomy of the Philippine Islanders* (Philadelphia: J. B. Lippincott, 1910), 8–9.

44. Ibid., 25–146 (quote, 145–46).

45. Ibid., 153 (quote), 217, 220.

46. "Baseball in the Islands," *New York Times*, May 11, 1913, part 5:1, in Dean C. Worcester Papers, Box 3, folder 8, newspaper clippings, in the Bentley Historical Library, University of Michigan.

47. David P. Barrows, "The Ilongot or Ibilao of Luzon," ms. for *Popular Science Monthly* (December 1910), in Fred Eggan Papers, University of Chicago, Special Collections.

48. Kidd cited in Warwick Anderson, "'Where Every Prospect Pleases and Only Man Is Vile': Laboratory Medicine as Colonial Discourse," *Critical Inquiry*, 18:3 (Spring 1992), 506–29 (quote, 512).

49. Rt. Rev. Charles H. Brent, *Religious Conditions in the Philippines*, 1904 pamphlet, Library of Congress.

50. Anderson, "'Where Every Prospect Pleases and Only Man Is Vile': Laboratory Medicine as Colonial Discourse"; Kramer, "Empires, Exceptions, and Anglo-Saxons," 1345–346; Wolff, *Little Brown Brother*, 254 (quote).

51. Karnow, *In Our Image*, 13–14; Mrs. Campbell Dauncey, *The Philippines: An Account of Their People, Progress, and Condition* (Boston: J. B. Millet Co., 1910), 110 (quote).

52. Gems, *The Athletic Crusade*, 178; Thomas Hines, "The Imperial Façade: Daniel Burnham and American Architecture in the Philippines," *Pacific Historical Review*, 41:1 (1972), 33–53; Thomas S. Hines, *Burnham of Chicago: Architect and Planner* (Chicago: University of Chicago Press, 1979), 203 (quote).

53. Brody, "Building Empire," 135.

54. Gems, *The Athletic Crusade*, 51; Burnham to J. G. White, April 10, 1905 (quote), in Daniel Burnham Papers, vol. 15, series 1, at the Chicago Art Institute.

55. Hines, *Burnham of Chicago*, 206–7 (quote); Gems, *The Athletic Crusade*, 52.

56. Hines, *Burnham of Chicago*, 209, 210, respectively.

57. Brody, "Building Empire," 133.

58. W. E. B. Du Bois, *The Souls of Black Folk* (New York: Random House, 1990), xii.

59. See Pakenham, *The Scramble for Africa*.

60. Bradley, *The Imperial Crusade*, 186–99.

61. Ibid., 214–52; Kramer, *The Blood of Government*, 296–97.

62. Gerald R. Gems, Linda J. Borish, and Gertrud Pfister, *Sports in American History: From Colonization to Globalization* (Champaign, IL: Human Kinetics, 2008), 207.

63. Hall, *World's Work* (1908), cited in Kim Townsend, *Manhood at Harvard: William James and Others* (New York: W. W. Norton, 1996), 207.

64. Theodore Roosevelt, "The Value of Athletic Training," *Harper's Weekly* (December 23, 1893), 1236.

65. W. Cameron Forbes, *Football Notebook*, 1901, 2 (quote), in Harvard Archives, HUD 10897.24; Gems, *For Pride, Profit, and Patriarchy*, 78.

66. Roosevelt quoted in *NCAA News*, January 6, 1993, 4.

67. Gems, *For Pride, Profit, and Patriarch*, 119–23. See Michael Oriard, *Reading Football: How the Popular Press Created an American Spectacle* (Chapel Hill: University of North Carolina Press, 1993) on depictions of the Carlisle team.

68. Colleen Aycock and Mark Scott, eds., *The First Black Boxing Champions* (Jefferson, NC: McFarland, 2011.

69. Gerald R. Gems, *Boxing: A Concise History of the Sweet Science* (Lanham, MD: Rowman & Littlefield, 2014), 73–135. The best biography of Johnson is Randy Roberts, *Papa Jack: Jack Johnson and the Era of White Hopes* (New York: Free Press, 1983). See Gerald R. Gems, "Jack Johnson and the Quest for Racial Respect," in David K. Wiggins, ed. *Out of the Shadows: A Biographical History of African American Athletes* (Fayetteville: University of Arkansas Press, 2006), 59–77 for an assessment of Johnson's character; and Theresa E. Runstedtler, *Jack Johnson. Rebel Sojourner: Boxing in the Shadow of the Global Color Line* (Berkeley: University Of California Press, 2012), on Johnson's peregrinations while abroad.

70. Lewis E. Gleeck, Jr., *The Manila-Americans (1901–1964)* (Manila: Carmelo & Bauermann, 1977), 86–87.

71. Michael D. Pante, "A Collision of Masculinities: Men, Modernity and Urban Transportation in American-Colonial Manila," *Asian Studies Review*, 38:2 (May 2014), 253–73.

72. Gerald R. Gems, "Whiteness, Sport, and American Imperialism in the Pacific," *Sportwissenschaft*, 2 (2006), 171–192.

73. www.asanet.org/about/presidents/Edward_Ross.cfm (July 22, 2015); Edward Alsworth Ross, *The Old World In the New: The Significance of Past and Present Immigration to the American People* (New York: The Century Co., 1914).

74. Madison Grant, *The Passing of the Great Race or the Racial Basis of European History* (New York: Charles Scribner's Sons, 1916), 197.

75. James B. Lubinskas, "A Warning From the Past: Lothrop Stoddard and the Rising Tide of Color," *American Renaissance* (January 2000), www.toqonline.com/blog/lothrop-stoddard-and-the-rising-tide-of-color/ (July 22, 2015); Linda Espana-Maram, *Creating Masculinity in Los Angeles's Little Manila: Working-Class Filipinos and Popular Culture, 1920s–1950s* (New York: Columbia University Press, 2006), 4, 19, 42.

76. Bulosan's birth date is disputed. Carlos Bulosan, *America Is in the Heart: A Personal History* (New York: Harcourt, Brace & Co., 1946), 68–69; E. San Juan, Jr., *On Becoming Filipino: Selected Writings of Carlos Bulosan* (Philadelphia: Temple University Press, 1995), 62; Espana-Maram, *Creating Masculinity in Los Angeles's Little Manila*, 41, 117–18.

77. San Juan, *On Becoming Filipino*, 191.

78. Ibid., 198–99; www.historylink.org/index.cfm?DisplayPage=output.cfm&file_id=5202 (quote) (July 24, 2015).

THREE
Military

INCULCATING A MARTIAL SPIRIT

The United States has been/is a warlike nation, built upon violence. Since its advent as an independent country in 1776 every American generation has fought in a war. The westward expansion of the country was believed to be its "manifest destiny," and even a religious obligation. As president, Thomas Jefferson bought the vast hinterlands of the Midwest and West from Napoleon in the Louisiana Purchase of 1803 for $15 million. After a second war against Great Britain in 1812, the US government began systematically removing Native American tribes from eastern lands by force and war. The Texas revolution of 1836 and the Mexican-American War of 1846–1848 resulted in the acquisition of the American Southwest. With the end of the Civil War US troops engaged in a series of Indian Wars to expel the natives from the frontier and consolidate the national territory from the Atlantic to the Pacific oceans. The Spanish-American War of 1898 afforded the United States an opportunity to expand beyond its territorial boundaries into the Caribbean and the Pacific.[1]

That opportunity coalesced with the military strategy devised by Alfred Thayer Mahan, a naval officer and historian, who taught at the new Naval War College, which had been established at Newport, Rhode Island, in 1884. Mahan was appointed the head of the institute in 1886. His most important publication, *The Influence of Sea Power upon History*, published in 1890, had a global influence. Mahan argued that great nations were created by their navies that not only defended the homeland, but acquired and safeguarded commercial shipping routes that built the economy. Hence, the necessity for naval bases around the world, an offensive strategy that initiated an arms race among the major powers and not only rationalized, but fostered colonialism. Mahan asserted that "imperialism is the extension of national authority over alien communities."[2]

Despite his knowledge and his celebrity Mahan did not have the power to enact his principles. Theodore Roosevelt did. A combination of intellect, wealth, social networks, overwhelming ambition, and sheer tenacity assured that Roosevelt would assume a prominent role in the society, but chance and fate determined his ultimate greatness. He proved a thorn in the side of the Republican Party bosses, who ensconced him in the vice presidency as a means to deter his power and influence. He complained that the president "does not intend that I shall have any influence of any kind, sort or description in the administration from the top to the bottom." With the assassination of President McKinley in September of 1901, Roosevelt assumed the office that allowed him to fulfill his national dreams.[3]

As an ardent supporter of Mahan and his theory, Roosevelt had already initiated the naval policy in his role as assistant secretary of the navy, which he assumed in April of 1897. He lobbied for the annexation of Hawaii as a naval base, and during his superior's absence on summer vacation he devised a war plan for combat with Spain, and had George Dewey appointed to command the ships in the Pacific, poised to invade the Philippines.[4]

Shortly after assuming his position as assistant secretary of the navy, Roosevelt addressed the Naval War College.

> All the great masterful races have been fighting races, and the minute that a race loses the hard fighting virtues, then, no matter what else it might retain, no matter how skilled in commerce and finance, in science or art, it has lost its proud right to stand as the equal of the best. Cowardice in a race, as in an individual, is the unpardonable sin, and a willful failure to prepare for danger may in its effects be as bad as cowardice. The timid man who cannot fight, and the selfish, shortsighted man who will not take the steps that will enable him to fight, stand on almost the same plane.[5]

A CRISIS OF MASCULINITY

Roosevelt cherished war as a means to practice, assert, and publicly demonstrate one's masculinity. Like many men of his time he lamented the increasing feminization of culture. Young boys spent their first years under the care of their mothers, then attended school under the tutelage of female teachers. For most, that would be the only schooling that they received. Feminists had been clamoring for suffrage and equality for half a century and women's clubs were assuming greater roles in the public sphere. The Woman's Christian Temperance Union, established in 1873, even crusaded to deny men their simple pleasures. Industrialization further threatened the independence of previously self-employed men, who could not compete with the productivity of factories and had to settle for wage labor and enforced working hours. Women had also found their way into the urban workplaces, usurping roles traditionally held by males and further demeaning masculine pride and privilege. By 1880 women accounted for one-third of all college students, and female graduates began taking the white collar professional positions previously reserved for men.[6]

The stress of such social transition produced a new malady, known as *neurasthenia*. Characterized by lethargy, weakness, pain, and anxiety, it especially affected the middle class who no longer engaged in traditional physical labor. Physicians founded sanitariums to administer a "rest cure" to beleaguered patients. Weakness did not bode well for a nation bent on world leadership.

Perhaps most disconcerting was women's incursions into the male domain of sport. Throughout the latter half of the nineteenth century women took up rowing, sailing, archery, tennis, shooting, golf, baseball, and even challenged men in such individual sports as pedestrianism and cycling. By the 1890s they engaged in the new sports of basketball and volleyball. Such activity required dress reform, including the degenerate bloomers. The deviant female cyclists even began to wear pants. Artist Charles Dana Gibson portrayed such "new women" as young, vivacious, and independent, a threat to male hegemony.[7]

> The New Woman as a figure who had simply followed a new dress fad was ultimately acceptable, because her frivolity was expected. The New Woman whose dress indicated a real change in lifestyle was considerably more threatening, not only because once she shifted her place in society everyone else had to make accommodation, but because she held the physiological key to the next generation.[8]

Moralists held particular concerns for female boxers, whose increasing numbers enabled them to declare world champions by the 1890s. It seemed that football remained the only sport still in the province of men. It held particular esteem for Theodore Roosevelt because it fostered the martial spirit espoused by Mahan and the courage that he deemed necessary for Americans to assume their rightful place as world leaders. The mass plays developed by coaches replicated military strategies and the game was often compared to warfare. While the brutality of football resulted in severe injuries and numerous deaths, it had surpassed the national game of baseball as the preferred sport on college campuses by the 1890s. One college president remarked that "I would rather see our youth playing football with the danger of a broken collar-bone occasionally than to see them dedicated to croquet," while another commentator proclaimed that "an able bodied young man who cannot fight physically can hardly have a true sense of honor, and is generally a milksop, a lady-boy or a sneak. He lacks virility his masculinity does not ring true."[9]

As casualties and deaths mounted, some college presidents banned the game or switched to rugby. During his presidency Roosevelt's son, Ted (1887–1944), had his nose broken in a game against Yale. When the abolition movement reached crisis stage Roosevelt invited the top football coaches to the White House to effect reforms in an attempt to save the game. College presidents soon convened to form the National Collegiate Athletic Association that still governs intercollegiate sport.[10]

THE PARTNERSHIP OF TEDDY ROOSEVELT AND LEONARD WOOD

Football had held particular significance for Roosevelt even before the Spanish-American War. Shortly after the hostilities commenced Roosevelt resigned his position as assistant secretary of the navy on May 6, 1898, in order to organize his own volunteer cavalry regiment, known as the Rough Riders. A journalist stated that "sport is merely artificial work, artificial adventure, artificial colonizing, artificial war," and Roosevelt felt compelled to test his own masculinity.[11] Roosevelt largely recruited cowboys and Ivy League athletes for his troop, gushing over "the best quarterback who played on a Harvard eleven, and a former national tennis champion; a Yale high jumper, and the captain of the Columbia crew"; as well as Colonel Leonard Wood (1860–1927), a former football player and Medal of Honor winner. Roosevelt considered such "real men" to be the masculine ideal, the cream of American manhood. He deferred command of the unit to Leonard Wood, a veteran of the Indian wars. Roosevelt assumed the rank of lieutenant colonel as second in command, a partnership which resulted in a lifelong bond.[12]

As a young boy in Massachusetts Wood relished the outdoor life: hunting, fishing, sailing, and running throughout the environs of Buzzard's Bay. As a young man he studied to become a physician at Harvard, but was dismissed from his Boston internship for overstepping his authority in performing an unauthorized surgery, an indication of his future confrontations with subordination. In 1885 he joined the army as a contract surgeon, sent to the Southwest in pursuit of Geronimo and his warriors. Reassignment to northern California enabled him to meet and marry Louise Condit-Smith (1869–1943), the niece of a Supreme Court justice, and to join the San Francisco Olympic Club football team in 1892. A year later Wood was transferred to Fort McPherson in Georgia, where he organized, coached, and starred on the Georgia Tech team.[13]

> Football satisfied a fundamental need in Wood's make-up. He ceaselessly sought a direct challenge, an opportunity to engage in a contest of physical strength and will. Except for horseback riding and hiking, sports that did not require brute physical strength rarely interested

him. It was the physical aspect of army life that seemed to draw Wood into the service in the first place. The almost compulsive need to test his physical endurance impelled him along during the arduous Geronimo campaign, and it remained an essential characteristic of his personality.[14]

Both Roosevelt and Wood also practiced "the manly art of self-defense," the upper-class euphemism for the working-class sport of boxing. Roosevelt employed Mike Donovan (1847–1918), former middleweight champion, as his instructor in the White House, and he and Wood fenced and contended with cudgel sticks. Wood had also sparred with his commanding officer, General Nelson Miles (1839–1925), in California and even knocked out his superior on one occasion.[15]

Wood transferred to Washington, DC, as physician to the president in 1895, where he and Roosevelt became hiking and dining partners, reinforcing their mutual ambitions and extending their political networks.[16] Biographers described Wood as brusque and humorless, intense and aloof, haughty and confrontational, even imperious, with a sense of superiority. He did not drink, smoke, gamble, or chase women, and was scrupulously honest and forthright, with an attention to detail, for which he was respected and admired. He displayed intense energy, endurance, ambition, and impatience, not unlike Roosevelt himself.[17] Both saw the world through a similar lens based on their social class and upbringing, but in their quest for physical prowess they resembled the working class habitus, where sport not only enhanced their physicality, but provided an outlet for their naturally pugnacious attitudes.[18]

THE CONQUEST OF CUBA

Both men would be tested in the Spanish-American War. Roosevelt's prescience as assistant secretary of the navy resulted in a quick victory for the American navy at Manila Bay on May 1, 1898, only days after formal declarations of war by both countries. The battle for Cuba proved more difficult. Cubans had staged a number of revolts from their Spanish overlords throughout the nineteenth century due to the oppression of the natives. Slavery was not abolished on the island until 1886, but brought little change for the indigenous Cubans. By 1895 a rebel army confronted the Spanish once again and declared the island to be an independent republic on September 13, 1895. The war of liberation was still underway when the American army embarked for the invasion of Cuba.[19]

Roosevelt commandeered supplies and a ship to insure that his Rough Riders would not miss out on what was expected to be a quick triumph. The determined Spanish and a malaria epidemic, however, slowed American progress and success. The Rough Riders did engage in the battles of Kettle Hill and San Juan Hill, suffering a 20 percent casualty rate, as Roosevelt distinguished himself as a military leader. A photo of the regiment atop San Juan Hill (which excluded the African-American soldiers who had also been instrumental in the victory), media accounts, and Roosevelt's own self-promotion made him a war hero. He unsuccessfully campaigned for bestowment of a Medal of Honor, but was soon elected governor of New York.[20]

Wood won appointment as the military commander of Cuba in 1899, a role in which he flourished. He reformed the courts, penal system, and prisons, while addressing corruption. He greatly improved the Cuban infrastructure and sanitation as he promoted research on the cause of malaria. He promoted schools and education, even sending more than one thousand Cubans to Harvard University in order to become teachers in their homeland. As governor general of the island, Wood imposed a ban on gambling and the Spanish sports of bullfighting and cockfighting; although as a jai alai player he allowed the construction of a fronton in 1901. He secured a promotion to brigadier general through his political contacts as a reward, surpassing more than five hundred more senior officers who viewed the appointment as a breach of military etiquette. With the granting of Cuban independence in 1902 Wood left the island to first observe the exercises of the German army in Europe and then for his new post as military governor of Moro Province in the Philippines.[21]

WAR IN THE PHILIPPINES

Despite Dewey's overwhelming conquest of the Spanish fleet, land operations did not proceed as smoothly. Without an army to consolidate a victory over the Spanish, Dewey had to stall the revolutionary leader, Emilio Aguinaldo, and his rebel army, which had the Spaniards surrounded in Manila, until American troops arrived. Dewey had transported Aguinaldo to the Philippines from his exile in Hong Kong and supplied the rebel army with guns and ammunition. Aguinaldo declared Filipino independence on June 18, 1898, and installed himself as the first president. The US army arrived on June 30 after stopping on the way to annex the island of Guam in the Pacific, still held as an American territory today.[22]

Despite Aguinaldo's objections the American army moved in to positions around the capital city in conjunction with the Filipino rebels. American leaders began their own surrender negotiations with the besieged Spanish as tensions heightened between Filipino and American forces. The Americans conducted house searches without warrants, frisked Filipino women, and knocked down Filipino males who they felt did not show them the proper respect. Filipino storeowners had their goods "confiscated," while others were paid with Confederate money. Some received IOUs signed by the likes of George Washington, Thomas

Jefferson, and Andrew Johnson. Sentries shot indiscriminately at residents. One soldier wrote to his father that "we have to kill one or two every night."[23] In mid-August a sham battle was arranged between the Americans and Spaniards to enable the latter to deny surrender to Aguinaldo's insurgent forces. Sensing subterfuge the Filipino army joined the attack on Manila and the resulting confusion concluded with five Americans killed and another thirty-five wounded. American authorities' refusal to recognize the Aguinaldo government continued in a stalemate and joint encirclement of the city until the night of February 4, 1899. While details differ, historians agree that Private William Grayson (1876–1941) of the First Nebraska volunteer regiment fired the shots that ignited the war in the Philippines. Grayson and a Private Miller were on guard duty with orders to keep the Filipinos from encroaching up on American defenses. When four Filipino soldiers ventured within fifteen feet of the roadway, Grayson challenged them, then he and Miller opened fire, killing three of Aguinaldo's rebels. The excited Americans ran back to their colleagues shouting that "the niggers are all through the lines," which engendered a wholesale eruption of gunfire along a ten-mile front and an American attack on Manila over the next twenty-four hours that resulted in 3,000 deaths, including 55 Americans and another 300 wounded. The war had begun.[24]

Aguinaldo's army consisted of more than twenty regiments, well-organized, well drilled, and well clothed. "The people in all the different towns took great pride in this army. Nearly every family had a father, son, or cousin in it."[25] Unable to match the superior firepower of the Americans, Aguinaldo resorted to guerrilla warfare by November of 1899 with greater success. Despite the growing insurrection, General Elwell Otis (1838–1909), commander of the American forces, rarely left his Manila office. Described as a portly insomniac, with mutton-chopped whiskers, and a fussy, pompous micromanager obsessively detailed, Otis continually dispatched rosy messages of American successes to Washington, neglecting to admit any reversals and substantial casualties. With the replacement of Otis by General Arthur MacArthur (1845–1912), the Americans supplanted their pacification efforts in favor of more offensive strategies. MacArthur admitted "when I first started against these rebels, I believed that Aguinaldo's troops represented only a faction. I did not believe that the whole population of Luzon was opposed to us, but I have been reluctantly compelled to believe that the Filipinos are loyal to Aguinaldo and the government which he represents." In the first four months of 1900 the Americans suffered 442 attacks on US troops, which killed 130 and wounded another 322. The attacks only increased during the summer months with fighting spreading throughout the archipelago, and the number of engagements surpassing 1,000. By August the Americans had suffered nearly 1,000 deaths from various causes. Secretary of War Elihu Root urged "methods that have proved successful in our Indian campaigns in the West."[26] By the end of 1900 the United States employed 70,000 troops in the Philippines, headed by 30 generals, 26 of whom were veterans of the Indian wars.[27]

Americans considered guerrilla warfare to be immoral, "treacherous and cowardly," and contrary to civilized means of conducting combat. MacArthur declared that practitioners "divest themselves of the character of soldiers, and if captured are not entitled to the privileges of prisoners of war."[28] MacArthur undertook drastic measures, declaring martial law on December 20, 1900, executing seventy-nine captives, deporting another thirty-two to Guam, including Apolinario Mabini (1864–1903), the prime minister in the revolutionary government. Hundreds more were imprisoned and nationalistic newspapers suppressed. When General Franklin Bell (1856–1919) lectured Mabini on the criminal and uncivilized nature of guerrilla warfare, Mabini replied that might does not make right, and that the strong should not impose on the weak; therefore guerrilla warfare was fair to both sides and that the Filipinos were only protecting their homes from the American invaders.[29]

In 1901 the Americans established a Filipino Constabulary and the Filipino Scouts, both under the command of American officers, in an attempt to gather intelligence by greater integration with the local populace. Members of the Scouts were drawn from the Macabebe tribe, who were enemies of the Tagalogs that formed the backbone of the revolutionary movement. Such military service gave some Filipinos the opportunity to assert their masculinity as the American occupation diminished it in so many other ways. The Constabulary, which served as a local police force, gave the appearance of the indigenous population enforcing itself, rather than succumbing to the dictates of the American occupiers, a tactic still employed by American authorities in the Mideast.[30]

The Constabulary even preceded the Federal Bureau of Investigation established in Washington, DC, in 1908, making it the first federal agency to conduct covert operations. It would eventually employ two hundred spies and keep hundreds of thousands of files, photos, and fingerprints, including psychological profiles on suspects, and even monitored private mail.[31] On one occasion the operatives discovered that a social-athletic club founded by the wily Filipinos in Manila actually served as a storage point for uniforms and bolo knives. The initial intervention in espionage and intelligence operations came too late to alert American troops to avoid suffering their worst defeat of the war.[32]

THE ATROCITIES OF WAR

On September 28, 1901, the police chief, local priest, and disguised infiltrators in the village of Balangiga on Samar Island collaborated in an attack on Company C of the Ninth Infantry Regiment, which composed the American garrison stationed there. A friendly priest had warned the Americans of a plot weeks before he left the area, but they paid no heed to his warning. On the morning of the occurrence the soldiers were at breakfast without their weapons. Upon the ringing of the church bells the infiltrators, who had masqueraded as street cleaners, brandished their bolos and charged the Americans waiting in their service line or enjoying their breakfast. A few Americans grabbed baseball bats in their own defense, while others had only pots, rocks, and assorted clubs. The hand-to-hand combat was brutal, and most were hacked to death, while some of the wounded and other escapees scurried for boats, chased down by the pursuing Filipinos. Of the seventy-four soldiers stationed at Balangiga forty-eight were killed or missing, another twenty-two were wounded but managed to escape to the island of Leyte, and only four survived unscathed. Village women dispatched the wounded with daggers and mutilated the corpses. The hatred was clearly palpable.[33]

Aside from their political differences the Filipinos felt that the American occupiers had violated their human rights and religious beliefs. The Americans had commandeered the sacred space of the church plaza for their baseball games, and local villagers had been forced to labor on infrastructure projects due to a recent earthquake, which made their plot less noticeable as the attackers toiled nearby.[34]

The Ninth Infantry Regiment and a contingent of US marines from the Philippines had participated in the rescue of Americans and other foreigners trapped in China during the Boxer Rebellion only four months earlier. The Boxers, Chinese nativists spurred to violence in reaction to foreign land grabs, missionary proselytism, and loss of their culture, lashed out at the invaders, killing Christians and besieging the foreign legations in Tientsin and Beijing until they were relieved by international military forces. Among the foreign troops, an American officer admitted that "the Japs, in my humble opinion, are the best soldiers in China. Only the Japs can equal Americans and I hope we will never have to find out which is better." The Chinese retaliation proved to be a harbinger of Asian retribution over the course of the twentieth century.[35]

Only a few years later Japan attacked Russia in 1904 igniting a brief war over conflicting aspirations in Asia, a confrontation that Japan won decisively. The United States then had to seriously consider Japan as a rival in the Pacific. The US military devised a potential war plan, and Teddy Roosevelt launched the Great White Fleet of sixteen battleships on a worldwide cruise as a demonstration of American might, which was warmly received with a monumental, five-day, festive celebration in Japan. Still Leonard Wood wrote that "Japan is going ahead in a perfectly methodical philosophical way to dominate the Far East and as much of the Pacific and its trade as we and the rest of the world will permit. When she has a good excuse she will absorb the Philippines unless we are strong enough to prevent it."[36]

Racism lay at the core of many atrocities perpetrated by both sides in the Philippines, but the Americans, who had pledged "benevolent assimilation," drew the most ire. At least fifty-seven cases of murder, torture, rape, and torching of civilian homes and another sixty cases of aggravated assault were documented and hundreds of accusations leveled.[37] American soldiers freely looted Filipino homes, businesses, cemetery vaults, and the gold in churches for souvenirs. A Boston newspaper reported that "the 1st Colorado Company from Cripple Creek . . . got off the boat at New York with enough church goods to fill a large store."[38] A soldier of a Washington regiment admitted that "some of the boys made good hauls of jewelry and clothing. Nearly every man has at least two suits of clothing, and our quarters are furnished in style," and a captain claimed "enough plunder for a family of six."[39] Major Edwin Glenn (1857–1926) did not deny the charge that he made forty-seven prisoners kneel and 'repent their sins' before ordering them bayoneted and clubbed to death." Such carnage seemed typical. In another unit "some Tennessee boys were ordered to escort 'thirty niggers' to a hospital in the rear and 'get there with about a hundred chickens and no prisoners.'" A Missouri trooper remarked that "I don't know how many men, women and children the Tennessee boys did kill. They would not take any prisoners."[40] The Filipinos were considered less than human and indiscriminate killing resulted. A soldier from Utah stated that "the old boys will say that no cruelty is too severe for these brainless monkeys . . . and fill the blacks full of lead before finding out whether they are friends or enemies." When official reports indicated that five Filipinos were killed for every one wounded, a clear reversal of normal averages, General Otis claimed that it was due to the superior marksmanship of the soldiers who emanated from the American South and West. General MacArthur further rationalized the minimal American casualty rates compared to Filipinos by stating that "men of Anglo-Saxon stock do not succumb as easily to wounds as do men of 'inferior races.'"[41]

Perhaps another reason was the discovery in 1900 that Americans were using dum dum bullets, which expand upon impact to create greater trauma. A sergeant in the 43rd Infantry also provided an explanation for the high death count among Filipinos in a letter to his hometown newspaper in Maine. "On Thursday, March 29, eighteen of my company killed seventy-five nigger bolo-men and ten of the nigger gunners. . . . When we find one that is not dead, we have bayonets."[42]

Senator Albert Beveridge offered support for the Americans by claiming that the wounded Filipinos were "as carefully, tenderly cared for as our own. . . . Senators must remember that we are not dealing with Americans or Europeans. We are dealing with Orientals. . . . They mistake kindness for weakness, forbearance for fear."[43] One of the techniques used to extract information from prisoners involved the "water cure," which was still employed in Vietnam and during the American wars in the Mideast. It involved suppressing or tying down the prisoner before placing a bamboo tube in his mouth (optional), and forcing water down his throat, which can be forced from the stomach and repeated. Other versions place a cloth over the victim's mouth and pour water on to his face to simulate drowning. Both cases can be fatal. One soldier claimed that he administered such torture to 160 Filipinos and only 26 survived the ordeal.[44]

Mary Cole, an American teacher in the Philippines, wrote home about the torture conducted on the mayor of her town in 1902.

> As he told of the cruelty with which he had been treated I felt disgraced. They pounded him over the head with bottles, striking his shaven spot because he was a padre. We saw the great sores they made. His neck was very sore, showing where ropes had been, also on his wrists and ankles. He would be drawn up by ropes and let down with a thud, bruising his body dreadfully. There are great sores all over his body. They tied his hands and feet, then filled him with water and then jumped on him with their feet. They also cut the chord [sic] under his tongue and he was given nothing to eat. Wouldn't such treatment make insurrectos of anybody?[45]

The mayors of two towns had earlier been beaten to death with rattan rods. In another case a Private Jones of the 11th Cavalry related how

> his troop, upon entering a wedding party, fired into the throng, killing the bride and two men, and wounding another woman and two children. A captain and a lieutenant of the 27th Regiment were tried for hanging six Filipinos by their necks for ten seconds "causing them to suffer great bodily pain." After the words were changed to "mental anguish," the officers were found guilty and sentenced to reprimands.[46]

A soldier from California related the means of policing a town. "We make everyone get in the house by seven p.m. and we only tell a man once. If he refuses we shoot him. We killed over 300 natives the first night. They tried to set the town on fire. If they fired a shot from a house we burn the house down and every house near it, and shoot the natives, so they are pretty quiet in town now." Another regaled in the killing, stating that "this shooting human beings beats rabbit hunting all to pieces." Another admitted "I am probably growing hard-hearted, for I am in my glory when I can sight my gun on some dark skin and pull the trigger." When an American unit was ambushed every town within a twelve mile radius was incinerated; when an American was killed, an entire town of 1,000 men, women, and children was annihilated.[47]

General Otis claimed such occurrences as only isolated incidents in retaliation for Filipino atrocities. The army censored dispatches from Manila and noncompliant journalists faced deportation. Although Aguinaldo ordered his soldiers to treat any American prisoners with care, some were castrated and their genitals stuffed in their mouths, which only further incensed the Americans.[48]

General J. Franklin Bell (1856–1919) managed to pacify the southern area of Luzon by engaging in a war of extermination in which 54,000 civilians died in Batangas alone in 1901. Bell created concentration camps, similar to the incarceration stockades that the Spanish authorities used in Cuba that brought outcries from American activists. Bell characterized his enclosures as safe military zones, where people were herded into vastly overcrowded structures that fostered cholera. In areas where an American or friendly Filipino was killed, prisoners of war, including town officials and other citizens, would be chosen at lot and executed in retaliation. In Batangas 1,300 prisoners were forced to dig their own graves and a priest was commandeered to hear their confessions, which took two days. Then the priest was hanged before the prisoners met their fate. In another case an entire village was wiped out, only a beautiful mestiza mother was spared, only to be raped by the American officers and their troops.[49]

The American revenge for the attack on Balangiga proved so extreme that it generated a Congressional investigation in 1902. General Jacob Smith (1840–1918) ordered the soldiers to turn Samar into a "howling wilderness" and kill anyone over the age of ten capable of carrying a weapon. "I want no prisoners. I wish you to kill and burn; the more you burn and kill the better it will please me."[50] He further explained that "Every native, whether in arms or living in the pueblos or barrios will be regarded and treated as an enemy until he has conclusively shown that he is a friend. This he cannot be by mere words or promises, nor can it be done by aiding us in ways that do no material harm to the insurgents." Smith was court-martialed for his directives, but only admonished for his use of imprudent language. President Roosevelt forced him to retire.[51]

A marine major, Tony Waller (1856–1926), conducted an ill-fated and poorly led expedition across Samar after the Balangiga massacre in which he lost a substantial number of men. Waller accused his Filipino porters of plotting against him and harboring their own food as the marines starved. He ordered eleven of the porters to be executed, resulting in a highly publicized court martial in which he was exonerated. A junior officer, Lt. Preston Brown (1872–1948), was convicted of killing a prisoner and sentenced to five years, but Roosevelt commuted his sentence to half pay for nine months and a demotion on the seniority list for promotion. General Bell was promoted to army chief of staff.[52]

Despite abundant evidence of Americans' criminal behavior, most cases were whitewashed and dismissed, rationalized as necessary when fighting "savages." A doctor who served as a witness claimed that the Americans' minds were impaired by the tropical climate. David Barrows, head of the Manila school system, asserted that the water cure injured no one and that the concentration camps were voluntary and even provided a higher standard of living for their residents. Secretary of War Elihu Root offered that the atrocities "were few and far between—exceptions in a uniform course of self-restraint, humanity, and kindness."[53]

The evident racism shown in the investigation permeated the army, and affected the African American soldiers. Whites refused to salute black officers, and blacks served in segregated units. The 25th Infantry Regiment was the first to arrive on July 31, 1899, and was met at the docks by a white who yelled "what are you coons doing here"; to which a witty black replied "we have come to take up the white man's burden." Additional black units followed: the 24th Infantry Regiment, the 48th and 49th Volunteer Infantry, and the 9th and 10th Cavalry.[54] Service in the Philippines presented a dilemma for the black soldiers, torn between their intent to show their own hard won American citizenship and its implied patriotism versus their sympathy for an oppressed people of color like themselves. Only a few months after arrival, John Galloway, a member of the 24th Infantry, wrote to the *Richmond Planet*. "The whites have begun to establish their diabolical race hatred in all its home rancor in Manila, even endeavoring to propagate the phobia among the Spaniards and Filipinos so as to be sure of the foundation of their supremacy when the civil rule that must necessarily follow the present military regime, is established."[55] Galloway predicted that the Filipinos would suffer the same fate as southern blacks in the United States. Some of the black press even hailed Aguinaldo as a hero.[56]

Black soldiers mixed freely with the natives, some even marrying Filipinos. In the most extreme cases, some black soldiers defected to the rebel army. The most famous of them, David Fagen, achieved widespread celebrity, even becoming an officer in Agunaldo's army. Fagen had previously served in the Cuban campaign and had been promoted to corporal, but became alienated in the Philippines, joining the guerrillas on November 17, 1899, and leading raids and taking a number of American captives, all of whom reported benevolent treatment. The US army employed bounty hunters and offered a $600 reward for Fagen, and on December 5, 1901, a native hunter produced a partially decomposed head and some artifacts purportedly belonging to Fagen, whom he claimed he mortally wounded after befriending the fugitive in the Luzon wilderness. He claimed that Fagen's Filipino wife drowned in the encounter while trying to escape the onslaught. The army, however, continued to pursue Fagen for another ten months without capture.[57]

Black soldiers who married Filipinos were discharged and sent home, and Governor General Taft complained to the US government that the blacks "got along too well with the native women" and recommended their reassignment to America. Before their normal rotation date the black regiments were sent to Hawaii in 1902. Miscegenation concerns arose again in the summer of 1904 as a melee involving hundreds erupted when whites attacked Filipino Scouts, whom they accused of fraternizing with white women.[58]

Another story, perhaps apocryphal, claimed that one of the black deserters brought along a pair of boxing gloves, with which he tutored the Filipino revolutionaries. In any case the Filipinos had to be aware of the Social Darwinian athletic struggles that took place among the American military forces. Soldiers were allowed one day per month for sports that reinforced martial spirit and camaraderie, resulting in baseball, boxing, and track competitions, where the skills of black athletes were undeniable. As early as 1901 the YMCA also requested the need of a swimming pool and a weight room. The next year a baseball park was built in Manila and a city league ensued thereafter. The African-American regiments were eventually returned to the Philippines, where the 25th Infantry Regiment perennially won the army baseball championship, and blacks' victories over white teams provided particular joy. The Manila League also produced perhaps the greatest of all black ballplayers, Oscar Charleston (1896–1954). Charleston entered the army at the age of fifteen, serving with the 24th Infantry, and first starred in the Manila Baseball League. In the track and field competition Charleston covered the 220 yards in 23 seconds, before returning to the United States and a Hall of Fame career in the Negro Leagues.[59]

The US Army had greater visible success in capturing Aguinaldo than it did with David Fagen. Aguinaldo hid out in the mountains of northern Luzon for fifteen months, eluding the American forces, fending off attacks from tribal adversaries, and planning military operations until his capture on March 23, 1901, by means of a spectacular ruse devised by Colonel Frederick Funston (1865–1917). Eighty Macabebe Scouts, loyal to the Americans, masqueraded as Filipino guerrilla fighters, who delivered Funston and a few colleagues to Aguinaldo at his secret headquarters. After being fed and cared for, the "prisoners of war" and their accomplices then turned on their captors, taking Aguinaldo as their own hostage, and delivering him to the American authorities in Manila. President McKinley promptly rewarded Funston with a promotion to brigadier general.[60]

Aguinaldo acquiesced to American dominion and called for a cessation of hostilities, but fighting continued for another year on Luzon and sporadically thereafter. As president, Theodore Roosevelt declared a formal end to the war on July 4, 1902, at a cost of 4,234 US dead and 2,818 wounded, with an estimated 20,000 Filipino guerillas and 200,000 civilians killed. By 1903 the number of American troops in the Philippines was reduced to 17,748 from a peak of 71,528 in 1901. Despite Roosevelt's proclamation, violence persisted on Luzon until 1911, and most earnestly in Mindanao until 1916.[61]

MORO WAR

The Muslims of the southern archipelago resented the American administrative practices, construction projects, policies, and taxes as not only intrusions, but as the decimation of their own culture. The cholera epidemics that attacked the population were also attributed to the American occupation. Captain John Pershing (1860–1948), a white officer who led a black cavalry unit in Cuba, was then assigned to Mindanao. He noted that "the Moro considers himself the rightful owner of the country he has inhabited for generations. This assumed lordship, acknowledged from time immemorial by surrounding peoples and tribes, has become so deep-rooted in his mind that he resents the slightest indication of encroachment or interference." Such differences resulted in attacks on Americans, leading to the Battle of Bayan in May of 1902 that cost twelve American and as many as five hundred native lives, the first major encounter in a long war with the Muslims. The lax governance of the Moros up to that point changed abruptly with the appointment of General Leonard Wood as governor of the territory in 1903. Wood abolished the Moro practice of slavery, invited Christian immigrants from the northern islands, built roads and schools with taxes on the locals, and undermined the power of local chiefs by creating a constabulary and western style court system.[62]

Wood tried to introduce the Moros to agriculture and capitalism and his taxation system made the Moro Province the most profitable in the islands by 1905, but not all the *datus* (chieftains) proved receptive to the wholesale transition. In Wood's thirty-two months as governor more than one hundred battles ensued, with the Battle of Bud Dajo on the island of Jolo from March 5–8, 1906, being the most critical. Wood's troops, assisted by the Moro Constabulary, assaulted hundreds of Moros holed up in the rim of an extinct volcano. A fierce battle ensued with bayonets and hand-to-hand combat, but superior American technology prevailed. A survivor related that "they turned that machine gun on them and they'd stand there, the Moros would, and just look like dominoes falling." The American charge up the mountain eventually became a slaughter. Among the Americans and their allies, twenty-one lay dead and seventy wounded, but as many as nine hundred Moro men, women, and children were piled in trenches, documented by ghastly photos that were published by the anti-imperialist media in America. Wood censored his report of the carnage and claimed that the killing of women and children was "disagreeable," but "unavoidable."[63] Pershing wrote his wife, "I would not have [that] on my conscience for the fame of Napoleon." The reports set off a firestorm in the United States, but the colonial administrators, the military, and Roosevelt closed ranks in support of Wood, who covered his own tracks with falsehoods that diminished his faults.[64]

Wood showed little remorse, trap shooting shortly after the battle at a gun club. Despite the deprivations of life in the Philippines, Wood lived lavishly in an exquisite residence in Zamboanga, horseback riding, hunting, and playing tennis to maintain his fitness. He wrote that "troops are energetic and efficient in accordance with the energy of the officer who commands them, and his energy and efficiency depend very much upon his physical fitness." His soldiers followed his lead with baseball and football games and monthly field days.[65]

Wood had already been promoted to military commander of the Philippines before the battle of Bud Dajo, and he took the same attitude to Manila once the media refocused its attention on the great San Francisco earthquake of 1906. The further task of "civilizing" the Moros fell to Jack Pershing, who experienced a rapid rise in the army and returned to Mindanao as governor of the Moro Province in 1909. Like Wood, he managed to stay fit with daily rides throughout the countryside, which would be helpful as he dispersed his troops among the local population (yet another strategy employed in Vietnam). One of Pershing's directives, however, proved highly unpopular, resulting in the last big battle of the Moro War. He had ordered all Moros to disarm and relinquish their bolos, a symbol of masculinity, which caused a revolt in 1911 and another in 1913. A constabulary officer explained "it was a terrible thing to take the barong (knife) away from a Joloano Moro. You were taking away his visible masculine characteristics. You made him a woman and less than a woman. . . . When they (the constabulary) met a Moro wearing a barong they called for the blade. If he resisted or started to run, they shot him and entered it into their report." The crisis erupted once again in Jolo when the recalcitrant Moros gathered atop Bud Bagsak, a series of mountain fortresses in June of 1913. It took five days for the Americans and their Filipino allies to conquer the besieged warriors, but the results were inevitable: 15 American dead and 25 wounded. The estimate of Moro slain exceeded 500 (although Pershing only recorded 200–300), and an unknown number of wounded. It proved to be the bloodiest year of the Moro War.[66]

The Moros persisted in their defiance, but ultimately they lacked a united effort and consistent leadership, making it easy for the Americans to play off rivals against one another. They even defrayed Moro nationalism into sports competition by inviting northern Filipinos to the province to challenge their religious and political opponents in baseball games. Moro land was sold off to Christian settlers and American corporations. By 1924 the Moros felt compelled to petition the US Congress. "You have left us defenseless, and it is your duty to protect us or to return to us the weapons you took from us, and which we freely gave you, relying on your promise."[67]

INTERWAR YEARS

The American entry into World War I provided Filipino males with an opportunity to reassert their smothered masculinity under the American administration. The Philippines raised a National Guard Division and more than 28,000 volunteered, but the war terminated before their activation. Filipinos were allowed to serve in the US Navy, but only as stewards in the mess hall as servants to white officers. General Leonard Wood returned to the Philippines as governor general in 1921 and initiated military departments in the universities and officer training programs, where many of the future politicians received their leadership schooling. He particularly wanted "Filipino youth to master the manly arts of self-defense—wrestling and boxing—[to] develop he-men who become high class citizens." With commonwealth status granted in 1935 the autonomous Philippine government under Manuel Quezon (1878–1944) established a national army with a draft in 1936, resulting in 40,000 trainees a year later. The Philippines Military Academy, modeled on the American version at West Point, denied entry to any whose physical appearance did not measure up to acceptable standards, eliminating any applicants who were physically repulsive, ugly, featured large birthmarks or moles, or any disfigurements caused by injury or surgery. Students received lessons in dancing, ballroom etiquette, and gymnastics, and other sports as a means to develop a westernized version of masculinity.[68]

While Filipinos built their military forces their American tutors lived quite well during the interwar years. The Army and Navy Club in Manila contained a bar, a barber shop, a swimming pool, tennis courts, rooms for dining and playing cards, a library, a ladies' room with a beauty specialist, and a gym with fitness equipment. The club hosted dances in addition to the less formal social events, but exclusive membership required the personal recommendation of at least two of the club directors. A branch of the club also existed in the mountain retreat of Baguio by 1931, but the continued segregation between Americans and Filipinos throughout the interwar era grated on the locals.[69]

At Fort McKinley, six miles southeast of Manila, the soldiers had 1,800 acres of land with bowling alleys, billiard tables, a gym, and athletic fields to pass their time. Personnel at Fort Mills on the island of Corregidor in Manila Bay, had their own golf course, tennis courts, bowling alleys, basketball courts, and regular boxing matches for entertainment.[70]

Manila provided a host of activities for both military personnel and American employees or ex-patriates. In addition to the cabarets and vaudeville and movie theaters, and numerous fraternal clubs, the Manila Hotel offered upscale musical shows. The Manila Yacht Club was established in 1927, followed by the Wack Wack Golf Club. The elite Polo Club also offered Sunday baseball games that drew big crowds.[71]

World War II

The Japanese conquest of the Philippines in 1942 replaced an American occupier with an Asian one. In the process Manila was destroyed, Baguio bombed, the English language banned, and an Asian nationalism promoted, but much stayed the same, and ultimately, the United States assumed the role of liberator. Filipinos served in the American military, but within segregated units. They continued to contend in the American sports of baseball and boxing even while incarcerated in prisoner of war camps. In Manila the Japanese replaced the American baseball league with one of their own. The infamous Bataan Death March, in which as many as 2,000 American and 25,000 Filipino captives perished, forged an emotional and national bond that had not previously existed between the occupier and the occupied. In the aftermath of the war the Filipinos finally achieved their cherished independence in 1946.[72]

THE LEGACY OF MILITARISM

Despite independence, the nearly half century of American rule greatly affected Filipino society. The traditional Malay society that had practiced gender equality gave way to the American emphasis on masculinity. The promotion of the western military model, heroic soldiers, and its faith in male leadership resulted in decades of dictatorial rule, only allayed with the ascension of Corazon Aquino to the office of president in 1986. Women were not admitted to the Philippine Military Academy until 1993.[73]

The United States' involvement in the Philippines proved to be only an initial venture into Asian hegemony, as it soon fought wars in Korea and Vietnam to safeguard its markets and values, employing some of the same tactics, strategies, and policies developed earlier. Despite acknowledgement of the Philippines as an independent nation, the United States maintained its hold on the Filipino economy, and secured ninety-nine-year leases on its massive naval base at Subic Bay and Clark Air Base for its air force to enable further operations in Asia. Between 1952 and 1964 thirty-one Filipinos were killed by Americans on US bases, but no Americans were tried for their deaths. After a century of political, economic, social, cultural, and military intercourse, relations were still characterized as "mutual suspicion, distrust, contempt, and hostility. After six decades, the American still feels that if he goes into the Filipino community he will be gypped, clipped, stripped; and the Filipino is still a stranger in the American community."[74] That sense of alienation and segregation permeated social and political relations throughout the American occupation.

NOTES

1. Gerald R. Gems, "Sports, War, and Ideological Imperialism," *Peace Review*, 11:4 (Winter 1999), 573–78.

2. Miller, *"Benevolent Assimilation,"* 5; Bradley, *The Imperial Crusade*, 69–70; Karnow, *In Our Image*, 83; Zimmerman, *First Great Triumph*, 13 (quote).

3. Zimmerman, *First Great Triumph*, 401.

4. Ibid., 238–44.

5. Ibid., 239.

6. Lynn D. Gordon, *Gender and Higher Education in the Progressive Era* (New Haven, CT: Yale University Press, 1990), 2; Ann Douglas, *The Feminization of American Culture* (New York: Anchor Books, 1977), 80–117; Gems, *For Pride, Profit, and Patriarchy*, 47–49; Michael S. Kimmel, "Men's Response to Feminism at the Turn of the Century," *Gender and Society*, 1–3 (September 1987), 261–83; see Mark C. Carnes and Clyde Griffen, eds., *Meanings for Manhood: Constructions of Masculinity in Victorian America* (Chicago: University of Chicago Press, 1990), 195, on males' attempts to bar women from the professions.

7. Gems, *For Pride, Profit, and Patriarchy*, 49–50.

8. Patricia Marks, *Bicycles, Bangs, and Bloomers: The New Woman in the Popular Press* (Lexington: University Press of Kentucky, 1990), 208.

9. Gems, *For Pride, Profit, and Patriarchy*, 21–22, 56 (quote); 71–109.

10. Ibid., 82–83.

11. Price Collier, "Sport's Place in the Nation's Well-Being," *Outing* (July 1898), 382–88; Zimmerman, *First Great Triumph*, 268–312.

12. Gems, *For Pride, Profit, and Patriarchy*, 75; Millis, *The Martial Spirit*, 217–19; Zimmerman, *First Great Triumph*, 273–76, 297; H. W. Brands, *American Colossus: The Triumph of Capitalism 1865–1900* (New York: Doubleday, 2010), 518 (quote). Wood's Medal of Honor was conferred for his participation in the long chase to capture Geronimo, the Apache warrior and chief.

13. Jack C. Lane, *Armed Progressive: General Leonard Wood* (Lincoln: University of Nebraska Press, 2009 [1978]), 1–21. Wood was born in Montpelier, Vermont, but raised in Massachusetts.

14. Ibid., 20.

15. boxrec.com/media/index.php?title=Human:88547 (August 1, 2015); Gems, *Boxing*, 56; Lane, *Armed Progressive*, 20, 117.

16. Jeffers, *Colonel Roosevelt*, 34–35,

17. Lane, *Armed Progressive*, xv–xvi; Zimmerman, *First Great Triumph*, 372, 374.

18. See Pierre Bourdieu, *Outline of a Theory of Practice* (Cambridge, MA: Cambridge University Press, 1972), 72–87, on the concept of habitus.

19. Gems, *Athletic Crusade*, 82–98; Howard Zinn, Mike Konopacki, and Paul Buhle, *A People's History of American Empire* (New York: Metropolitan Books, 2008), 31–53.

20. Zinn, et al., *A People's History of American Empire*, 49; Zimmerman, *First Great Triumph*, 278–80, 296–97. President Bill Clinton awarded the Medal of Honor to Roosevelt posthumously in 2001. Theodore Roosevelt, Jr. received the same honor for his World War II service on D-Day.

21. Zimmerman, *First Great Triumph*, 375, 386, 413; Lane, *Armed Progressive*, 102–31; Gems, *Athletic Crusade*, 86–87.

22. Millis, *The Martial Spirit*, 81, 223–54, 330–36.

23. Wolff, *Little Brown Brother*, 320; Bain, *Sitting in Darkness*, 76–77, 77 (quote).

24. Ibid., 333–36, 354–60; Anderson and Cayton, *The Dominion of War*, 332, offers approximate casualty figures; Wolff, *Little Brown Brother*, 9–11; Karnow, *In Our Image*, 106–30; Donald Chaput, "Private William W. Grayson's War in the Philippines, 1899," *Nebraska History*, 61 (1980), 355–66.

25. Millis, *The Martial Spirit*, 384.

26. David J. Silbey, *A War of Frontier and Empire: The Philippine-American War, 1899–1902* (New York: Hill & Wang, 2007), 142; Hixson, *American Settler Colonialism*, 171(quote).

27. Zimmerman, *First Great Triumph*, 386–87; Gregg Jones, *Honor in the Dust: Theodore Roosevelt, War in the Philippines, and the Rise and Fall of America's Imperial Dream* (New York: New American Library, 2013), 98, 137, 195. Jones lists 254 deaths from combat, 20 suicides, 40 drownings, and 653 deaths from disease by the end of July, 1900.

28. Hixson, *American Settler Colonialism*, 173; Welch, "American Atrocities in the Philippines," 237.

29. Kramer, *The Blood of Government*, 134–36.

30. McCoy, "Philippine Commonwealth and Cult of Masculinity," 320; Zimmerman, *First Great Triumph*, 389; Anderson and Cayton, *The Dominion of War*, 372; Wolff, *Little Brown Brother*, 311 (quote), 317, 330, 334; Kramer, *The Blood of Government*, 113–14; Alfred McCoy, "Philippine Commonwealth and Cult of Masculinity," *Philippine Studies*, 48:3 (2000), 315–46, argues that the Constabulary, which required American officers until 1917 was yet another means to emasculate Filipino males.

31. Alfred W. McCoy, "Policing the Imperial Periphery: Philippine Pacification and the Rise of the US National Security State," in Alfred W. McCoy and Francisco Scarano, eds., *Colonial Crucible: Empire in the Making of the Modern American State* (Madison: University of Wisconsin Press, 2009), 106–15.

32. Ibid.; Wolff, *Little Brown Brother*, 176.

33. Stephen Bonsal Papers, Library of Congress, "Philippines, Balangiga, 1901–1945" file; Silbey, *A War of Frontier and Empire*, 190–93; Wolff, *Little Brown Brother*, 354–57; Welch, "American Atrocities in the Philippines," 238; William T. Sexton, *Soldiers In the Sun: An Adventure in Imperialism* (Freeport, NY: Books for Libraries, 1971 [1939]), 270. Gregg Jones, *Honor in the Dust*, 219–40, 407, disputes the mutilation claims, stating no such remarks in the initial report, and that Filipinos' belief in desecration of the body would bring bad luck and that lack of time precluded the possibility. Such reasoning fails to consider that many of the American deaths throughout the war resulted from being hacked to death with bolos, and the American relief force only arrived after the town had already been evacuated. Jones, 314, indicates survivors later testified relative to the mutilation.

34. Wolff, *Little Brown Brother*, 354–57.

35. Jones, *Honor in the Dust*, 175–85; Edward M. Coffman, *The Regulars: The American Army, 1898–1941* (Cambridge, MA: Belknap Press, 2004), 33 (quote).

36. W.M. Hoeger to Leonard Wood, November 7, 1904; Admiral George Dewey to My Dear President, August 4, 1904, Leonard Wood to Dear Bishop Brent, March 24, 1910 (quote), all in Library of Congress, Leonard Wood Papers, Philippines Box; Jim Rasenberger, *America, 1908: The Dawn of Flight, the Race to the Pole, the Invention of the Model T, and the Making of a Modern Nation* (New York: Scribner, 2007), 40–48, 65–66, 156–57, 242–44.

37. Welch, "American Atrocities in the Philippines," 234.

38. Wolff, *Little Brown Brother*, 254.

39. Hixson, *American Settler Colonialism*, 173; Miller, *"Benevolent Assimilation,"* 187–88 (quote).

40. Ibid., 189; Wolff, *Little Brown Brother*, 252.

41. Ibid., 189 (all quotes).

42. Wolff, *Little Brown Brother*, 305 (both quotes). Dum dum bullets are prohibited in modern warfare.

43. Zimmerman, *First Great Triumph*, 347.

44. Ibid., 406–12; Miller *"Benevolent Assimilation,"* 213.

45. Alidio, "When I Get Home, I Want to Forget," 112.

46. Wolff, *Little Brown Brother*, 306 (quote), 307.

47. Bain, *Sitting in Darkness*, 83–84 (all quotes).

48. Ibid., 83–85; Zimmerman, *First Great Triumph*, 405; Karnow, *In Our Image*, 178.

49. Wolff, *Little Brown Brother*, 358; Miller, "*Benevolent Assimilation*," 207–8, 238–39, 241, 243; 245; Welch, Jr., "American Atrocities in the Philippines." American strategists resurrected the concept of "'free fire zones' in Vietnam, in which civilians were removed to safe territories and anyone who remained was presumed to be an enemy.

50. Welch, Jr., "American Atrocities in the Philippines"; Zimmerman, *First Great Triumph*, 410–12; Kramer, *The Blood of Government*, 145–51, Miller, "*Benevolent Assimilation*," 213–41, 261; Wolff, *Little Brown Brother*, 357 (quote).

51. Alidio, "When I Get Home, I Want to Forget," 108 (quote); Silbey, *A War of Frontier and Empire*, 201–6.

52. Jones, *Honor in the Dust*, 253–66, 282–95; Miller, "*Benevolent Assimilation*," 218, Zimmerman, *First Great Triumph*, 409. Both Waller and Brown retired as major generals.

53. Welch, Jr., "American Atrocities in the Philippines," 243 (quote), 247; Miller, "*Benevolent Assimilation*," 216, 261. Root's excuse was made in September, 1902, several months after the inquiry.

54. Miller, "*Benevolent Assimilation*," 193; Silbey, *A War of Frontier and Empire*, 107 (quote), Daylen and Hammond Moore, "Senator John Tyler Morgan and Negro Colonization in the Philippines," 70; Runstedtler, "The New Negro's Brown Brother," 105.

55. Willard B. Gatewood, Jr., "*Smoked Yankees*" *and the Struggle for Empire: Letters from Negro Soldiers, 1898–1902* (Fayetteville: University of Arkansas Press, 1987), 4, 14, 21, 244–45, 252 (quote).

56. Runstedtler, "The New Negro's Brown Brother," 109–11.

57. Ibid., 241–42; Michael C. Robinson and Frank N. Schubert, "David Fagen: An Afro-American Rebel in the Philippines, 1899–1901," *Pacific Historical Review*, 44:1 (February 1975), 68–83; Miller, "*Benevolent Assimilation*," 192, asserts that of the 200,000 who served in the islands, 15 deserted, among them 9 of the more than 5,000 African Americans. Robinson and Schubert provide a figure of 29 black desertions and agree on the 9 defectors. They report that 20 defectors were sentenced to death, but Roosevelt commuted the sentences of all except 2 black deserters.

58. Miller, "*Benevolent Assimilation*," 193; Kramer, *Blood of Government*, 276; Gatewood, "Smoked Yankees," 241–43; 15–16 claims that approximately 500 black soldiers remained in the islands to form an African-American colony; Runstedtler, "The New Negro's Brown Brother," 113, claims more than 1,200 who stayed in the Philippines.

59. Second Conference of the Secretary of the Army-Navy Department of the YMCA, Manila, Philippine Islands, September 14–23, 1901, YMCA Archives, Philippines Box, 1901–1973; Runstedtler, "The New Negro's Brown Brother," 112; Gems, *The Athletic Crusade*, 177; Coffman, *The Regulars*, 111: coe.kstate.edu/annex/nlbemuseum/history/players/charleston.html (August 3, 2015).

60. Bain, *Sitting in Darkness*, 13, 278, 283; Zimmerman, *First Great Triumph*, 393.

61. Zimmerman, *First Great Triumph*, 393; Karnow, *In Our Image*, 194; Guerrerro, *Philippine Society and Revolution*, 35; Vince Boudreau, "Methods of Domination and Modes of resistance: The U.S. Colonial State and Philippine Mobilization in Comparative Perspective," in Julian Go and Anne L. Foster, eds., *The American Colonial State in the Philippines: Global Perspectives* (Durham, NC: Duke University Press, 2003), 256–90, 265 on troop reductions. Hixson, *American Settler Colonialism*, 169, 238, estimates total Filipino deaths as high as 400,000.

62. Lane, *Armed Progressive*, 120–31; James R. Arnold, *The Moro War: How America Battled a Muslim Insurgency in the Philippine Jungle, 1902–1913* (New York: Bloomsbury Press, 2011), 14, 27–39, 62, 48 (quote), 87–98. Pershing would rise to commander of the American forces during World War I.

63. Ibid., 104–5, 147–69, 177.

64. Ibid., 171 (quote), 169–77.

65. Ibid., 86, 97, 134–135, 143, 191 (quote) 202.

66. Ibid., 217–43, 241 (quote).

67. Ibid., 13–14, 246, 254 (quote).

68. Stanley, *A Nation in the Making*, 255; Silbey, *A War of Frontier and Empire*, 209; Kramer, *Blood of Government*, 384–85, 398; McCoy, "Philippine Commonwealth and Cult of Masculinity," Celia Bocobo-Olivar, *History of Physical Education in the Philippines* (Quezon City: University of the Philippines Press, 1972), 123–25; Runstedtler, "The New Negro's Brown Brother," 117 (quote).

69. Annual Report, Army and Navy Club, December 31, 1931, in the National Archives, Record Group 350, Box 1074; Gleeck, Jr., *The Manila-Americans*, 147, 157, 195, 232.

70. Gleeck, Jr., *The Manila-Americans*, 245, 248.

71. Ibid., 25, 32, 64–73, 122–24, 136, 169–71, 226.

72. Ibid., 131–40, 145–46, 264; Erlyn Ruth E. Alcantara, "Baguio Between Two Wars: The Creation and Destruction of a Summer Capital," in Angel Velasco Shaw and Luis H. Francia, eds., *Vestiges of War: The Philippine-American War and the Aftermath of an Imperial Dream, 1899–1999* (New York: New York University Press, 2002), 201–23; Espana-Maram, *Creating Masculinity in Los Angeles's Little Manila*, 4, 11, 136–37, 150, 154–57; Lou Antolihao, "From Baseball Colony to Basketball Republic: Post-Colonial Transition and the Making of a National Sport in the Philippines," *Sport in Society*, 15:10 (2012), 1396–412; Miller, *"Benevolent Assimilation,"* 385; Anderson and Cayton, *The Dominion of War*, 385.

73. McCoy, "Philippine Commonwealth and Cult of Masculinity," 316.

74. Michael H. Hunt and Steven I. Levine, *Arc of Empire: America's Wars in Asia from the Philippines to Vietnam* (Chapel Hill: University of North Carolina Press, 2012); Julian Madison, "American Military Bases in the Philippines, 1945–1965: Neo-Colonialism and Its Demise," in Richard Jensen, Jon Davidann, and Yoneyuki Sugitaa, eds., *Trans-Pacific Relations: America, Europe, and Asia in the Twentieth Century* (Westport, CT; Praeger Press, 2003), 125–45, 135 (quote).

FOUR
Politics

THE PHILIPPINES UNDER THE SPANISH

Spaniards originally encountered the Philippines on the first voyage to circumnavigate the world, led by Ferdinand Magellan (1480–1521), a Portuguese navigator in the service of the Spanish crown. Magellan lost his life in the Philippines to warlike natives, but the Spanish returned in 1565 under Miguel Lopez de Legazpi (1502–1572), who managed to consolidate Spanish authority to some degree and initiate the conversion of the natives to Catholicism.

Under Spanish rule hereditary chiefs, known as *datus*, headed villages composed of family units, but *datus* might also own slaves. Villages expanded to become towns with an elected official, and a territory with a significant number of towns was designated as a province with an appointed governor. A governor general officiated over the entire archipelago. Unlike other Spanish colonies, such as Puerto Rico and Cuba, the Philippines were not represented in the Spanish Cortes in Madrid, but remained subject to the governor general of Mexico until 1820. Women enjoyed considerable liberty such as property ownership and the ability to separate from their spouses if desired. In reality, power rested with the Spanish friars, Dominican, Augustinian, and Franciscan priests, who owned much of the land in the northern islands, with peasants reduced to the role of sharecroppers. Under Spanish Catholic rule, slavery and divorce were prohibited.[1]

In time, a social class system developed with *peninsulares*, those born in Spain; *insulares*, those born in the Philippines of Spanish parents; and half-breed *mestizos*, considered to be of the upper class. At the local level government officials assumed the role of overlords, able to impose fines and fees. A portion of the taxes paid their salaries, but many overpaid themselves. Such officials financed the local schools, churches, and public markets with villagers supplying labor, services, and crops similar to the feudal system of Europe. As early as the sixteenth century the Spanish friars established schools of higher education. Many educated Filipinos, known as *ilustrados*, had knowledge, but lacked political power, which resulted in uprisings against the Spanish authorities. The Americans arrived in the midst of such a revolt which had started in 1896.[2]

Jose Rizal (1861–1896), an *ilustrado* studying in Europe, formed an association with like-minded peers to resist Spanish dominance in their homeland. Rizal's 1887 novel, *Noli me Tangere (Don't Touch Me)*, adopted American ideals of liberty and democracy as a basis for revolution. Rizal, a multilingual surgeon, scholar, athlete, and nationalist represented the epitome of Filipino manhood. Upon returning to the Philippines he was exiled to Mindanao and later imprisoned in Manila and executed in 1896. In the islands a number of fractious groups adopted the revolutionary zeal, but disagreed on issues. Andres Bonifacio (1863–1897), head of the Katipunan movement founded in 1892, was co-opted by Emilio Aguinaldo, who had Bonifacio tried and executed for treason in 1897 when he assumed leadership of the mutiny. Although he did not possess the multiple gifts of Rizal, Aguinaldo, an anticlerical Mason, studied law, but did not complete his degree. A poor orator, he possessed physical talents as a marksman, swimmer, rider, and a street fighter, combined with leadership abilities. Where Bonifacio's troops suffered in their battles against the Spanish, Aguinaldo succeeded. After the denial of his independent government by the Americans his guerrilla war against the colonizers endured for three years until his capture in 1901, and sporadically thereafter.[3]

THE SCHURMAN COMMISSION

The First Philippines Commission, headed by Jacob Schurman (1854–1942), president of Cornell University, operated in the newly acquired territory from March 4 to September 15 of 1899. The group had only investigatory and advisory powers and spoke only to foreign and local residents who favored American annexation. General Elwell Otis, the military commander in Manila, resented any civilian intrusion on his authority, but he allied with Dean Worcester, another member of the commission, who proved to be its dominant personality. Worcester wrote much of the commission's report, which stated that "only through American occupation . . . is the idea of a free, self-governing and united Philippine commonwealth at all conceivable."[4] Worcester also won appointment to the Second Philippines Commission, led by William Howard Taft.

THE TAFT COMMISSION

Taft was a Cincinnati native, a Yale graduate, a lawyer, and a conservative judge before accepting the leadership of the commission with directives from Secretary of War Elihu Root to prepare the Filipinos for self-government, provide education, and develop the economy. Consequently, Taft fostered New England–style town governments, but the social elites retained local power, resulting in the formation of political factions. Taft also introduced American teachers into the public school system to better instill a sense of democracy, but the Filipinos were slow to transfer their allegiance. In the provincial capital of Bangued in northern Luzon, only 26 of the 13,000 residents registered to vote in 1900, and only 21 actually cast a ballot.[5] In the Visayan islands of the central Philippines, with more than 2.5 million inhabitants, General Robert Hughes (1839–1909) managed to establish only two civil courts, as he could find few lawyers willing to cooperate with the American occupiers.[6]

In May of 1900 General Arthur MacArthur replaced General Otis in Manila, signaling a change in strategy as MacArthur took the offensive in military campaigns, while Taft worked on greater incorporation of Filipinos in the governance of the islands. Taft built the infrastructure and schools, redistributed the lands previously held by the friars, and encouraged American investment. On July 28, 1900 MacArthur and Taft organized a banquet and offered amnesty to the recalcitrant nationalists, only to be foiled by Filipinos who decorated the hall with their own flag and pictures of Aguinaldo, and then delivered speeches calling for independence. With the continuation of the war the American administration clamped down on revolutionary propaganda by censoring the media. By the end of the year MacArthur declared martial law, and imprisoned hundreds of Filipinos, seventy-nine of which were executed, and another thirty-two banished to Guam.[7]

The American administrators cultivated the Filipino elites, who formed the Federalist political party, which advocated statehood and representation in the American Congress, in opposition to the guerrilla warfare. The Federalists and their American collaborators marked the occasion with a celebration that included brass bands and American flags waving at the Luneta, the seaside park in Manila. Dean Worcester, who assumed the role of Secretary of the Interior in addition to his place on the Taft Commission, claimed responsibility for the Federalist Party. He wrote to his brother that a friend (Frank) "Bourns and I nursed the thing along between us until it was big enough to stand alone." Taft provided $6,000 for *La Democracia*, the Federalist newspaper, while banning oppositional media, and loyal party members soon held a monopoly on the many civil service jobs offered by the American administration.[8]

A Supreme Court decision further incensed Filipinos in 1901 when the American jurists ruled in the Insular Cases that residents in the newly acquired territories accrued no constitutional rights afforded to American citizens. The sedition law outlawed freedom of speech by banning any advocacy of independence. Suffrage was limited to Spanish and English speakers who paid at least $15 per year in taxes, thus excluding the vast majority of Filipinos. Americans retained absolute power, as they filled the roles of all provincial governors and treasurers, and the governor general held veto power over all Filipino initiatives. When the Federalists appealed to Elihu Root in quest of statehood he replied that "statehood for Filipinos would add another serious problem to the one we have already. The Negroes are a cancer in our body politic, a source of constant difficulty, and we wish to avoid another such problem."[9]

Racism continually undermined the American efforts in the islands as well. While Taft purportedly liked the Filipinos, he took a dim view of their abilities. He quickly learned that the US military officers and their wives "regard the Filipino ladies and men as 'niggers' and as not fit to be associated with. We propose so far as we are able to banish this idea from their mind."[10] Taft and his wife both conspicuously danced with Filipinos at joint social functions; Edith Moses, wife of Commissioner Bernard Moses (1846–1930), stated that "When General Bell danced with the daughters of elite Lipa families, he did more 'pacifying' that night than he had accomplished during his entire campaign. . . . It was difficult to make the Filipinos believe in our theory of political equality when so many Americans are disposed to emphasize by their conduct the idea of social inequality." Such occasions proved the exception as both American men and their wives consistently excluded Filipinos, even from such institutions as the Woman's Hospital board and the library, even though the latter was built with funds from the Philippines treasury.[11]

Elsie Clews Parsons (1875–1941), an early feminist sociologist, later an anthropologist and wife of a US senator, claimed that "Race snobbishness seems to be the source of much of the present discontent in the Philippines with the American administration. Between this native aristocracy and the Americans in Manila there is at present little or no social intercourse although the natives have a deep sense of hospitality and are devoted to social festivity."[12] The native aristocracy to which she referred were the *ilustrados* who held much of the wealth of the islands and whatever political power the Americans were willing to delegate.

Filipinos were excluded from most American clubs and leisure activities. Taft, despite his huge girth in excess of three hundred pounds, had been a baseball player in his youth, and his brother owned a professional team, but as he aged he became an avid golfer and served as the first president of the Manila Golf Club. Despite his cordiality and references to "his little brown brothers," Filipinos were not permitted to join the club. Nor were they welcome in the elite Manila Polo Club, the Army and Navy Club, or in American fraternal organizations.[13]

The inclusion of Filipinos in governmental positions and in the numerous civil service jobs did, however, present at least an illusion of democracy. Three Filipinos joined the Taft Commission, but their voices could be overridden by the five American members. There simply were not enough Americans to fill all positions, but English speakers among the Filipinos got preferential selection. Taft indicated the difficulty in attracting suitable Americans for the desired objectives in an early letter to Secretary of War Elihu Root. "Here Oriental corruption, through gambling, prostitution and other vices flourishes in its most luxuriant form, and it is so easy for an American in authority to acquire a great deal of money . . . the real danger in the administration is the inability to secure, not honest Americans, but honest Americans who will not become dishonest under the temptations."[14] Between June of 1903 and June of 1904 the civil service was forced to fire 10 percent of its employees for theft and embezzlement.[15] By 1914 fifteen Americans who served as provincial treasurers had been convicted of embezzlement and sent to prison.[16]

Dean Worcester faced continual attacks on his integrity. As early as 1902 there were allegations of corruption, and a year later it was charged that beside his $15,000 annual salary as a commissioner he had "many business interests, and is becoming wealthy." He sold rice to his friend, Frank Bourns, who then resold it to the government for famine relief at an inflated price.[17] When a Filipino newspaper publically exposed his alleged transgressions, he successfully sued for libel. Yet his biographer described him as "ambitious, tireless, 'scientific,' unscrupulous in pursuit of what he considered right, and ruthless in riding over those who opposed him."[18] Imperious by nature and feared by his underlings, he was treated as a visiting monarch upon his annual tours to the hinterland. Large attendance by townspeople was assured under penalty of beatings. An American teacher who failed to arrange a suitable welcome was soon unemployed, and a Filipino who refused to transport his cargo was killed. Worcester's relatives found ready employment in the government or in American corporations operating in the islands. Aware of government intentions, Worcester, his brother, and a nephew purchased land in Baguio before the commencement of construction for the summer capital, and his land sales, in which he awarded public lands to his nephew and those containing gold to himself, drew a congressional inquiry in 1910–1911. He was exonerated when the vote split along party lines.[19]

While aspiring *ilustrados* felt hampered by Worcester in their economic and political goals, the masses blamed him for their living conditions. As secretary of the interior he addressed the regular cholera epidemics that decimated the islands. The scourge of 1902–1904 killed 109,461, among them 4,386 in Manila, while the 1908 occurrence forced the shutdown of the Manila Carnival. Worcester published a book in which he blamed the cause on the "ignorance and superstition of the common people," while the American-owned *Manila Times* blamed the unsanitary conditions of the poor due to their ignorance. Worcester hired five thousand health inspectors, almost all of them Americans due to his distrust of Filipino competence. Vaccines were tested on Filipino prisoners, ten of whom died in the process. Vaccinators injected Manila residents without warning or compliance, and Worcester's more draconian directives violated Filipino cultural norms. The sick were extracted from their houses without agreement, notification, or accompaniment of kin, who got no updates on their family member until a death notice informed them to retrieve the body. Funerals, Catholic masses, and religious processions were forbidden, and bodies were cremated, drawing the ire of family members. When neighborhood quarantines failed to alleviate the suffering Worcester ordered the wholesale incineration of homes and property without notice, hardly endearing himself to the residents who had little else.[20]

After the Democratic victory in the presidential election of 1912, Worcester submitted his resignation and returned to the United States, where he addressed the National Geographic Society, describing the Filipinos as "peculiarly treacherous, vicious, and savage" and incapable of self-governance.[21] He soon returned to the Philippines as a top executive for an American corporation. In 1923 he still carried enough political capital to assure that his son, who had shot and killed a Muslim employee in an alleged robbery, would gain acquittal. Worcester wrote to then governor general of the Philippines, Leonard Wood, "I, of course, wish to arrange things that my son will not be dragged through the streets of Zamboanga by policemen, a thing which a certain element in this country is very fond of doing with Americans."[22]

Taft had considerably more success as an administrator. Named the first civilian governor general in 1901, he assumed the duties on July 4. Municipal elections for Filipinos who held suffrage ensued soon thereafter, and provincial governors were elected the following year. Taft conducted a census in 1903, but one that adhered to racial categorizations and limited voting rights. Christians were listed as "civilized," while non-Christians were deemed "wild." A census allowed for greater data for taxation and surveillance purposes, and called for an election within two years, but Filipinos did not willingly acquiesce to such intrusions. Census workers—7,627 of them, and all but 125 of whom were Filipinos—were hired at high wages, but they faced assaults by the local residents of whom they inquired. Despite the inclusionary intentions of the American administrators, an American chaplain complained that "the census only regarded as literate those who knew what we term as modern language, English or Spanish. The percentage of literacy among Filipinos, if you include those who know how to read and write their own native language is greater than the percentage of literacy in the United States." Less than 2 percent of the population qualified for suffrage.[23]

The *pensionado* program, initiated in 1903, provided greater benefits for largely *ilustrado* families, by sending their offspring to the United States for education, where they resided with American families. Upon return they were required to serve five years in the civil service. The program served dual purposes by forging closer ties with the American government and insuring that the recipients would return to the Philippines with American values to be instilled in the next generation of national leadership.[24] The United States continues a similar strategy today.

Taft left the Philippines in late 1903 to assume duties as secretary of war in Teddy Roosevelt's cabinet. That same year General Leonard Wood arrived as governor of Moro Province, which consisted of five districts and fifty-one tribal wards in Mindanao and other southern islands inhabited by the Muslims. Wood considered the Muslims to be "religious and moral degenerates." He further stated that "the Moros and other savage peoples have no laws—simply a few customs . . . many of them revolting and practically . . . utterly and absolutely undesirable from every standpoint of decency and good government." The army, rather than civilian officials, governed all Muslim territories and had free license to enact reforms. Army officers considered the civilian leadership in Manila to be weak, corrupt, and too accommodating to the Filipinos. They thought they could convert Muslims' beliefs through education and acceptance of a capitalist economy. To that effect, Wood established a Moro Exchange in Zamboanga that promoted trade and customs duties, built roads and bridges, and encouraged the immigration of whites to Mindanao.[25]

Tasker Bliss (1853–1930) succeeded Wood as military governor. He required the district governors to learn the local dialects, to be tested after eighteen months. Failure to pass the exam meant a discharge from their post. Bliss dispersed American troops more widely throughout the province, but the violence continued. John Pershing followed Bliss as governor and he favored a more diplomatic approach to negotiate with the Moro chiefs, but they remained recalcitrant, resulting in the last major battle of the Philippine War in 1913.[26]

While the Moros continued to befuddle the American administration in the southern islands, the *ilustrados* in the north also pursued a new strategy. By 1904 even the Federalist Party members, who had previously advocated statehood, called for independence. Nationalistic plays fanned the sentiments for liberation until the colonial Supreme Court declared them to be seditious and ordered a ban, along with the symbolic display of the Filipino flag. By 1906 three political parties emerged, all with the common goal of independence. The Independistas argued for a peaceful separation from the United States, the Unionistas saw no need to cooperate with the Americans, and the Urgentistas opted for violent overthrow if necessary. A year later the three factions joined in their common cause as the Nacionalista Party, calling for an independent and democratic government. The first election for a Filipino assembly took place in July of 1907, with the Nationalistas winning 58 of the 80 seats, and they would extend that majority in succeeding elections. Two Filipino representatives were sent to the US House of Representatives in Washington, but they had no voting power. After nearly ten years of American occupation, the Filipinos achieved a voice in the American Congress, albeit a muted one.[27]

The National Assembly authorized funds for the needs of local municipalities, whose administrators determined the means of dispersal. Without any centralized oversight of the funds, such an arrangement allowed local officials to maintain their roles as feudal overlords and a patronage system that had been established under the Spanish. Hiring of family and friends was commonplace and the police force served as their personal servants. American officials derided such practices as corruption, but Filipinos considered it to be a cultural norm.[28]

While the *ilustrado* families managed to consolidate social, economic, and political power in the hands of a few, they also contested with each other for laurels, prestige, and prominence. Two of the elected officials, Sergio Osmena (1878–1961) and Manuel Quezon, had been provincial governors before their election to the assembly in 1907. Osmena became the first Speaker of the Assembly and Quezon the first Senate president in a rivalry that would continue throughout the American occupation.[29]

LIMITED FILIPINIZATION

While the cordial and jovial William Howard Taft had some success in co-opting the Filipino nationalists and initiated their inclusion in the government, his successors demonstrated less initiative. Luke Wright (1846–1922), a former Confederate soldier in the American Civil War, corporate lawyer from Tennessee, and the only Democrat on the Taft Commission, succeeded him as governor in 1904. As governor, Wright and his wife, though a Catholic, refused to socialize with Filipinos, required all government positions to be manned by English speakers, and placed Americans, Spaniards, and the hated friars in such roles. During his early administration, one of Aguinaldo's former generals, Artemio Ricarte (1866–1945), who refused to take the oath of allegiance to the Americans, tried to reignite the Filipino uprising. Editorials in Filipino newspapers excoriated Wright as he increased taxes on land, tobacco, alcohol, and businesses, which alienated even the *ilustrado* collaborators. Wright's inability to work with the *ilustrados* forced his retirement and appointment as US Ambassador to Japan.[30]

Henry Ide (1844–1921), a Vermont judge and civil servant in Samoa, who had been another member of the Taft Commission, briefly succeeded Wright in 1906, but served less than a year. His major accomplishment was a ruse to capture Macario Sakay (1870–1907), another of Aguinaldo's generals who continued to fight the guerrilla war against the Americans after Aguinaldo's apprehension. Sakay even declared himself president of a Tagalog Republic and found support among the proletariat on Luzon. Ide offered him amnesty and invited him to a celebratory event, but when Sakay accepted the offer he was seized, imprisoned, and hanged in 1907.[31]

James F. Smith (1859–1928), a lawyer who joined the army for the Spanish-American War and rose to the rank of general, was appointed to the Philippines Supreme Court, and to the Taft Commission as a replacement in 1903. He served as governor general in his own right from 1906 to 1909. During Smith's reign the Filipinos elected their first national assembly and sent representatives to Washington, but had their national flag banned as a seditious symbol. The imposition of the American flag further substantiated an American rather than a Filipino identity on the occupied country.[32]

During the administration of William Cameron Forbes, who served as governor general from 1909 to 1913, sport became a primary means of Americanization. Forbes emanated from a distinguished background. Ralph Waldo Emerson (1803–1882), an American poet and intellectual leader of the Transcendentalist movement during the nineteenth century, was his maternal grandfather. His paternal ancestors made their money in railroads and the opium trade in China, and his father, William H. Forbes (1840–1897), was a founder and president of the Bell Telephone Company. His son, W. Cameron Forbes, became an accountant, an investment banker, and a diplomat, but his original profession was that of a football coach at Harvard University.[33]

Forbes placed considerable faith in the powers of sport as a means to health, character building, and racial superiority. He claimed that "football is the expression of strength of the Anglo-Saxon. It is the dominant spirit of a dominate race, and to this it owes its popularity and its hopes of preeminence."[34] The Philippines proved too hot for football, but Forbes continued to play baseball, hiked, and spent a part of his own immense fortune to build polo fields and a golf club. A lifelong bachelor, described as a humorless, yet sentimental authoritarian, sport provided the means for him to assert his masculinity. While he necessarily associated with Filipinos, he did not endear himself to them. He would, however, have a great influence upon the Filipino culture.[35]

Forbes first served as Secretary of Commerce and Police and acting governor before assuming the office of governor general on November 24, 1909. During his tenure in office Filipino nationalism continued to assert itself. The Philippine Assembly had already passed a bill that aimed to provide instruction in the schools in local dialects rather than English, which the commission vetoed. When the assembly tried to postpone the use of English in the court system until 1917, Forbes also rejected that proposal in his adherence to Americanization of the Filipino culture. Given the multiplicity of languages in the islands, the Americans deemed the common use of English to be a unifying force in the creation of a nation. Forbes did greatly enhance the infrastructure, building roads and railroads in accordance with the American plan to build the economy. He also attempted a novel experiment to teach democracy and self-government, which started when he was Commissioner of Police. When overcrowding in the Manila prison required construction of a new penitentiary on Palawan Island, Forbes introduced individual land plots for prisoners, who policed themselves, and had their own council and court system. The experiment had limited success as prisoners fashioned their own underground power structure, managed liaisons with women, and expected wages for their work. Still, they largely managed themselves, but the American warden of the enterprise had to resign after misappropriating funds for his own benefit.[36]

Forbes had much more visible success in transforming the Manila Carnival, which originated in 1908 as an exposition for businesses, into a regional athletic festival that emulated the Olympic Games. Forbes did so in conjunction with Elwood Brown (1883–1924), who arrived in 1910 to direct the YMCA in Manila. Brown founded the Philippines Amateur Athletic Federation in 1911 with Forbes as the president of the organization to promote its concept of fair play. Brown predicted "that a great many of the evils that grew up in athletics in the States before definite control was established will never find a foothold in the Philippines or in the Far East." By 1913 the Manila Carnival included national championships for schools, colleges, military and government teams, as well as international competitions with teams from China and Japan. The Filipinos were drawn to the pomp and pageantry of the occasion and the playing of both the anthems of the United States and the Philippines expressed separate national identities that nationalists craved. Moreover, the integrated competition allowed Filipinos to test their physical prowess against other Asians and the precepts of Social Darwinism. At the provincial level Forbes offered prizes and uniforms as regional rivalries developed within the Philippines to further stir a common interest in sport as a national unifier. The emphasis was on American games, such as baseball, basketball, softball, volleyball, swimming, tennis, rowing, golf, polo, soccer, football, bowling, track and field, and boxing. Girls, too, were included in the events, with competition in basketball, foot races, softball, and dancing. By 1913 authorities claimed that 95 percent of schoolchildren were engaged in sports and games. Brown's organization of the Far Eastern Games, to be held every two years, only expanded the participants and the rivalries thereafter.[37]

American officials deemed sport to be an antidote to social ills. J. M. Groves, secretary general of the YMCA in 1911, claimed sport to be a "substitute for the false ideal of a gentleman as a perfumed dandy, afraid of soiling his fingers, an ideal grafted on an Oriental stock." Playing time was determined by individual ability rather than family connections, representative of the American belief in the self-made man and equal opportunity. O. Garfield Jones (1884–1957), who had been an official of the Bureau of Education, stated that "self-governing ability in athletics has now been established, because the reactionary influences of priests and old-line politicians has been nil on the baseball field. . . . The older generation of Filipinos will probably never learn to lose a ball game or a political contest; the younger generation not only will, but in many cases have learned it."[38]

Sport also served a distinct social control function. The Americans engaged in a campaign to ban dance halls and brothels, as the soldiers in the Philippines had the highest rate of venereal disease in the US Army. The surgeon general blamed the poor hygiene among Filipino prostitutes and the minimal cost of procurement (25¢) as the cause rather than the immorality of the soldiers. American policemen were also implicated in a 1912 scandal for accepting graft from such locations. As a result Forbes banned liquor sales and white prostitutes from the red light district, only to have them move elsewhere. The chief of police resigned and the head of the secret police was replaced. The large number of *mestizo* children produced by illegitimate liaisons as well as legal marriages resulted in the formation of the American Mestizo Association in 1914 and a home for destitute children.[39]

Both the American soldiers and the Filipinos gambled on the weekly cockfights and American sports were meant to replace what was perceived to be an abhorrent and uncivilized practice. Elwood Brown reasoned that

> the Filipinos are great imitators. When they see the constabulary soldiers playing . . . and engaging in all sorts of races, it is entirely possible that they will in turn take the games up and substitute them as rapidly as possible for their foolish *sipa* [in which an object is juggled with the feet as in hacky sack or played as a game similar to volleyball, but a rattan ball can only be kicked over the net] and cockfighting.

Americans thought that they could also rid the savage tribes of headhunting, as sport might be an alternative means of demonstrating one's masculinity.[40]

When the American government officials made their annual summer trek to Baguio in the cooler mountains of Luzon, their Filipino servants and employees were unwillingly obliged to accompany them, leaving their families behind. The disconsolate Filipinos retaliated with aggression, defacing buildings and vandalizing plumbing, destroying government papers, and dismantling the bed netting in sleeping quarters. The Americans introduced sports and games to placate their charges and reported that "this year [1911] not one malicious mischief was reported, due to the athletic program which absorbed their attention completely."

Further benefit derived when the employees returned to their provinces and promoted their new interests among the populace.[41]

The cooling breezes of Baguio served as a refuge for Americans, the only municipality designed by and for Americans. The Benguet Road to Baguio was completed in 1905 after five years of construction at a cost of almost $3 million. Forbes rewarded the soldiers with a bounty of ten kegs of beer, a keg of whiskey for the supervising colonel, 3,000 packs of cigarettes, and 21,000 cigars. Baguio reflected American society in its racial and social distinctions. The upper classes only associated with those of the working class who served them. Forbes used his own money to build a polo club and a golf course, where Igorot boys served as caddies. Bishop Brent, head of the Episcopalians in the islands, built a private school in the city, but *mestizos* were not accepted. American laborers were confined to seeking out local Igorot women for their libidinal pleasures, a practice which the good bishop railed against. A major difference, however, was the inclusion of Filipino *ilustrados* as members of the Baguio Country Club as early as 1910. Forbes found it a necessity to reach out to the wealthy *ilustrados* in order to sell all the plots of land in the city and to justify the expense of the magnificent club, which included a bar, a dining room, lockers, showers, reading rooms, a billiards room, sleeping quarters, cottages, a stable for twenty horses, four tennis courts, the polo field, which also served for baseball games and cricket matches, a swimming pool, a croquet site, and the eighteen-hole golf course. Forbes invited the *ilustrados* to Baguio for trapshooting and co-opted Emilio Aguinaldo with American largesse, stating that "General Aguinaldo had his first game of golf and had become a convert at Baguio."[42]

Not all Filipinos catered to American tastes and dictates, however. The Igorot caddies refused to adopt pants and toted golf bags in their customary loincloths, and the waiters who served the Americans in their restricted dining room wore the required white jackets, but sans pants. The local baseball team also kept their loincloths, but accepted the caps and jerseys which gave them a visible distinction during their games.[43]

The widespread adoption and adaptation of sport during Forbes' governorship did promote Americanization among the Filipinos, but American land grabs continued to incite Filipinos. Americans were allowed to buy the confiscated church lands of the friars and encouraged to do so. Despite the seeming conflict of interest Forbes endorsed such incentives for Americans to serve in the islands. Filipinos perceived it as exploitative, but Forbes was generally shielded from criticism as his brother owned the *Manila Times*.[44]

A Turning of the Tide

With the ascension of a Democrat, Woodrow Wilson (1856–1924) to the United States' presidency in 1912, the process of self-government for

Filipinos increased pace. Francis Burton Harrison (1873–1957) replaced Forbes as governor general and served from 1913 to 1921. A New York politician, an anti-imperialist, and a serial bridegroom (six wives), Harrison proved to be the most popular American governor; although he largely remained sequestered in Manila during his term. Unlike his predecessors, he forbid government employees from engaging in private business and discontinued the summer hiatus in Baguio. In 1916 the national assembly became a bicameral legislature, similar to the American Congress. Between 1913 and 1919 he reduced the number of American governmental employees from 29 percent to 6 percent, and turned administration of Moro Province over to the local population. The Philippines faced a banking crisis during his term and he reasoned that it was cheaper to employ Filipinos than Americans. In Manila, he reversed the American dominance on the Philippines Commission by appointing five Filipinos and only four Americans. The assembly responded by replacing the original art in its chambers, which had previously reflected American domination, with a heroic portrait of Jose Rizal.[45]

The athletic endeavors of W. Cameron Forbes, however, continued, as American professional baseball teams toured Asia during the winter months, competing in Manila, Japan, and China. Harrison assured a warm welcome with a greeting by the constabulary band, a parade, closing all colonial offices and banks, and providing free passes to military personnel, while the Filipinos were charged $7 for a grandstand seat, twice the price of spectators in the United States. The American players also toured the Bilibid Prison, considered to be the largest and most modern structure of its kind in the world, holding three thousand prisoners. While the New York Giants and the Chicago White Sox split two games, rain cancelled the contest with the Manila League all-stars, which featured Oscar Charleston (1896–1954), then serving with the US Army in the islands, but destined to become a Hall of Fame player in the American Negro Leagues.[46]

WOOD-FORBES REPORT

General Leonard Wood campaigned for the US presidency in 1916, but failed to gain the candidacy of the Republican Party. In late 1917 and early 1918 he toured the Allied military units in France during World War I, where he was wounded; a year later he suffered the loss of his friend and advocate with the death of Theodore Roosevelt. Nevertheless, he continued to pursue the presidency, but lost the nomination to the eventual winner, Warren H. Harding (1865–1923). In April of 1921, he and W. Cameron Forbes returned to the Philippines to investigate the Filipinos' progress toward independence.[47] Their report proved to be highly critical, admitting the great desire of the Filipinos for self-government, but citing great inefficiency and claiming the continued necessity for American supervision and greater authority for the governor general. They approved of the widespread employment of sports, particularly Filipino victories against the Japanese and Chinese, but lamented the lack of American teachers, the decreased number of children attending schools, and the limited use of the English language.[48]

Interwar Years

Consequently, Wood returned to the Philippines as governor general, a post he held from 1921 until his death during surgery for a brain tumor in 1927. Wood embarked on a retrenchment of the Filipinization of the government, resulting in severe clashes with the *ilustrados* who had gained a greater measure of power under Harrison. Wood's quarrels with Senate president Manuel Quezon and his cabinet were exacerbated by a scandal. The American administration initiated a crackdown on practices it deemed to be immoral, closing gambling halls and opium dens in 1922. The following year Ray Conley, head of the vice squad, was indicted for accepting bribes. Conley had shielded Americans from conviction, including Wood's son, who had been involved in sexual peccadilloes and had managed to amass a bank account of $490,000 on an annual salary of $2,000. Quezon and his cabinet demanded Conley's dismissal, but Wood permitted his retirement with full pension, which led to the resignation of Quezon and his cabinet in 1923. Wood later co-opted Quezon's American friend, George Malcolm (1881–1961), a Supreme Court justice, by threatening to expose Malcolm's own illegitimate children, in gaining the deciding vote which upheld Wood's authority in a 1926 case.[49]

Americans' strong racial attitudes continued to linger in the islands. When young *pensionados* returned from the United States they embarked on a crusade to integrate white clubs, but failed to accomplish their goal. One, who had been chosen captain of the water polo team at the University of Chicago, faced continued exclusion in his homeland. In the United States the Welch bill sought to ban Filipino migration. Though it failed to pass, such sentiments convinced even more Filipinos that only full independence might grant them equality.[50]

During the depression of the 1930s Filipinos began to form labor unions and organized protests against the machinations of the *ilustrados* manning the government. Other nationalists chose a more radical solution, forming the communist party in 1930. The communists and socialists later merged in 1938, but the Hukbalahap communists of Mindanao continued their insurgency throughout the century, and communists served as the primary liberators of Luzon from the Japanese during World War II.[51]

Sport, however, remained a strong component of Americanization under Wood's successors. Dwight Davis (1879–1945) served as governor general from 1929 to 1932. He had been a national tennis champion at the turn of the century and established the Davis Cup trophy awarded to international match victors before embarking on a political career. He constructed public tennis courts in his native St. Louis and served as Secretary of War before appointment to the Philippines.[52] Theodore Roosevelt, Jr. (1887–1944) succeeded Davis in a brief tenure as governor general from 1932 to 1933 after serving in the same capacity in Puerto Rico from 1929 to 1932. Frank Murphy (1890–1949) followed as the last governor general from 1933 to 1935. During the decade American companies fielded baseball teams, and the YMCA allowed for integrated basketball squads, while maintaining separate dormitories for Americans and Filipinos.[53]

The Philippines gained commonwealth status and its own president in 1935 under the Tydings-McDuffie Act, passed by the US Congress the previous year. The Philippines House of Representatives celebrated with a speech presented in Tagalog rather than English.[54] The legislation provided for an autonomous government, but required allegiance to the United States, which retained ultimate authority, veto power, review of court decisions, the maintenance of a tariff on Filipino products, and supervision of all foreign affairs. The United States retained its large military bases in the islands and strategic control of the Filipino military. The Philippines' new government was saddled with the debts of the previous American administration. Its first president, Manuel Quezon, soon began the establishment of a national army. In the schools and officer training academies, military drills and sports became essential markers of Filipino masculinity to be publicly displayed in pageantry and spectacles such as the annual Manila Carnival.[55]

The cult of masculinity proved so strong that it cost one American administrator his job. James Fugate (1877–1938), provincial governor of the Sulu islands, succumbed to a nervous breakdown in 1931 and sought relief in a California retreat. A year later he sought to return to his post, but then Governor General Theodore Roosevelt, Jr., dismissed him from his office. Fugate had previously served in the occupying American army in 1900 and as one of the first teachers before gaining the position of governor of Siquijor in the Negros Oriental province. He pleaded with Roosevelt that he was "noble, selfless, committed, and only truly alive in his role as a colonizer," to no avail. Others perceived him as an invalid and a liability, but his political connections won a brief reinstatement to office in 1934. He was murdered in Sulu in 1938.[56]

Such internecine quarrels plagued the new Filipino government as well. Quezon defeated the aging Emilio Aguinaldo for the presidency, but "the bright, charismatic, self-important Quezon governed more like a patriarch than a democrat and ignored widespread economic problems that fueled social unrest."[57] Aguinaldo, the revolutionary hero, no longer posed a threat, having been co-opted by Dean Worcester several years earlier. Aguinaldo accepted a role as vice-president of US corporations operating in the islands with a substantial salary, a house, and an American education for his son.[58] Other *ilustrados*, however, whose wealth largely depended on favorable trade relations with the United States, feared the loss of their economic capital with independence. Among them, Sergio Osmena emerged as a rival to Quezon.[59]

World War II and Its Aftermath

With the Japanese invasion of the Philippines, both Quezon and Vice President Osmena fled with American commander, General Douglas MacArthur (1880–1964), while the *ilustrados* that remained behind began collaborating with the occupying Japanese forces. Emilio Aguinaldo even made speeches on behalf of the Japanese, but with the end of the war, he and others were granted amnesty. Another collaborator, Manuel Roxas (1892–1948), won election as the first president of the independent Philippines in 1946 through the auspices of his friend, Manuel Quezon. The *ilustrado* rivalries intensified without American oversight, as families began to enlist their own militias. The 1949 presidential election resulted in victory for Elpidio Quirino (1890–1956), who had taken office upon the death of Roxas a year earlier. Both the election and his term were marred by corruption and violence, as well as a resurgent communism. Ramon Magsaysay (1907–1957) succeeded Quirino and proved more successful in curtailing the insurrection, and restoring a measure of integrity, but he died in a plane crash in 1957.[60]

The Marcos Regime

The power struggles between the elite families was interrupted with the ascendance of Ferdinand Marcos (1917–1989) in 1965. Marcos portrayed himself as a war hero, a heartthrob, and a nationalist to win the presidential election. With a two term limit on the presidency the elites bided their time until they might assume the reins of power. Few paid taxes and a handful of Filipinos controlled most of the national economy. One commentator claimed that "nobody in the Philippines has ever heard of a successful prosecution for graft."[61] In the 1969 presidential election Sergio Osmena, Jr. (1916–1984) lost to Marcos, claiming that "we were outgunned, outgooned, and outgold." In 1972 Marcos nullified the two term limit by declaring martial law. He abolished the Congress and Osmena, Jr., and a host of others, would be imprisoned. Lands and businesses of his rivals would be confiscated. The military forces became his private army and the United States fueled his dictatorship by providing high rental fees for the use of their military bases in order to conduct their war in Vietnam.[62]

Marcos also employed sport as a means to exert social and economic control over his enemies and the general populace. His allies owned the television channel that broadcast games as well as the professional basketball teams that so enthralled the general populace. He terminated the Philippines Amateur Athletic Federation and established his own ministry for youth and sports development to promote nationalism and gain international recognition. The Philippines Basketball Association became the first professional league in Asia in 1975, largely mimicking the National Basketball Association in America, creating mass media spectacles and local sports celebrities as entertainment to assuage the poverty and horrendous living conditions of the masses, while he and his wife, Imelda (1929–), lived lavishly.[63]

Marcos' blatant usurpation of power began to unravel in 1983 when opposition leader Benigno Aquino (1932–1983), who had been imprisoned for eight years and then resided in the United States, decided to challenge the dictator after martial law was lifted in 1981. Two years later he returned, but was assassinated as he disembarked from the airplane in an arranged murder that shocked the global community. In a revolution of the common people that would be mirrored three decades later in the Mideast, Filipinos erupted in retaliation. Marcos was eventually forced to abandon the Philippines as the rebellious populace installed Corazon Aquino (1933–2009), the widow of the assassinated challenger, in the presidential Malacanang Palace. Marcos repaired to Hawaii, where the United States continued to support him until his death in 1989, despite the obvious abuses heaped upon his people. Historian Walter Hixson charged that Marcos had donated $10 million to Ronald Reagan's (1911–2004) election campaign in 1984 to assure his asylum in Hawaii.[64]

There was, however, no happy ending. Corazon Aquino faced repeated coup attempts by a military disgruntled over their loss of social, economic, and political capital. In the local and provincial elections of 1988 no less than forty-one candidates were assassinated and the country remained mired in poverty with massive numbers of Filipinos migrating to the Mideast in search of employment. The People Power movement chased President Joseph Estrada (1937–) from power in 2001, and a crowd of 50,000 poor soon confronted the police and his successor, President Gloria Macapagal-Arroyo (1947–). Amidst widespread corruption, she faced yet another army mutiny in 2003. An estimated twenty million occupy some of the worst slums in Asia, while wealth is conspicuously concentrated in the Makati district of Manila. Still, the elite dominance of politics remains, as Benigno Aquino III (1960–) assumed the Filipino presidency in 2010, and Marcos' children have reinserted themselves in the political leadership and contemplate their own presidential ambitions.[65]

Conflicted Nationalism

The Philippines "suffers from cultural schizophrenia, it is a forced union of the East and the West."[66] The transition from a rural, clan-based, tribal society began with more than three hundred years of colonial occupation under the Spanish empire, but greatly accelerated in the nearly half century of American rule. The United States promoted a greater sense of nationalism among disparate tribes, and linguistic and religious groups. It fostered an urban, industrialized, commercial economy to supplant a rural, agricultural, subsistence lifestyle; yet the Philippines remains one of the largest recipients of American aid and United States' corporations are among the biggest extractors of the country's resources. "The U.S. still enjoys the economic and cultural privileges of neo-colonial domination, and that the Philippine Republic, despite vociferously anti-American nationalism, continues to be culturally and economically subordinate to American interests."[67]

It could not, however, alleviate religious and social strife. Muslims still feel excluded, Protestant factions introduced by the American missionaries still contend with the Catholic majority, and the enormous socioeconomic gaps breed despair and foment rebellion, as a communist insurgency continues to operate.

The American intentions to unify the islands through education, the use of the English language, and the inculcation of democracy has had mixed results. While considerably more Filipinos have access to basic education, the use of English only intensified class differences. The *ilustrados* who mastered English had greater access to US capital and American leadership, amassing wealth and influence. English remains one of the two official languages of the country; yet only slightly more than half of the Filipinos speak it and many have adapted it to their own form of Tagalog slang, as it represents a colonial mentality.[68] Filipinos have eschewed the imported American heroes for their own, especially Jose Rizal and Benigno Aquino, but the Americans never inculcated a true democracy. Their co-optation and cultivation of the *ilustrado* elites produced an oligarchy that continues to rule the country, effectively disenfranchising the majority.

The Americans had considerably more success in the inculcation of their sports. The Philippines continues to send baseball teams to the Little League championship, and basketball has supplanted indigenous games as the national sport. American NBA stars remain heroes in the Philippines. A Filipino journalist recently determined that "today's Filipino is basically a man of two religions. He is a God-fearing Christian and an irrepressible basketball devotee."[69]

The culmination of such cultural interplay continues to be a conflicted sense of nationalism, part American, part Filipino, not completely one nor the other. It might be likened to siblings in a family, one born of the same parents, while the younger other was adopted and may always feel a sense of difference and subordination, continually in need of guidance and reassurance, while desperately seeking independence. Sport had served as a means of social control, but cultural and religious differences had thwarted full assimilation of the WASP values.

NOTES

1. Bonifacio S. Salamanca, *The Filipino Reaction to American Rule, 1901–1913* (Norwich, CT: The Shoe String Press, 1968), 6–10; Kramer, *Blood of Government*, 36–39; Wolff, *Little Brown Brother*, 17–18; Eva-Lotta E. Hedman and John Thayer Sidel, *Philippine Politics and Society in the Twentieth Century* (London: Routledge, 2000), 7; Lynn T. White III, *Philippine Politics: Progress and Problems in a Localist Democracy* (New York: Routledge, 2014), 12–19; Fernando N. Zialcita, "State Formation, Colonialism, and National Identity in Vietnam and the Philippines," *Philippine Quarterly of Culture and Society*, 33:2 (June 1995), 77–117.

2. Julian Go, *American Empire and the Politics of Meaning* (Durham, NC: Duke University Press, 2008), 96–97; Salamanca, *The Filipino Reaction to American Rule*, 12–16; Benedict Anderson, "Cacique Democracy in the Philippines: Origins and Dreams," *New Left Review*, 88 (1988), 3–31.

3. Silbey, *A War of Frontier and Empire*, 12–14; Wolff, *Little Brown Brother*, 23–25, 28–30, 340–46; www.joserizal.ph/bg01.html (August 10, 2015).

4. Rodney J. Sullivan, *Exemplar of Americanism: The Philippine Career of Dean C. Worcester* (Ann Arbor: University of Michigan Press, 1991), 64–95; Kramer, *Blood of Government*, 112; Wolff, *Little Brown Brother*, 255; Zimmerman, *First Great Triumph*, 388 (quote).

5. Glenn May, *Social Engineering in the Philippines: The Aims, Execution, and Impact of American Colonial Policy, 1900–1913* (Westport, CT: Greenwood Press, 1980), xvii–xviii, 8–12; Karnow, *In Our Image*, 14, 228; Jones, *Honor in the Dust*, 196.

6. Jones, *Honor in the Dust*, 208.

7. Zimmerman, *First Great Triumph*, 389–93; Wolff, *Little Brown Brother*, 322–24.

8. Karnow, *In Our Image*, 176; Sullivan, *Exemplar of Americanism*, 121 (quote). While Worcester may have masterminded the organization of the Federalists, Protestant missionaries, and Felipe Buencamino, Aguinaldo's secretary of foreign affairs who defected to the American side, were also instrumental, see Clymer, *Protestant Missionaries in the Philippines*, 115–16; and May, *Social Engineering in the Philippines*, 24–32.

9. William H. Taft, *Civil Government in the Philippines* (New York: The Outlook Co., 1902); Zimmerman, *First Great Triumph*, 394; Susan K. Harris, *God's Arbiters: Americans and the Philippines, 1898–1902* (New York: Oxford University Press, 2011); Karnow, *In Our Image*, 176–77 (quote).

10. Stanley, *A Nation in the Making*, 164.

11. Kramer, *Blood of Government*, 186–88, (quote, 186).

12. Ibid., 294.

13. Gleeck, Jr., *The Manila Americans*, 25, 64–67. Wealthy Filipinos did join the Baguio Golf Club about a decade later.

14. Kramer, *Blood of Government*, 166–67, 171–73; "My dear Secretary" (Taft to Root), October 21, 1900, in William H. Taft Papers, reel 463, Library of Congress (quote).

15. Kramer, *Blood of Government*, 168; Taft, *Civil Government in the Philippines*, 42.

16. Lewis E. Gleeck, Jr., *American Institutions in the Philippines* (Manila: Manila Historical Conservation Society, 1976), 279.

17. Sullivan, *Exemplar of Americanism*, 115–21, 121 (quote).

18. Sullivan, *Exemplar of Americanism*, 4.

19. Ibid., 130, 135–36, 157–58, 162–63, 195–97, 201–11; Virginia Benitez Licuanen, *Filipinos and Americans: A Love-Hate Relationship* (Manila: Baguio Country Club, 1982), 94–100.

20. Sullivan, *Exemplar of Americanism*, 106–14 (quote, 114).

21. Patrick M. Kirkwood, "'Michigan Men' in the Philippines and the Limits of Self-Determination in the Progressive Era," *Michigan Historical Review*, 40:2 (Fall 2014), 63–86 (74, quote).

22. Sullivan, *Exemplar of Americanism*, 163; 227–28 (quote, 228).

23. Wolff, *Little Brown Brother*, 350; Zimmerman, *First Great Triumph*, 389–93; Hedman and Sidel, *Philippine Politics and Society in the Twentieth Century*, 7, 39; Vicente L. Rafael, "'White Love': Surveillance and Nationalist Resistance in the U.S. Colonization of the Philippines," in Kaplan and Pease, eds., *Cultures of United States Imperialism*, 185–218; Kramer, *Blood of Government*, 220–25, 301; Christina Evangelista Torres, *The Americanization of Manila, 1898–1921* (Diliman, Quezon City: University of the Philippines Press, 2010), 137 (quote).

24. Kramer, *Blood of Government*, 204–5, 257–58, 274; Salamanca, *The Filipino Reaction to American Rule*, 76–77, 92.

25. Arnold, *The Moro War*, 126–28; Patricia N. Abinales, "The U.S. Army as an Occupying Force in Muslim Mindanao, 1899–1913," in McCoy and Scarano, eds., *Colonial Crucible*, 410–20, (quotes, 411).

26. Arnold, *Moro War*, 47–48, 203–6, 228–43.

27. Salamanca, *The Filipino Reaction to American Rule*, 158–163; Rafael, "'White Love,'" 206–14; Kramer, *Blood of Government*, 286, 301, claims 59 seats for the Nacionalistas.

28. Go, *American Empire and the Politics of Meaning*, 244–73.

29. Miller, *"Benevolent Assimilation,"* 264; May, *Social Engineering in the Philippines*, 32–36; Torres, *The Americanization of Manila*, 170.

30. Paul A. Kramer, "The Pragmatic Empire: U.S. Anthropology and Colonial Politics in the Occupied Philippines, 1898–1916," PhD Dissertation, Princeton University, 1998, 204; Stanley, *A Nation in the Making*, 63, 117–20; May, *Social Engineering in the Philippines*, 10; Kramer, *Blood of Government*, 275, 291; Salamanca, *The Filipino Reaction to American Rule*, 180–82; Go, *American Empire and the Politics of Meaning*, 191; kahimyang.info/kauswagan/articles/1449/today-in-philippine-history-february-1-1904-luke-e-wright-was-inaugurated-as-civil-governor-of-the-philippines (August 13, 2015); www.asj.upd.edu.ph/mediabox/archive/ASJ-09-02-1971/luna-general%20artemia%20ricarte%20y%20garcia%20filipino%20nationalist.pdf (August 13, 2015).

31. Salamanca, *The Filipino Reaction to American Rule*, 178–80; www.bibingka.com/phg/sakay/default.htm (August 13, 2015).

32. May, *Social Engineering in the Philippines*, 19–20; philippinesfreepress.wordpress.com/tag/james-f-smith/ (August 13, 2015). See Christine O'Bonsawin, "From Black Power to Indigenous Activism: The Olympic Movement and the Marginilization of Oppressed Peoples," *Journal of Sport History*, 42:1 (Summer 2015), 200–219, on the continued employment of such strategies in the twenty-first century.

33. Bradley, *The Imperial Crusade*, 290; Karnow, *In Our Image*, 216; Stanley, *A Nation in the Making*, 99; May, *Social Engineering in the Philippines*, 20–21; Gems, *The Athletic Crusade*, 54–55.

34. Oriard, *Reading Football*, 229.

35. Stanley, *A Nation in the Making*, 99; Karnow, *In Our Image*, 216; Benitez, *Filipinos and Americans*, 44, 66, 80.

36. Stanley, *A Nation in the Making*, 99, 102–6, 139; Salamanca, *The Filipino Reaction to American Rule*, 87; Michael Salman, "'The Prison that Makes Men Free': The Iwahig Penal Colony and the Simulacra of the American State in the Philippines," in McCoy and Scarano, eds., *Colonial Crucible*, 117–28.

37. Gems, *Athletic Crusade*, 59–61; Janice A. Beran, "Americans in the Philippines: Imperialism or Progress Through Sport?," *International Journal of the History of Sport*, 6 (May 1989), 62–87; Bocobo-Olivar, *History of Physical Education in the Philippines*, 55–59,

69–70; Elwood S. Brown, *Annual Report October 1, 1911 to October 1, 1912*, in YMCA Archives, Philippines Box, NP, Correspondence Reports, 1911–1968 (quote, n.p.). Brown would institute other regional games in South America and the Inter-Allied military games after World War I.

38. Lou Antolihao, *Playing with the Big Boys: Basketball, American Imperialism, and Subaltern Discourse in the Philippines* (Lincoln: University of Nebraska Press, 2015), 45 and 50 (quotes, respectively).

39. Gleeck, Jr., *American Institutions in the Philippines*, 118; Gleeck, Jr., *The Manila-Americans*, 88–100; Coffman, *The Regulars*, 67, 80.

40. Antolihao, *Playing with the Big Boys*, 24 (quote), 37.

41. Ibid, 38.

42. Benitez, *Filipinos and Americans*, 28–81 (81, quote).

43. Coffman, *The Regulars*, 54.

44. Torres, *The Americanization of Manila*, 35–36; Sullivan, *Exemplar of Americanism*, 130–31; Stanley, *A Nation in the Making*, 138; Salamanca, *The Filipino Reaction to American Rule*, 241–42.

45. Stanley, *A Nation in the Making*, 202–12; Hedman and Sidel, *Philippine Politics and Society in the Twentieth Century*, 7, 39; Sullivan, *Exemplar of Americanism*, 131; Alcantara, "Baguio Between Two Wars," 213; Karnow, *In Our Image*, 243–49; Kramer, *The Blood of Government*, 303, 352–53, 379; Torres, *The Americanization of Manila*, 38–41.

46. James E. Elfers, *The Tour to End All Tours: The Story of Major League Baseball's 1913–1914 World Tour* (Lincoln: University of Nebraska Press, 2003), xxii, 138–44.

47. Lane, *Armed Progressive*, 207–56.

48. Leonard Wood, *Report of the Special Mission to the Philippines Islands to the Secretary of War* (Washington, DC: Government Printing Office, 1922).

49. Lane, *Armed Progressive*, 257–73; Benitez, *Filipinos and Americans*, 101–14; Alfred W. McCoy, "Policing the Imperial Periphery: Philippine Pacification and the Rise of the U.S. National Security State," in McCoy and Scarano, eds., *Colonial Crucible*, 105–15. Malcolm was instrumental in the founding of the Philippines Law College. See Kirkwood, "'Michigan Men' in the Philippines," 80–83.

50. Benitez, *Filipinos and Americans*, 116–17; Kramer, *Blood of Government*, 350, 397.

51. Boudreau, "Methods of Domination and Modes of Resistance: The U.S. Colonial State and Philippine Mobilization in Comparative Perspective," in Go and Foster, eds., *The American Colonial State in the Philippines: Global Perspectives* (Durham, NC: Duke University Press, 2003), 256–90; Karnow, *In Our Image*, 336–55; Guerrero, *Philippine Society and Revolution*, 47, 52; Miller, *"Benevolent Assimilation,"* 264; Hixson, *American Settler Colonialism*, 182.

52. www.britannica.com/biography/Dwight-F-Davis (September 1, 2015).

53. Benitez, *Filipinos and Americans*, 132–36.

54. *School News Review*, September 1, 1934, 8, in National Archives, RG 350, Box 1187.

55. Kramer, *Blood of Government*, 424–25; McCoy, "Philippine Commonwealth and Cult of Masculinity"; see various issues of *School News Review*, February 15, 1933–January 15, 1937, on extensive athletic competitions.

56. Karen R. Miller, "'Thin, Wistful, and White': James Fugate and the Disavowal of Muscularity in the Colonial Philippines," paper presented at the Organization of American Historians Convention (April 2015); www.gov.ph/1938/12/16/statement-president-quezon-on-the-murder-of-ex-governor-james-fugate-december-16-1938/ (September 1, 2015).

57. Anderson and Cayton, *The Dominion of War*, 371.

58. Sullivan, *Exemplar of Americanism*, 203.

59. Anderson, "Cacique Democracy in the Philippines," 9, 12; Torres, *The Americanization of Manila*, 170.

60. Anderson, "Cacique Democracy in the Philippines"; asianhistory.about.com/od/philippines/p/Biography-of-Emilio-Aguinaldo.htm (September 1, 2015); www.biography.com/people/elpidio-quirino-37511#profile (September 1, 2015).

61. Anderson, "Cacique Democracy in the Philippines," 16 (quote), 17, estimates 5 percent of Filipinos controlled about 50 percent of the economy by the 1970s and income taxes derived largely from international corporations. McCoy, "Philippine Commonwealth and Cult of Masculinity," 323, 333–35.

62. Peter Krinks, *The Economy of the Philippines: Elites, Inequalities and Economic Restructuring* (London: Routledge, 2001), 41; Anderson, "Cacique Democracy in the Philippines," 18–22, 18 (quote).

63. Antolihao, *Playing with the Big Boys*, 97–103.

64. www.britannica.com/biography/Benigno-Simeon-Aquino-Jr (September 1, 2015): Hixson, *American Settler Colonialism*, 183.

65. McCoy, "Philippine Commonwealth and Cult of Masculinity," 336–39; McCoy, "Policing the Imperial Periphery," 106–7; Gavin Shatkin, "Colonial Capital, Modernist Capital, Global Capital: The Changing Political Symbolism of Urban Space in Metro Manila, the Philippines," *Pacific Affairs*, 78:4 (Winter 2005–2006), 577–600; Anderson, "Cacique Democracy in the Philippines," 26–30: White, *Philippine Politics*, 120, 158, 176–77, 189–91.

66. Zialcita, "State Formation, Colonialism and National Identity in Vietnam and the Philippines," 77.

67. Sharon Delmendo, "The Star Entangled Banner: Commemorating 100 Years of Philippine (In)dependence and Philippine-American Relations," *Journal of Asian American Studies*, 1:3 (1998), 211–44, (quote, 216).

68. Vicente L. Rafael, "The War of Translation: Colonial Education, American English, and Tagalog Slang in the Philippines," *Journal of Asian Studies*, 74:2 (May 2015), 283–302.

69. Antilohao, *Playing with the Big Boys*, 134.

FIVE
Religion

The Philippines represents an enigma as the only Christian country in Asia. It became so after three centuries of Spanish rule following the exploration and occupation of the islands in the sixteenth century. One of the primary purposes of Spanish imperial endeavors was the diffusion of the Catholic faith, but even temporal Catholic emperors had to acquiesce to the papal ruler of the church. Consequently, the Spanish clerics held undue influence in the islands, owning nearly half a million acres of land in the northern islands and more than 50 percent of the land in some provinces by the late nineteenth century, with indigenous sharecroppers serving their needs. The Spaniards had less success in subduing the southern islands, where Islam had spread from Indonesia by the end of the fourteenth century. Schools were run by the Spanish government, but supervised by priests who insured religious instruction. The Spanish friars thus converted the northern tribes to Catholicism, but uprisings were commonplace, and the Americans arrived in the midst of an ongoing revolt that had started in 1896.[1]

Religious issues proved to be a perplexing issue for the Americans as well, as they tried to replace Catholicism with their own brand of Protestant Christianity. Nativist backlash against Catholicism in the United States had surfaced with the rise of European immigrants in the early nineteenth century and gained prominence thereafter, greatly excluding Catholics from the mainstream culture. Protestants saw the Spanish-American War of 1898 as a religious crusade and an opportunity to garner souls in Asia and the Caribbean in the territories taken from the defeated Spanish. Senator Knute Nelson (1843–1923) of Minnesota announced that "Providence has given the United States the duty of extending Christian civilization, and we propose to execute it."[2] The *Baptist Union* proclaimed that "the conquest by force of arms must be followed by conquest of Christ." The *Methodist Review* stated that "by the direction of divine Providence (the policy of foreign colonization should be) the foreign policy of the U.S. is foreign missions," and the Congregationalist *Advance* opined that "morally and religiously, we should not shun an opportunity to lift up a barbarous people."[3] Presbyterian minister John H. Barrows (1847–1902) called on American missionaries to fulfill "the manifest destiny of the Christian Republic," and the *Religious Telescope* announced that "we would be selfish to decline ownership of the Philippines, to do so would be an actual crime in the eyes of God. . . . Religion had joined the great crusade, hand-in-hand with duty and destiny." Protestant denominations soon met to divide up the spoils among themselves in Cuba, Puerto Rico, and the Philippines, viewing the latter as an entry to the pagan hordes of Asia. Episcopalian chaplains and the YMCA accompanied the American troops to the islands in 1898, and the first missionaries soon traveled to Manila in March of 1899 with a load of bibles and a message of the gospel.[4]

Despite the zeal of the missionaries and the initial support of colonial administrators, the confiscation of church lands and the attack on Catholicism created a dilemma for the US government. The Catholic hierarchy in the United States had backed William McKinley in the presidential election of 1900 and Archbishop John Ireland (1838–1918) was a strong advocate of the Americanization of Catholics. Ireland complained that "as a plain matter of fact the only safety which the Catholic Church has at the present time in the Philippines for the possession of her properties and for the lives of our priests is the protection of the American flag and all this is fully recognized in Rome."[5] Emissaries were sent to Rome and McKinley eventually reconsidered the confiscation of church lands in the Philippines. The church properties were consequently bought in 1904 and resold.[6]

The colonial administrators soon realized that the American Catholics could be useful in their Americanization efforts. Taft indicated as much when he wrote to Secretary of War Elihu Root in 1900 that he intended to import five American Catholics to teach English and an American Catholic archbishop to replace the Spanish one in Manila, and in doing so he hoped that "half the religious battle here would be won."[7] In 1903 Pope Leo XIII (Vincenzo Pecci, 1810–1903) named Archbishop Jeremiah Harty (1853–1927) the first American Catholic archbishop in Manila. The American Catholic hierarchy viewed cooperation in the islands as an opportunity to assert their own Americanization and a means to greater acceptance in American society. Doctrinal differences, however, continued to plague religious harmony. Protestants charged that Catholics worshiped idols in their statuary and religious rituals. Indigenous cockfighters even took their roosters to church to sip the holy water for fortification before a match, while others fed Holy Communion wafers to their birds. Protestants also decried the pecuniary efforts of Catholic priests who charged rent for cemetery plots. Catholics retaliated to the Protestants' defamation by harassing or even attacking Protestant converts and boycotting Protestant businesses.[8]

Catholics took particular exception to the Protestant missionaries' efforts to convert their church members who already professed Christianity. In 1905 Francis Kelley (1870–1948), an American Catholic priest who had served as a chaplain during the Spanish-American War, established the Extension Society as a fundraising organization to supply priests, nuns, and goods for missionary efforts. Filipino priests appealed to Kelley to combat the Protestant preachers who distributed anti-Catholic materials and openly proselytized on street corners. Archbishop Harty countered the Protestant efforts by importing more priests, especially the zealous Jesuits.[9]

Catholics pronounced particular concerns about the use of the public schools for such evangelism. Most of the early American teachers recruited for duty in the Philippines were Protestants, and the Protestant missionaries also volunteered to serve in such a capacity. Protestants claimed that "every public school can be counted as an evangelical force in a Roman Catholic country," and used the Catholics' own initiatives to their advantage.[10] Archbishop Ireland had managed to institute the Faribault Plan in Minnesota, which forbid religious criticism in the schools, but allowed for thirty minutes of religious instruction three times per week if requested by a student's parents. Protestant schoolteachers in the islands invoked the ruling as a license to preach in the schools. A Catholic prelate registered his opposition with President Roosevelt in 1904. "Complaints were made to be in nearly every town that the native teachers were exercising a perverting influence religiously and parents came to me with tears rolling down their faces, begging that I try to do something to have Catholic teachers placed in the schools so that the faith might not be taken from their little ones." The colonial administrators' emphasis on secular schools in itself deviated from the norm of private religious instruction under the Spanish, and Filipinos were slow to accept the transition. In 1903 General James Smith, a Catholic, was named Secretary of Public Instruction (and served as governor general of the islands from 1906 to 1909).[11] Still, a Catholic priest complained in 1913 that "the public schools through the length and breadth of the Philippine Islands are Godless, and now they are consequently drawing away from the Holy Church the rising generation of Filipinos."[12]

Various Protestant groups formed their own private schools, including universities, and they petitioned the colonial administration for dormitories, which provided them with a captive audience. Dormitories were a necessity at provincial schools, but the secular University of the Philippines, perceived as an American antidote to the University of Santo Tomas established by the Catholic Spanish, also included dorms with American supervisors by 1912. Murray Bartlett (1871–1949), the first president of the University of the Philippines, and an Episcopalian minister, initially served as a chaplain and as head of the Episcopalian Cathedral in Manila.[13]

The Protestants introduced vocational schools as well to teach practical skills such as tailoring, carpentry, shoemaking, printing, and auto repair for employment in the promotion of a capitalist economy, but also to instill discipline and a work ethic that Americans valued and found lacking in Filipinos.[14]

The Protestant efforts extended beyond educational institutions to include the establishment of hospitals, settlement houses, libraries, community centers, and social clubs to augment their evangelical work. Bishop Charles Brent, head of the Episcopalians in the Philippines, stated that "I do not care to have a hospital, or a dispensary . . . where the mere exercise of scientific skill is the sum total of treatment. If we haven't physicians who can bring into play in an active manner the potent influences of divine power in connection with their operative skill, we had better not attempt medical missionary work." Rebecca Parrish (1869–1952), a Methodist Episcopal female physician, served in the Philippines over a period of four decades and founded a hospital in the Tondo slum to administer to the poor. Her care extended to religious matters, including daily Bible study, prayer services, spiritual songs and posters, as well as proselytism in the local schools.[15]

A rift in the Catholic Church of the Philippines appeared at the turn of the century when Gregorio Aglipay (1860–1940), a nationalist who had fought against the Americans, advocated for a greater Filipino presence in the clergy. As an excommunicated priest he established his own church independent of the Catholic hierarchy. Aided by American Protestant clergy, he attempted to ally with the Episcopalians by 1904, but the colonial administration was necessarily bound to support the Catholic Church due to its political leverage among the populace. Lands seized by the schizmatics were eventually returned to the Catholic Church in a Filipino Supreme Court ruling in 1906.[16]

The opposition of the American missionaries to the Filipino independence movement would eventually thwart their conversion efforts. Although the Methodists, Presbyterians, and Seventh Day Adventists initially secured some neophytes, the Filipino clerics who accepted Protestantism opted for their own nationalistic churches.[17]

AMERICAN SINNERS

While missionaries from various religious denominations chased souls throughout the islands; the Episcopalians largely limited themselves to the service of white Anglos and Chinese in the Philippines. They soon discovered that it was an ample task. Bishop Brent described many of his countrymen as "degenerate, criminal, immoral . . . [and] that the Orient is no fit place for persons, especially young men, who have not moral stamina. The Philippines are almost the sure undoing of the weak. . . . Anglos in Manila don't attend church . . . [and there is] an absence of that moral stimulation that is a concomitant of Anglo-Saxon civilization." As to the indigenous population he claimed that "the constitutional fault of the Filipinos, a fault common to all Orientals, is sensuality . . . laziness, concubinage and gambling."[18] Mary Fee, one of the early American school teachers, claimed that "gambling is a national vice," as the Filipinos bet on cards, dominoes, and horse races, and both men and women frequented the cockfights.[19]

Early in the campaign against the Filipinos cavalry officer Matthew Batson (1866–1917) noticed the psychological and moral damage incurred in warfare. In an 1899 letter to his wife he stated that "we come as a Christian people to relieve them from the Spanish yoke and bear ourselves like barbarians." Batson himself would later order the decimation of a town after his friend was killed in an ambush.[20] An American missionary also lamented that "as I look and see the flag of my country floating in the breeze which is the emblem of a christian [sic] government, and then look around me and see the men sent over here to represent us, I feel ashamed."[21]

The missionaries moaned that few of the soldiers went to church, and were given to drinking, gambling, and whoring. The clerics placed their faith in sport as an antidote and a means of social control. The YMCA had accompanied the first California contingent of troops to the war in 1898, enticing the men to their religious message by offering sports equipment and athletic competition. It continued to expand its operations in the Philippines throughout the remainder of the American occupation, building athletic facilities and dormitories in the cities, and organizing local, national, and international events on a grand scale.[22]

Local cockfights, however, raised both moral and political concerns for both the missionaries and politicians. The clergy decried the inherent gambling on the matches and the consequent bloodshed and death of the birds as inhumane and barbarian, while politicians feared the cultural symbolism as well. Filipinos viewed the activity as an adherence to their historical culture, and a right to self determination. Moreover, the participation of Americans seemed to grant tacit approval. When a smaller bird defeated a larger one it had particular symbolism for Filipino nationalists engaged in their own struggle with the United States. A missionary complained that Filipinos who had won a substantial amount at the Sunday cockfight refused to return to work until they had spent their profit, an attitude antithetical to the Protestant work ethic and the capitalist economic system. Consequently, General J. Franklin Bell issued an order banning the sport in 1902 under penalty of incarceration and fines as high as $500, but the directive proved futile and the colonial government eventually opted for regulation of the activity.[23]

Bishop Brent and other American reformers (including Catholic archbishop Harty) established the Moral Progress League in 1906 to address gambling with the intention of closing the cockpits and the racetracks. Gambling had previously been an institutionalized activity fostered by the Spanish government, which gleaned the tax revenue from card and dice games, billiard halls, and horse racing. The campaign to instill Protestant righteousness thus proved futile; especially since one of the organizers who intended to regulate morality, Judge W.A. Kincaid, had his own problems with alcohol. Kincaid founded the *Free Press* newspaper as a call to moral reform, but it fell on deaf ears and lasted only a year as Americans continued to pursue their pleasures unabated.[24]

American soldiers even bred a new strain of bird that came to dominate the avian battles. Known as the Texas, it possessed "flaming spirit and deep-seated courage ... [even though] hit and pierced right thru [sic] the heart, at times, with one last desperate thrust, this prodigious breed may still kill its foe." The American authorities even granted inclusion to the cockfighters in the Manila Carnival of 1908 despite the vehement protests of the Protestant missionaries. Such deep involvement of the Americans in an indigenous activity represents an example of reverse cultural flow, in which the colonizers are, to some degree, appropriated by the colonized.[25]

Missionaries believed that baseball could deter both American and Filipino men away from their attraction to the cockpit. The Reverend George Dunlap, who had played semipro baseball in the United States, became known as a "baseball evangelist" by introducing the game to students at the Cebu High School, the Presbyterian Silliman Institute in Negros Island "to kill the cockpit," and promoting international competition in Asia. David Hibbard (1868–1966), president of the Silliman Institute, stated that "a Silliman student would feel disgraced for life if he were caught at one of the cockpits by a member of his faculty, even during the long vacations."[26]

Baseball had some success in supplanting the cockpit because patrons might find even more ways to gamble on the game. The YMCA also promoted sport as a means to and a display of rugged "muscular Christianity" to thwart libidinal desires, but few accepted the call to celibacy. The US Army subscribed to the belief that sexual release was a necessity to assuage male needs, lest pent up energies result in attacks upon the general populace and even the white women of the colonial community. Prostitution remained legal in the United States itself until the late Progressive Era when moral reformers crusaded for municipal bans on the practice. Massachusetts became the first state to abolish prostitution in 1917. Nevertheless, throughout the twentieth century, the American military continued to turn a blind eye to the activity when it did not actively support brothels for the troops.[27]

Manila featured allegedly the world's largest licensed brothel, guarded by American soldiers and supervised by army doctors. In Davao, the American officials imported Japanese prostitutes to service the men. Among the migrants to the islands were hundreds of American, European, and Japanese prostitutes, and venereal disease soon accounted for 25 percent of the sick bay cases. From April to December of 1899 the naval hospital at Cavite treated sixty-two cases of venereal disease, which accounted for more patients than those afflicted by gunshot wounds, malaria, fevers, rheumatism, and dysentery. General Elwell Otis attempted to rectify the situation by registering the prostitutes and requiring weekly examinations. Despite the precautions venereal disease rates in the Philippines remained the highest of all American military forces into the 1930s.[28]

A further problem for the authorities resulted with the number of illegitimate children produced by such liaisons. Many soldiers who married or cohabited with Filipino women simply abandoned them and the resultant children upon their return to the United States. By 1914 the American Mestizo Association established a home for destitute children. *Mestizo* children faced rejection in American society and despite the declining number of Americans in the islands by 1921, then Governor General Leonard Wood and others saw the need for an American Guardian Association to meet the need of 18,000 such children in the provinces.[29]

Racist attitudes hampered the missionary efforts. Several of them wrote books about the Filipinos, often focusing on the more primitive tribes, sometimes praising their physical prowess or other qualities as noble savages, but generally denigrating them as backward and inferior beings. The Negritos were compared to apes and considered hopeless as converts. Only the Methodists attempted to Christianize them. James Thoburn (1836–1922), a Methodist bishop who spent only three weeks in the Philippines, testified at a US Senate committee in 1902 that Filipinos ranked above American Indians, but below Chinese, and rated them far below Anglo-Saxons.[30]

The Protestant clergy especially detested miscegenation, adhering to the separation of races as practiced in the United States. Even the more liberal Episcopalian Bishop Brent pronounced that "it grieves me whenever I see one of my fellow citizens tied for life to a Filipina; it seems to be unnatural, and ordinarily I cannot get away from a sense of degradation connected with it." Brent even denied the entry of Filipinos to his school in Baguio. Segregation of Filipinos followed that of African Americans in the United States, sanctioned by the Protestant clergy.[31]

By 1910 there were about five thousand Americans residing in Manila, but only an estimated 20 percent attended church services. Some declined because they refused to integrate with the Filipino patrons. Others disagreed with the Protestant campaigns to outlaw gambling and ban alcohol, while some American entrepreneurs felt that the aggressive proselytism fostered anti-American sentiments and hurt their businesses, especially the many saloons opened by former soldiers. Dean Worcester, too, as Secretary of the Interior, blocked Episcopalians' attempts to purchase lands in northern Luzon, possibly due to his own self-interests in more commercially lucrative ventures.[32]

The Protestants also impeded their own efforts due to factional disputes. As early as 1901 they had formed the Evangelical Union to divide up the Philippines into denominational territories, but the Episcopalians and the Adventists refused to join the association. Doctrinal differences further divided the factions as Episcopalians remained closer to Catholicism in their beliefs and practices, while Adventists, and Disciples preached a second coming of Christ. Methodists, United Brethren, and Disciples all prohibited dancing, but Episcopalians and others offered it as wholesome recreation to combat illicit leisure pursuits. The various denominations soon began accusing others of poaching on their assigned territories and forfeiting any uniform campaign for conversion.[33]

BISHOP CHARLES H. BRENT

The Episcopal Bishop Charles Brent did, however, wield considerable influence throughout the archipelago. Born at Newcastle in the Canadian province of Ontario in 1862, he attended public schools, entering Trinity College in 1880, where he played rugby. He earned his degree from the University of Toronto in 1884. Brent entered the priesthood in 1887 in Toronto, but spent his early ministry in the United States in Boston and became a US citizen. Elected bishop of the Philippines on October 11, 1901, he traveled to Washington, DC, to meet with President Roosevelt, Governor General Taft, and the presidential cabinet, consequently developing grand dreams for his foreign mission. He embarked for the islands in May of 1902 by way of Europe, where he traveled to Rome with William Howard Taft to address papal concerns over the American occupation of the Catholic country. Brent arrived in the Philippines on August 24, a post that would last until 1917.[34]

Brent held particular influence among the American authorities in the Philippines. He befriended several governors general, especially Taft and Forbes, although the latter generally distrusted the missionaries. When Brent chastised Forbes for his appointment of a person that Brent considered to be corrupt, Forbes gave the post to the bishop. In his ecclesiastical role Brent established schools, hospitals, settlement houses, and social clubs to meet the needs of his flock.[35]

Brent subscribed to a "muscular Christianity" and sport played a prominent role in his evangelism as a means to achieve discipline, self-control, and a rugged masculinity. In one of his many books, entitled *The Splendor of the Human Body* (1904), Brent argued that the body served as a Christian temple and believers had an obligation to maintain it. He led a crusade against the opium trade and its addiction, which resulted in international treaties to limit narcotic production.[36] Like many other missionaries who promoted sport as a means to spiritual and physical health, Brent played tennis, but his favorite game was golf. He also participated in polo matches and an occasional baseball game, although he did not particularly like the sport. He did like football, but preferred rugby, fishing, and chess.[37]

Many of Brent's social contacts revolved around sports. He particularly enjoyed his relationships with the military officers Leonard Wood and John Pershing. In 1904, he was one of the founders of the Columbia Club in Manila, which offered a clubhouse with bowling and billiards facilities as well as an indoor swimming pool and a library for its Anglo patrons. It later added a gym in 1914, but no hard liquor was served on the premises. The Supreme Court granted the club a tax exemption by accepting its athletic endeavors as religious work.[38]

Brent also founded a school for Anglo boys in Baguio, stating that "the aim of the school is to promote Christian character, intellectual vigor, and respect for the body.... Every boy will be required to bring a Bible." Sport played a prominent role in the curriculum, including horseback riding, golf, tennis, and swimming. Brent's friend, Governor General Forbes, contributed money for a gym at the school. Brent also established a school for Moro children in Jolo, where they were taught baseball and boxing. The baseball initiative proved so successful that by 1915 Frank Carpenter (1871–1945), Governor of Mindanao and Sulu, requested that more missionaries engage in baseball evangelism.[39]

Brent's engagement in sports led to him assume the duties as president of the Philippines Amateur Athletic Federation (PAAF), replacing Governor General Forbes in 1914. Though the PAAF was founded under the auspices of the YMCA, Brent and the YMCA soon found each other competing for the same souls as the Filipinization program under Governor General Harrison sent increasing numbers of Americans back to the United States.[40]

Brent and the other Protestant missionaries had less success with the Filipino nationalists. Even the Filipino Protestant clergy campaigned for both national and ecclesiastical independence from their American overseers, a call that was not supported by the missionaries. Brent, in particular, adhered to the belief that the Filipinos were not yet capable of self-government. The missionaries also continued to support the American military even in the face of public disclosure of the atrocities committed against the Filipino populace. Consequently, Bishop Brent faced disdain among Filipinos.[41]

THE YMCA AND THE POWER OF SPORT

Supreme Court Justice David Brewer (1837–1910) believed that the United States possessed the "purest form of Christianity." In a 1904 address to the YMCA he suggested that "here in the Republic, in the Providence of God, should be worked out the unity of the [human] race—a unity made possible by the influences of education and the power of Christianity."[42] The YMCA efforts to promote its brand of Protestant Christianity in the United States had already been underway for a half century, but it received considerable assistance from the government in its operations in the Philippines.

The work of the YMCA in the Philippines began slowly, as it offered only baseball games and an occasional boxing match for soldiers in 1901. It began offering its services to white civilians a year later. Activities increased considerably with the decision to construct two buildings in Manila in 1907, "one peculiarly American and the other peculiarly Filipino, for the development of their work." A year later, the resulting facility consisted of a seventy-five-room dormitory, a swimming pool, a gym, a social hall, a library, dining room, and tennis courts. The association soon requested a tax exemption as a religious organization.[43]

By 1909 the exclusion of Filipinos from the YMCA activities raised concerns. A Supreme Court Justice of the Philippines wrote to John Mott (1865–1955), head of the YMCA international division, that "already the question whether or not Filipinos will be admitted to the association is being discussed. . . . There are so many Southerners among the young people of the American population of Manila, that it will make it impossible, in my opinion, to unite the Americans and Filipinos in the present association."[44] Only a week later, Bishop Brent warned Mott that "it ought to be taken into consideration that never since the American occupation has there been more racial hatred between American and Filipino than now. The establishment of a separate building for the Filipinos side by side with that for Americans would tend to emphasize the breach."[45]

THE CATHOLIC RESPONSE TO THE YMCA

The Catholic Church embarked upon its own sports program in response to the YMCA's efforts. By 1915 a YMCA official reported that "the opposition of the Catholic Church . . . is proving to be more formidable than we anticipated . . . for the Association is regarded by them as purely a Protestant movement."[46] The Catholic perception proved accurate as the YMCA attempted to unite all the Protestant factions and promote their objectives. The Catholic Church sent increasing numbers of American priests to the islands to counteract the Protestant efforts, and threatened to excommunicate Catholics who joined the YMCA. Though it did not follow through with such a punishment, it did expel Catholic school students who frequented the YMCA. It also built its own Pope Pius XII Center with a swimming pool, sports facilities, and dormitories as an alternative to the YMCA. Catholic opposition proved so steadfast that the YMCA opened its doors to Catholic members in 1916 and it even appointed Catholics to its committees in a show of reconciliation, as well as a means to attract Filipinos (who were, nevertheless, assigned to a separate building). The Catholic Church protested when the YMCA was designated as the supplier of recreational activities for the US army in 1917, which resulted in greater inclusion of other religious organizations, including the Catholic Knights of Columbus (K of C). The Catholics perhaps had better success with the soldiers, who disdained the YMCA's haughty attitude and selling of cigarettes, which the K of C supplied at no charge.[47]

YMCA PROGRAMS

The YMCA, similar to the Progressive reformers' social work in the United States, attempted to address juvenile delinquency in Manila by recruiting children from the slums and cultivating the sons of gang leaders that they might shape into community heroes, a concept adopted by the Catholic Church in the United States with the establishment of the Catholic Youth Organization in 1930. The YMCA later introduced a Pioneers Club for youth, similar to the Boy Scouts organization.[48]

Despite the constitutional separation of church and state in the United States, the YMCA enjoyed a close association with the government in the Philippines. Elwood Brown (1883–1924), a former basketball coach at the University of Illinois, arrived in Manila in 1910 as the new director of the YMCA. He soon promoted the sports of basketball and volleyball, both games invented by YMCA instructors in the United States. Brown reasoned that "the Filipinos are great imitators. When they see the constabulary soldiers playing . . . and engaging in all sorts of races, it is entirely possible that they will in turn take the games up and substitute them as rapidly as possible for their foolish *sipa* [*sic*] and cockfighting." The Manila basketball league was established that same year with separate divisions for Anglos and Filipinos. Brown organized the Philippines Amateur Athletic Federation in 1910, with Governor General Forbes as its first president. The colonial administrators allowed Brown to prepare the official recreation manual and a member of the YMCA staff also directed public education, infusing the curriculum with sports and games as a means to greater assimilation with American cultural values. By 1913 Brown also served on the Playground Committee and trained the playground directors, but his biggest accomplishment was the transformation of the Manila Carnival, the site of interscholastic athletic championships and a business expo originally intended to promote commercial development in 1908, into an international sports spectacle similar to the Olympic Games.[49]

THE MANILA CARNIVAL AND THE FAR EASTERN GAMES

The Manila Carnival hosted the national athletic championships in track and field, baseball, basketball, tennis, swimming, rowing, golf, polo, soccer, football, and bowling under the auspices of the Philippines Amateur Athletic Association, but Brown transformed the festival into a regional competition by inviting China and Japan to participate, and forming the Far Eastern Athletic Association with inaugural competition to take place in Manila in February of 1913.[50] Frank L. Crone (1875–1960), Director of Public Education in the Philippines, claimed that "nothing previous to this meeting has shown so clearly the departure of the Oriental nations of the old conservative standards, for the interest of the East in organizing athletic sports is only recent." Even though Japan had already participated in the international Olympic Games in 1912 in Sweden, the American organizers of the Manila Carnival assumed credit for bringing the Asian nations into the modern world of athletics.[51] For East Asian countries steeped in historical traditions, the concept of modernity was a western one, promoted by foreign occupiers to reinforce their own cultural superiority. Nevertheless, international athletic competition offered the participants a means to gain greater recognition and even symbolically challenge western powers, or their regional lackeys (as the Filipinos were perceived to be by the Japanese).[52]

English served as the common language of the games, and the Philippines' team marched into the arena under the American flag, further symbolizing the Anglo dominance. Governor General Forbes opened the games with an admonition that "I hope all your contests will be carried on in the spirit of fair play, which in after years may govern your conduct in business and other vocations of grown-ups." The avuncular assumption of superiority and moral rectitude continued to characterize white relationships with Asian populations.[53]

The Philippines and Japan had engaged in baseball competition as early as 1905 and such contests helped to channel Filipino nationalist sentiments into the athletic rather than political sphere, as witnessed by the 18,000 spectators that attended the game between the two rivals at the 1913 carnival.[54] More than 150,000 attended the other athletic events, which included track and field, baseball, basketball, swimming and diving, football, tennis, volleyball, and girls' basketball. (The 1915 Games also included cycling.) The Filipinos and their American tutors rejoiced in their overall victory. An American journalist reported that "[up] to the time of American occupation the Filipino had done absolutely nothing in athletics. The race, in an athletic standpoint, was in very poor condition. They were, perhaps, the weakest of all Orientals. Today, they are at the head."[55]

The Japanese were further humiliated when the California legislature, supported by US President Woodrow Wilson, passed a bill banning foreign ownership of land in the state, eliciting a formal protest by Japan, only three months after the Manila spectacle. The law continued to fuel Japanese resentment of American hegemony in the Pacific and sport provided one means of confrontation.[56]

The Far Eastern Games were held every two years thereafter in the urban centers of Asia, and the Philippines continued to dominate the competition, winning the first five contests, and nine of the first ten basketball championships.[57] The YMCA continued to extol the value of the competition as a means to peaceful cooperation and friendship. A correspondent at the 1917 Far Eastern Games, hosted by Japan in Tokyo, wrote,

> The dust clouds of strife and hatred are uprising on the battlefields of Europe; the dust of furious but friendly conflict is ascending on the athletic field of Japan. As in Europe, the flags of three allied nations wave over the scene of action—without inspiring the lust of killing. The generals of the Japan field wear business suits, and troops are uniformed in white cotton suits, the armament are vaulting poles, discus plates, baseball clubs. The rifle-shot on the battlefield echoes in Japan; it is the report from a starter's pistol. . . . And while the finest youth of Western civilization are racing to see who can kill first, the choicest lads of the East are racing to determine who is the best runner and after that is settled they are seen standing before a camera, their arms around their opponent's shoulders.[58]

The correspondent apparently missed the soccer game between the Philippines and China, in which the Filipino goalkeeper slugged the Chinese player who scored on a penalty kick in a 4–0 rout by the Chinese. The Filipinos then marched off the field and refused to continue.[59] Such public displays of physical prowess and martial spirit enabled the Filipinos and their American occupiers to measure their development against Asian rivals, resurrected Filipino masculinity, and promoted national pride in a surrogate form of warfare that continued until 1934. The competitions were discontinued thereafter as Japan continued its military incursions into Chinese territory in a prelude to World War II.

The athletic confrontations carried over into the YMCA's efforts in the Philippines. Although the YMCA adhered to segregation policies in its facilities, it did permit integrated competition on its playing fields, and in the 1915 PAAF volleyball tournament a team of Filipino clerks defeated their American bosses in the semifinal round. The Americans, upset at their loss, claimed that the Filipinos had employed deceptive and unsportsmanlike tactics because they playfully volleyed the ball among themselves as many as fifty-two times before returning it to their American opponents, who promptly returned the ball with a single hit. The Americans consequently changed the rules to give themselves unlimited hits, while the Filipinos were limited to three. Sport thus provided one of the few areas of social contact between the occupiers and the occupied, which allowed the Filipinos to test Anglo notions of racial superiority.[60]

THE YMCA SCORESHEET

With the increasing Filipinization of the government under Governor General Harrison and the declining number of Americans in Manila the YMCA had to compete with Bishop Brent's Columbia Club for Anglo patronage. Elwood Brown reported less than 400 YMCA members in 1914. The next year both the YMCA and the Columbia Club offered dances to counter the attraction of the public dance halls and the numerous brothels. The YMCA offered numerous athletic teams, year-round basketball leagues, softball and baseball leagues, and gym classes for both males and females, and even initiated plans for a separate YMCA building for Chinese businessmen in an attempt to address gambling, opium smoking, and the prostitution trade, estimated at a million pesos per year from the Chinese alone.[61] Americans, too, succumbed to the pleasures of the flesh, and Brown reported that "young fellows who were staunch and steadfast at home find that in some subtle way their ideas have undergone a change and almost before they realize it they are fighting the battle of their lives to keep clean and true, to stand up straight."[62] The brothel owners circumvented the morality crusades by simply designating their establishments as "dancing schools," in which the dancing "teachers" were required to undergo examinations for venereal disease.[63]

The YMCA continued to offer athletic alternatives as a means of social control and moral uplift. It proceeded with plans for a new student building, a quarter-mile track, a baseball field, eleven tennis courts, a handball court, a swimming pool, a gymnasium with a second floor indoor track, and an exercise room. Despite the grand facilities and extensive programs the YMCA began to lose its leadership role in the islands. With the transfer of Bishop Brent to France with the American entry into World War I, Manuel Quezon, president of the Philippines Senate, assumed the presidency of the PAAF, and Filipinos assumed greater roles in the organization thereafter. Elwood Brown, too, heeded the call to serve the American troops in World War I, providing an instrumental role in the organization of the postwar Interallied Games, a military Olympics held in Paris in 1919. By 1922 the executive secretary at the Manila YMCA reported that "as for the work that we came out here to do, there seems little likelihood of its immediate accomplishment."[64]

RELIGIOUS AFTERMATH

With the onset of the Protestant missionary crusade in the Philippines, the Catholic Church responded by sending increasing numbers of American priest to the islands. The Vatican replaced the Spanish bishops with Americans and created more Filipino bishops by 1910. In contrast, the Protestant churches in the Philippines remained under the control of the American hierarchy, much to the chagrin of Filipino Protestant clergy. The US colonial administration also needed the assistance of the Catholic Church to control the Filipino populace, thereby limiting its overt support to their Protestant brethren. Furthermore, the Protestant emphasis on individualism and sterile rituals held little appeal for the more communal and emotional Filipinos. Only the more emotional Methodists had a modicum of success, registering about one-third of the conversions. More problematic for the missionaries and the converts, such novitiates faced ostracism, harassment, and even murder.[65]

The Protestants also had little success among the Muslims of Mindanao. As early as 1903 General Samuel Sumner (1842–1937) determined that "they are essentially different people from us in thought, word and action and their religion will be a serious bar to any efforts towards Christian civilization. So long as Mohammedanism prevails, Anglo-Saxon civilization will make slow headway." The Christian concept of monogamous marriage also differed greatly from the multiple wives that gained social capital among Muslim *datus*. Nor did the Muslims even recognize the sovereignty of the United States, as they had never recognized the Spanish as their rulers. They continued to practice jihad, the holy war against infidels, and John Pershing noted that "he (a Muslim) generally looks upon it as a meritorious thing to kill and rob Christians."[66]

The American faith in the power of sport, while beneficial to the creation and sense of a national identity, also had some detrimental repercussions for religious endeavors. Filipinos who watched American soldiers co-opt and play their baseball games on the church or municipal plazas considered such usurpation a desecration of holy land and it produced resentment. Among the more secular denizens a Filipino scholar has stated that the great success of "baseball attracted a sort of 'religious following' that challenged the power of the church as the main proponent of most local public congregations." With the increase of baseball leagues and Sunday double headers, fewer people attended church services. Indeed, contemporary sociologists and anthropologists have made the case of sport as a new secular religion, complete with saints, shrines, and fervent followers as an alternative to organized denominations.[67]

The overt racism of some missionaries and the segregation practices of many only hampered their efforts, as Filipinos judged such practices as hypocritical to their preaching about fraternity, righteousness, and godliness. By 1920 the Episcopal bishop reported to the church board that "we have to record more failure than success." Other congregations face similar results, counting only 105,000 converts by 1925, and by 1985 only 3 percent of Filipinos remained Protestant.[68] The power of sport thus largely failed as a mechanism of religious conversion, but its competitive characteristics did augment the transition to a capitalist economy.

NOTES

1. Wolff, *Little Brown Brother*, 18; Kramer, *Blood of Government*, 39–42, 50–81; Anderson, "Cacique Democracy in the Philippines," 5–6; Krinks, *The Economy of the Philippines*, 23; Salamanca, *The Filipino Reaction to American Rule*, 6–16.

2. Susan K. Harris, *God's Arbiters: Americans and the Philippines, 1898–1902* (New York: Oxford University Press, 2011), 26.

3. Pratt, *Expansionists of 1898*, 291–301 (quotes, 291–92, 295, 301, respectively).

4. Gleeck, Jr., *The Manila-Americans*, 6; Gleeck, Jr., *American Institutions in the Philippines*, 57–58; Clymer, *Protestant Missionaries in the Philippines*, 5–7; Wolff, *Little Brown Brother*, 85 (quote).

5. Miller, *"Benevolent Assimilation,"* 138.

6. Ibid., 139; Salamanca, *The Filipino Reaction to American Rule*, 21, 97–107, 151–52.

7. William Howard Taft to My dear Secretary, August 11, 1900, Taft Papers, reel 463, Library of Congress.

8. Anne M. Martinez, *Catholic Borderlands: Mapping Catholicism onto American Empire, 1905–1935* (Lincoln: University of Nebraska Press, 2014), 73–74, 238; Clymer, *Protestant Missionaries in the Philippines*, 95–100.

9. Martinez, *Catholic Borderlands*, 33–39, 74–75, 81, 84; Gleeck, Jr., *The Manila-Americans*, 48–49; Gleeck, Jr. *American Institutions in the Philippines*, 81–82.

10. Clymer, *Protestant Missionaries in the Philippines*, 163.

11. Salamanca, *The Filipino Reaction to American Rule*, 77–82, (quote, 79).

12. Martinez, *Catholic Borderlands*, 84.

13. Gleeck, Jr., *American Institutions in the Philippines*, 36–38, 48–54, 61–63; opinion.inquirer.net/inquireropinion/columns/view/20080122-114113/Three-American-presidents-of-UP (September 7, 2015). Bartlett later served as president of Hobart and William Smith College, 1919–1936.

14. Clymer, *Protestant Missionaries in the Philippines*, 86–87.

15. Ibid., 18–19 (quote, 18).

16. McCoy, "Policing the Imperial Periphery," 8; Salamanca, *The Filipino Reaction to American Rule*, 110–13; Jones, *Honor in the Dust*, 141–45; Clymer, *Protestant Missionaries in the Philippines*, 194; Kenton J. Clymer, "The Methodist Response to Philippine Nationalism, 1899–1916," *Church History* (December 1, 1978), 421–33.

17. Joseph P. McCallus, *The MacArthur Highway & Other Relics of American Empire in the Philippines* (Washington, DC: Potomac Books, 2010), 76.

18. Rt. Rev. Charles H. Brent, Religious Conditions in the Philippines, pamphlet, 1904, Library of Congress; Clymer, *Protestant Missionaries in the Philippines*, 6.

19. Mary H. Fee, *A Woman's Impression of the Philippines* (Chicago: A. C. McClurg & Co., 1910), 270.

20. Karnow, *In Our Image*, 154; Hixson, *American Settler Colonialism*, 173 (quote).

21. Clymer, *Protestant Missionaries in the Philippines*, 182.

22. Remson B. Ogilvy to My dear Bishop, September 5, 1910 (Box 9); and Private Carmi L. Williams, Company G, 13th Infantry to Right Reverend Charles H. Brent, November 19, 1914 (Box 10), on complaints regarding soldiers, both in Bishop Charles H. Brent Papers, Library of Congress. See Kenneth L. Latourette, *World Service: A History of the Foreign Work and World Service of the Young Men's Christian Association of*

the United States and Canada (New York: Association Press, 1957) on the role of the YMCA.

23. Le Roy, James A., *Philippine Life in Town and Country* (New York: G. P. Putnam's Sons, 1905), 56–65; Davis, "Cockfight Nationalism," 548–49, 556–60. See Clifford Geertz's classic study "Deep Play: Notes on the Balinese Cockfight," *Daedalus* 101, (Winter 1972), 1–38.

24. Dean C. Worcester, *The Philippines Past and Present* (New York: Macmillan Co., 1914), 515; Gleeck, Jr., *American Institutions in the Philippines*, 97; Clymer, *Protestant Missionaries in the Philippines*, 167–68; philippinesfreepress.wordpress.com/tag/moral-progress-league/ (September 27, 2015).

25. Ibid., 561.

26. Clymer, *Protestant Missionaries in the Philippines*, 85; Beran, "Americans in the Philippines," 78.

27. Lenore Kuo, *Prostitution Policy: Revolutionizing Practice through a Gendered Perspective* (New York: New York University Press, 2001), 73; Roberts, *What Soldiers Do*; Jarvis, *The Male Body at War*, 82–83, 145–46.

28. Wolff, *Little Brown Brother*, 178, 299; Clymer, *Protestant Missionaries in the Philippines*, 186; Jones, *Honor in the Dust*, 400; Coffman, *The Regulars*, 344, 355, 369.

29. Clymer, *Protestant Missionaries in the Philippines*, 181–82. Gleeck, Jr., *The Manila-Americans*, 96–100.

30. Clymer, *Protestant Missionaries in the Philippines*, 66–75.

31. Ibid., 75 (quote), 223.

32. Ibid., 160, 175–79.

33. Ibid., 16, 25–61.

34. Alexander C. Zabriskie, *Bishop Brent: Crusader for Christian Unity* (Philadelphia: Westminster Press, 1948), 1–50. Brent served Canadian and American soldiers in France during the latter part of 1917 and then became the bishop of western New York.

35. Ibid., 74–76; Clymer, *Protestant Missionaries in the Philippines*, 107, 160, 183; Clifford Putney, *Muscular Christianity: Manhood and Sports in Protestant America, 1880–1920* (Cambridge, MA: Harvard University Press, 2001), 185; Arthur S. Pier, *American Apostles to the Philippines* (Boston: Beacon Press, 1950), 145.

36. David T. Courtwright, "The Cycles of American Drug Policy," *The American Historian* (August 2015), 24–29; Putney, *Muscular Christianity*, 56–57; Zabriskie, *Bishop Brent*, 83–85, 97–102, 134, maintains that Brent wrote twenty books, fourteen of them during his stay in the Philippines.

37. Putney, *Muscular Christianity*, 131–32; Zabriskie, *Bishop Brent*, 94–96; Pier, *American Apostles to the Philippines*, 149–50.

38. Pier, *American Apostles to the Philippines*, 100; Putney, *Muscular Christianity*, 185; Clymer *Protestant Missionaries in the Philippines*, 70; Zabriskie, *Bishop Brent*, 77; Gleeck, Jr., *The Manila-Americans*, 67–68; J. M. Groves to Mr. Mott (copy of memorandum to Mr. Haussermann), July 12, 1913, in YMCA Archives, Box Philippines, Int. Div. 167, local association, 1907–1973, file Manila, 1906–1907.

39. Pamphlet on Baguio School for American Boys, Brent Papers, Box 47, Philippine Islands folder; Remson B. Ogilvy to George Wharton Pepper, December 19, 1912 in Brent Papers, Box 10; Zabriskie, *Bishop Brent*, 70–72; Clymer, *Protestant Missionaries in the Philippines*, 161.

40. Elwood Brown, Annual Report, October 1, 1913–October 1, 1914, 17; Elwood Brown, Annual Report, October 1, 1914–October 1, 1915, in YMCA Archives; Bocobo-Olivar, *History of Physical Education in the Philippines*, 56; Remson B. Ogilby to My dear Bishop. September 15, 1910 in Box 9, Brent papers.

41. Clymer, *Protestant Missionaries in the Philippines*, 114–53.

42. Linda Przybyszewski, "Judicial Conservatism and Protestant Faith: The Case of Justice David J. Brewer," *Journal of American History*, 91:2 (September 2004), 471–96, (quotes, 484–85).

43. Second Conference of the Secretaries of the Army and Navy Department of the YMCA, Manila, Philippines, September 14–23, 1901, in Box Philippines, 1901–1973; William H. Taft to James F. Smith, Governor General of the Philippines, December 31, 1906 (quote), in Box Philippines, International Division 167, Manila, 1906–1907 file, both in the YMCA Archives; Gleeck, Jr., *American Institutions in the Philippines*, 72–73; Antolihao, *Playing with the Big Boys*, 56.

44. E. Finley Johnson, Supreme Court of the Philippine Islands, to John R. Mott. April 22, 1909, in correspondence file 1906–1909, YMCA Archives.

45. Charles H. Brent, Bishop, to Mr. Mott, April 30, 1909, in correspondence file, 1906–1909, YMCA Archives.

46. E.S. Turner, Preliminary Report, Filipino Association, 1915; correspondence file, 1906–1908, YMCA Archives.

47. Clymer, *Protestant Missionaries in the Philippines*, 37, 99–104; Antolihao, *Playing with the Big Boys*, 57; Gleeck, Jr. *American Institutions in the Philippines*, 74, 81–82; Putney, *Muscular Christianity*, 187–91.

48. Gleeck, Jr., *American Institutions in the Philippines*, 81–82, 95. See Gerald R. Gems, "Sport, Religion, and Americanization: Bishop Sheil and the Catholic Youth Organization," *International Journal of the History of Sport*, (August 1993), 233–41 on the national scope of the program and its effectiveness.

49. Governor General Harrison, Executive Order 79, September 16, 1914, National Archives, R 35, Box 931; Gleeck, Jr., *American Institutions in the Philippines*, 74–75; James Naismith, *Basketball: Its Origin and Development* (New York: Association Press, 1941), 147; Philippines Correspondence Reports, 1911–1968, YMCA Archives, Administrative Reports file, n.p.; Antolihao, "From Baseball Colony to Basketball Republic," 1398; Antolihao, *Playing with the Big Boys*, 24 (quote), 74–75. Naismith invented the game of basketball while teaching at the Springfield, Massachusetts, YMCA in 1891, and William Morgan, who headed the Holyoke, Massachusetts, YMCA, created volleyball in 1895.

50. Elwood S. Brown, *Annual Report*, October 1, 1911–October 1, 1912; and Brown, *Annual Report*, October 1, 1912–October 1, 1913, n.p., Brown, *Annual Report*, October 1, 1916–October 1, 1917, 13, all in YMCA Archives, Philippines Box, NP, Correspondence Reports, 1911–1968. Malaysia, Thailand, Indonesia, and Hong Kong later joined the Far Eastern Athletic Association.

51. Brown, *Annual Report*, October 1, 1912–October 1, 1913, n.p.

52. See Ying Chiang and Tzu-hsuan Chen, "Adopting the Diasporic Son: Jeremy Lin and Taiwan Sport Nationalism," *International Review for the Sociology of Sport*, 50:6 (September 2015), 705–21, on sport and modernity in East Asia.

53. Brown, *Annual Report*, October 1, 1912–October 1, 1913, n.p.; Brown, *Annual Report*, October 1, 1911–October 1, 1912, n.p (quote).

54. Brown, *Annual Report*, October 1, 1912–October 1, 1913, n.p.

55. Brown, *Annual Report*, October 1, 1912–October 1, 1913, n.p.; Antolihao, *Playing with the Big Boys*, 59, 61–62 (quote).

56. John M. Blum, Edmund S. Morgan, Willie Lee Rose, Arthur M. Schlesinger, Jr., Kenneth M. Stampp, and C. Vann Woodward, *The National Experience: A History of the United States* (New York: Harcourt, Brace, Jovanovich, 1981), 584–85. See Gems, *The Athletic Crusade*, 30–44, on the series of baseball games between Japanese and American teams starting in 1896.

57. Antolihao, *Playing with the Big Boys*, 63. The hosting Japanese delayed the 1929 Games until 1930.

58. Edith Wildes cited in Elwood S. Brown, *Annual Report*, October 1, 1916–October 1, 1917, 13–14.

59. *Bojan Jovanovic* for the Rec.Sport.Soccer Statistics Foundation at www.rsssf.com/tablesf/fareastgames17.html (September 24, 2015).

60. Elwood S. Brown, *Annual Report*, October 1, 1914–October 1, 1915, n.p.

61. Brown, *Annual Report*, October 1, 1913–October 1, 1914, n.p.; Clymer, *Protestant Missionaries in the Philippines*, 38; E. J. Mazurkiewicz, *Annual Report of the Physical*

Department, American Branch YMCA, Manila, Philippine Islands, September 30, 1917, in YMCA Archives, NP, Correspondence Reports, 1911–1968; Chengting T. Wang to My dear Fletcher, February 19, 1915, and *Report on the Chinese in Manila and the Philippines*, both in YMCA Archives, Philippines Box, International Division 167, local associations, 1906–1973.

62. Clymer, *Protestant Missionaries in the Philippines*, 177.

63. Karnow, *In Our Image*, 214.

64. YMCA Archives, Manila file, 1918–1922; Bocobo-Olivar, *History of Physical Education in the Philippines*, 56; J. Truitt Maxwell to Elwood S. Brown, April 18, 1922, YMCA Archives, correspondence reports, 1920–1923 (quote); 1930–1936.

65. Salamanca, *The Filipino Reaction to American Rule*, 109–20.

66. Arnold, *The Moro War*, 15–58, (quotes, 15, and 58, respectively).

67. Antolihao, "From Baseball Colony to Basketball Republic," 1398; Antolihao, *Playing with the Big Boys*, 69 (quote). Among the numerous works that treat sport as a secular religion, see Michael Stein, "Cult and Sport: The Case of Big Red," *Mid-American Review of Sociology*, 2:2 (1977), 29–42; Charles S. Prebish, "'Heavenly Father, Divine Goalie': Sport and Religion," *The Antioch Review*, 42:3 (Summer 1984), 306–18; Shirl J. Hoffman, *Sport and Religion* (Champaign, IL; Human Kinetics, 1992); William J. Baker, *Playing with God* (Cambridge, MA: Harvard University Press, 2007); and Rebecca T. Alpert, *Religion and Sports: An Introduction and Case Studies* (New York: Columbia University Press, 2015).

68. Clymer, *Protestant Missionaries in the Philippines*, 194, 195 (quote).

SIX

American Capitalism in the Philippines

The United States experienced an economic boom in the wake of the Civil War. Railroad companies constructed more than 50,000 miles of track between 1865 and 1879, including the completion of a transcontinental line in 1869. Southern agriculture, which faced an abrupt decline after the war, rebounded dramatically. Only three million bales of cotton were produced in 1870, but that figure surpassed nine million by 1900. Less than 75 million pounds of tobacco were harvested in 1870, a figure that reached nearly 325 million pounds by 1900. Sugar production bottomed out below 90 million pounds in 1870, but totaled nearly 325 million pounds by 1900. Gold and silver mining drew adventurers to the American West, while homesteaders populated the Midwestern farmlands that produced immense quantities of wheat, corn, beef, pork, and mutton. Manufacturing output measured at 1.8 billion in 1859 surpassed 13 billion by 1899. Iron production of 920,000 tons in 1860 reached 10,300,000 tons in 1900. Steel production reached almost 11,400,000 tons by the turn of the century as skyscrapers began to reshape the teeming urban landscapes across the nation. New technology produced the telephone and electric lighting as corporate competition spurred innovation and growth. Despite the depressions of 1873 and 1892, US exports tripled between 1860 and 1897, and by 1893 the United States trailed only Great Britain with its global empire in world trade.[1]

Within such an explosive economy the titans of industry amassed huge personal fortunes and rationalized their capital attainments in Social Darwinian terms as the survival of the fittest in the war of accumulation. Protestant clergy supported the quest for materialism, and Russell Conwell (1843–1925), a Baptist minister and the first president of Temple University, preached that "It is your duty to get rich. It is wrong to be poor."[2] Historian Susan Harris has noted that "the principle of Free Trade came to be associated with Protestantism itself and . . . honesty, self-control, and orderliness became identified as Protestant values. . . . 'Christian civilization,' (meant) an American way of life in which the practice of Christianity means consumerism and civil liberties means unrestricted commerce."[3] Many of the Americans who traveled to the Philippines adopted such precepts wholeheartedly.

By 1890 a culture of consumption had taken hold in the United States, but the quest for material goods was disrupted by the economic depression of 1893. The US Treasury Department was forced to solicit the aid of financier J. P. (John Pierpont) Morgan (1837–1913) and other bankers to replenish the national gold supply. That same year Professor Frederick Jackson Turner delivered a speech at the Chicago World's Fair on the closing of the American frontier and the expiration of free land. Labor unrest in 1894 resulted in almost 1,400 strikes, including a shutdown of the national rail lines. The need for external markets became a necessity. In 1897 Senator Albert Beveridge stated that "American factories are making more than the American people can use; American soil is producing more than they can consume. Fate has written our policy for us; the trade of the world must and shall be ours."[4]

The competition for commercial supremacy reached global proportions in the latter nineteenth century, as England and Germany built huge navies to pursue advantageous trade locations and shipping stations. Japan fought wars with China (1894–1895) and Russia (1904–1905) to extend its control over Asian territories, and President Theodore Roosevelt sent the Great White Fleet of sixteen battleships with more than 13,000 sailors on a fourteen month voyage around the world to demonstrate American sea power.[5]

THE ECONOMIC VALUE OF THE PHILIPPINES

The Spanish-American War and its resultant colonies offered one means of expanding the American economy, and the Philippines provided an entrée into the vast Asian markets, already dominated by the British. English merchants had operated in the Philippines as early as 1878, and by the time of the Americans' arrival in 1898 they controlled the three largest banks, much of the export trade, and considerable internal commerce through their Chinese intermediaries. Dean Worcester, Secretary of the Interior in the Philippines, promoted Manila as a trade rival to the British colony of Hong Kong, and Senator Albert Beveridge emphasized the importance of the Asian market. "Our largest trade henceforth must be with Asia. That Pacific is our ocean . . . China is our natural customer. . . . The statesman commits a crime against American trade—against the American grower of cotton and wheat and tobacco, the

American manufacturer of machinery and clothing—who fails to put America where she may command that trade." When critics claimed that the Philippines would never return a profit, Beveridge pulled a gold nugget from his pocket, a souvenir from his trip to the islands.[6]

In 1900 Beveridge predicted that "most future wars will be conflicts for commerce. The power that rules the Pacific, therefore, is the power that rules the world. And, with the Philippines, that power is and will forever be the American Republic." As early as 1898 Mobil Oil Company had already opened an office in Manila, and Benguet province in northern Luzon held the promise of gold and copper. Beveridge alluded to the rice, coffee, sugarcane, tobacco, hemp, coconuts, bananas, wood, and coal deposits in the Philippines. In the following decade *National Geographic* continually extolled the rich resources available in the islands, highlighting its minerals, forests, farmlands, fisheries, products, and available workforce. By 1907, an article by William Howard Taft claimed that trade with the Philippines increased from $5 million in 1895 to $18 million in 1906.[7]

The Philippines also offered the American administration in the United States a laboratory for research unencumbered by the internecine political quarrels stateside. In 1902 Gifford Pinchot (1865–1946) took leave of the US Forestry Service to spend six weeks in the Philippines to plan the scientific management and sustainable harvesting of the vast tropical forests. In Davao on the southern island of Mindanao, more than forty hemp plantations produced 35 percent of that product in the Philippines, and from 1910 to 1913 revenues for hemp, rubber, pearls, and coconuts tripled.[8]

In addition to the development of the Philippines' resources the colony served as a repository for American goods. Senator Henry Cabot Lodge wrote to William Howard Taft in 1900 that "it has been my firm belief that the Philippines would not only become an important market for us for our finished goods but what is still more important would furnish a large opportunity for the investment of surplus capital," which might achieve a better return than investments in the United States.[9] Dean Worcester claimed that American teachers were quick to discover the entrepreneurial opportunities by organizing and commercializing the Filipino handicraft trade in embroidery, basketry, and hat making. Schools soon introduced manual training and vocational education, introducing competitions and rewarding the best work, and selling the handicrafts produced by the students. Frank White (1875–1913), Director of Education in the Philippines from 1909 to 1913, asserted that "it will be our purpose to operate every trade school and every school farm on a business basis."[10] Governor General Forbes obliged by creating a Sales Agency "to correlate the work of the Bureau of Education with the industrial markets of the world," and to sell the products created in the schools. By 1911 half a million children were engaged in such work, not unlike the sweat shops of immigrant youth in the United States, with the expectation of limiting lace imports from Europe, which amounted to $10 million by 1912.[11] The agency was disbanded in 1915 after reaching annual sales of $480,000. Limited sales of the school handicrafts at the Manila Carnival still produced 45,000 pesos in 1916, but reached 180,000 pesos within two years. By 1920, the handicrafts accounted for the fifth highest export at $7.5 million, providing goods to department stores in the United States. Educational historian Anne Paulet has charged that "by altering the lifestyles . . . to more closely resemble that of Americans, the United states could maintain control without the use of force and could achieve economic success without the appearance of exploitation."[12]

Americans considered it their intent and duty to raise Filipinos to a higher level of civilization, and with that outcome would come a higher standard of living. Such an endeavor also contained an economic motive as explained by David Barrows, superintendent of the school system from 1903 to 1909. "Development of markets and of trade only accompany higher standards of life, and higher standards of life proceed no where so quickly as from an advance of education."[13] Americans believed that education would increase Filipinos "contentment as it increased his independence, and as it raise[d] his standard of life and comfort and increase[d] his desires, it [would] make him a better producer and a larger purchaser." For Filipinos who acquired such tastes, Americans gladly supplied furniture, kitchen utensils, western clothing, sporting goods, and any other needs advertised in the *Manila Times*, an American newspaper established in 1900.[14]

THE BURNHAM PLAN

On October 13, 1904, Daniel Burnham, famed architect of the 1893 Chicago World's Fair, left the United States for a four-month trip to the Philippines, during which time he planned the reconstruction of Manila and the proposed summer capital at Baguio in the mountains of Luzon. Burnham's charge included the development of the waterfront through reclamation, the Luneta, a large central park in Manila, the improvement of the street system, the improvement of waterways, and the construction of parks, plazas, and boulevards, all of which was intended to facilitate greater trade and increase real estate values. The plans included a customs house along the Pasig River and another building designated for the Chamber of Commerce. A new world-class hotel was to be built on the waterfront to attract the tourist trade. Construction of government buildings copied those that Burnham had planned for Washington, DC, and he stated that "the two capitals of the Philippines, even in their physical characteristics, will represent the power and dignity of this [US] nation." The bones of revered national hero Jose Rizal were interred in a memorial on the Luneta, similar to the national mall in Washington, DC. While such public monuments intended to instill deference and homage to American rule among the Filipinos, Burnham's improvements were largely meant to benefit the American residents of Manila.[15]

Baguio served as a summer refuge for American officials and wealthy foreigners. Lot sales began in 1905 and W. Cameron Forbes reported to Burnham that he had secured a prominent spot for his own home and that "the sale was a tremendous success, Americans, Englishmen, Spaniards and Filipinos all united in buying and 89 lots in all were disposed of for residence purposes." Baguio thus formed an enclave of the rich and powerful, segregated from the working class who served them.[16]

William Parsons (1872–1939), Burnham's associate, spent eight years in the Philippines enacting the plans of the master architect and developing his own designs for Cebu in the central Philippines and Zamboanga in southern Mindanao. Among the primary concerns were the treatment of water supplies that carried deadly cholera and dysentery. Until public water facilities were treated Americans were forced to drink distilled or boiled water. The American administrators issued bonds to cover the cost of installing a new sewer system, drilling of deep wells, fluoridation treatments to purify water supplies, and the construction of a new reservoir. W. Cameron Forbes established a Bureau of Public Works and street vendors were chased from their locales and daily markets, subjected to inspections, and disinfected.[17] Despite such improvements, at least one historian considered the Burnham Plan neglectful in its concentration on American comforts and its disregard of the general Filipino populace. Gavin Shatkin declared such "social inequities inherent in the colonial experience had transformed Manila into a symbol of the failures of American rule."[18]

BUILDING THE PHILIPPINES INFRASTRUCTURE

The first act of the Philippines Commission in September of 1900 was the allocation of funds to build roads, in particular the Benguet Road to Baguio in the mountains of Luzon, considered to be the source of gold and copper, and later to be designated as the summer capital. The second act of the commission authorized the construction of a railroad to Baguio, a task that was never accomplished. Despite an original estimate of $75,000, the Benguet Road took five years to build at a final cost of $2,754,281.05, more than 10 percent of the total purchase price of the archipelago. Wagon traffic on the road commenced in 1905 and gold mining began two years later.[19]

In Manila, the commissioners concentrated on upgrading the commercial infrastructure and sanitation facilities. By 1903 direct cable service was established between the islands and the United States. The governing body hired US contractors and army officers to construct the public works, but the assignees soon sublet the work to local Chinese at half the cost and pocketed a large profit. Still, road building proceeded apace with 303 miles of first-class roads by 1907 and 1,303 by 1913. Secondary roads pushed the latter figure to 4,505 by 1913, with railroads adding 608 miles of track connecting the regional centers. Within Manila, the Escolta shopping district catered to Americans, providing ice cream establishments and English-language newspapers. The city was policed by a staff of 705, numbering both American and Filipino officers, and an American sheriff, and his two American and seven Filipino deputies. The municipal fire department had seven stations manned by 146 men, 63 of which were Filipinos. By 1914 no less than 700 automobiles in the city began replacing the horse-drawn coaches, and the city derived its revenue from ever increasing taxes, which included real estate and entertainment taxes, as well as the sale of occupational and vehicle licenses.[20]

The *cocheros*, male drivers of the city's many horse-drawn vehicles, did not take kindly to the modernization of the city. Americans perceived the relaxed pace of Filipino life as a detriment to the capitalist work ethic, and the *cocheros* received particular blame, adding to the congestion of the city and displaying aloof and even disdainful attitudes to foreigners. American media characterized them as "scheming, irresponsible, unreliable, and rude." The civil authorities enacted local ordinances that required drivers to be at least sixteen years of age, "of intelligence and good character, and free from infections and contagious disease." Still the *cocheros* refused to yield to the automobiles and failed to give way on blocked city thoroughfares. The *cocheros* viewed such modernization and American criticism as assaults on their masculinity and retaliated by foiling the foreigners' vision of progress. Similar to laborers in the United States, Filipino workers organized strikes in 1903, demanding a 25 percent increase in their wages. In March of 1909 the Manila Railway Company employees bonded with the *cocheros* in organizing another labor strike to boycott the streetcars and buses in favor of the horse-drawn vehicles, and the *cocheros* "would make special rates to enemies of the street railway company." The workers further denounced their employers as imperialists and enemies of the nationalist independence efforts.[21]

CLIMATE AND RACE

Americans often based their needs on racial differences. Anglos believed that "in climatic conditions which are a burden to him; in the midst of races in a different and lower stage of development; divorced from the influences which have produced him, from the moral and political environment from which he sprang, the white man . . . tends himself to sink slowly to the level around him." A US Army surgeon stated that whites could not live closer than within fifty degrees of the equator and that exposure to the sun for lengthy periods resulted in degeneration of the body and eventual death. The lab workers of the Manila Bureau of Science tested such assertions as germ theory, which gained greater credence in the late nineteenth century, resulting in better sanitation and hygiene to thwart microorganisms. It also had a negative effect, however, reinforcing racist beliefs and segregation patterns as whites feared that native bodies carried harmful bacteria.[22]

From 1907 to 1910 the army conducted a study of five hundred American soldiers wearing orange or red underwear as a means to adapt to tropical conditions versus those who wore only white underwear, assuming that darker colors, as in one's skin, provided greater protection from the sun. Copious records measured age, height, weight, nativity, hair and eye color, skin color, length of service in the islands, and blood pressure, only to discover that those with the colored underwear suffered more so than those without, and sweated more profusely. Other studies found no variation in body temperature regardless of season or skin complexion from American citizens back in the United States. The belief in "tropical anemia" was also disproven, as further studies showed the cause to emanate from hookworms or malaria. By 1914 scientists could report that "by far the larger part of the morbidity and mortality in the Philippines is due to nostalgia, isolation, tedium, venereal disease, alcoholic excess, and especially to infections with various parasites."[23]

The research had the detrimental effect of labeling the native Filipinos as unsanitary, unhygienic carriers of such parasites. Cholera, dysentery, and smallpox epidemics occasionally ravaged the population. In December of 1899 the Bureau of Health offered five centavos for every rat tail produced by the local residents in an attempt to eradicate the pestilence. Enterprising Filipinos, however, took to breeding rats and delivering their tails to the Americans to increase their incomes. As a result of the diseases, "sanitary squads" under the direction of Victor Heiser (1873–1972), health commissioner in the Philippines, conducted housing inspections with the authority to remove anyone considered sick from the community. Filipino patients became the subjects of medical research without their consent. Heiser's mandates offended Filipinos, whose culture dictated the care of one's own and they proved reluctant to surrender their family members to government care. The Americans constructed the Philippines General Hospital in 1908, but the Philippine Bureau of Science, established in 1901, also addressed health concerns. Heiser believed that, due to such efforts, by 1914 "the Archipelago [sic] had become a healthful place for the white man to live."[24]

American capitalists further decried the psychological characteristics of Filipinos, deeming them unfit for the modern workforce. Americans identified a "lack of thrift, of industry, of foresight, of the habit of saving" among the indigenous population.[25] Andrew Draper (1848–1913), president of the University of Illinois, claimed that the Filipinos "pass their time in loafing and smoking and fishing and cock-fighting."[26] Episcopalian Bishop Charles Brent went so far as to state that the natives were "sick physically and morally, and so ignorant that they exist rather than live."[27]

The Manila Electric Railroad and Light Company (Meralco) introduced electric streetcars in 1905, but initially hired only American motormen. Among the laborers it was claimed that it took three to four Filipinos to lay as much track as one white man. A manager complained that Filipino mechanics worked only half as fast as Americans and "they can not use figures or calculate and must have white foremen over them. In 14 years we have not been able to train up a traffic inspector from their numbers."[28]

In the southern province of Mindanao, Dean Worcester labeled the Moros "unexcelled pirates and slave traders, treacherous and unreliable to the last degree," and the Bagobo tribe of Davao as "effeminate, the boys and girls being indistinguishable and the latter having the vigor of the former."[29] The Americans introduced baseball as an antidote to produce a competitive spirit and turn effeminate males into manly men, capable of participating in the capitalist economy.

Americans believed that physical activity would not only wrest the Filipinos from their lethargy, but promote physical growth. W. Cameron Forbes stated that, after a decade of American rule, "one of our great movements was the upbuilding of the physique of the Filipino people, who were too poorly nourished, and too much weakened by disease to do the work which an able-bodied and healthy people ought to do."[30] Even Dean Worcester, no admirer of Filipinos, felt that "baseball is one of the really important things which the Bureau of Education has taught the boys . . . it brightens them up and increases their activity and alertness. Keen interest is taken not only by the boys themselves, but by their fathers and mothers, in competitive games between different settlements."[31] He further stated that baseball strengthened both muscles and wits, and admitted that "when well fed, properly directed and paid a reasonable wage, the Filipino makes a good field labourer [sic]."[32]

THE EXPLOITATION OF LABOR

American authorities commandeered local labor forces to effect their infrastructure projects. Construction of the Benguet Road started in 1901 with the impressment of Igorot tribesmen under the supervision of American overseers. By 1903 a report indicated that the Igorot is "'a vastly superior animal' that could be trusted to earn his wages without the necessity of a white foreman to watch him." Workers slept in railroad cars and had no shelter in torrential downpours during the rainy season.

Cholera, dysentery, and malaria took a toll, and by April of 1903 the authorities were forced to hire 173 American laborers at $2 per day. Within two months another 1,000 Filipinos were hired at 25¢ per day, plus food and sleeping quarters with the promise of increased wages "if they showed ability to perform the same amount of work as laborers of other nationalities and races." Wages, however, were paid to foreman for distribution to the workers, and the overseer often took a 20 percent appropriation for himself. Recruiting agents implied wages of $1 to $2 per day, but when such expectations fell short 200 workers walked out of camp in July, disgusted with the conditions, their treatment, and the low wages. As many as 1,000 men occupied camp sites, segregated by race, with separate quarters for Americans, Filipinos, and other Asians. The polyglot contingents included American Indians, Europeans, South Americans, Mexicans, Hawaiians, Hindus, and Chinese, and relationships were not always cordial. They worked in squads of twenty to twenty-five, harassed by harsh and racist foremen, who cajoled, ridiculed, coerced, and shamed them into completing assigned tasks. Laborers retaliated by feigning work, shoveling already loose dirt, and sleeping on timber parties that returned with little firewood in time to receive their evening meal. Others stole tools, vandalized sites and even attacked the timekeepers who determined their hourly rates.[33]

The striking workers began a march back to Manila joined by more than four hundred others who were enroute to the worksite, forced to beg for food along the way, some perishing before they reached their destination. They established a camp at the Manila city hall, where they beseeched Governor General Taft to provide food and passage back to their homes. The authorities responded by compelling two hundred shackled prisoners from the Manila penitentiary to replace the striking laborers. The shackles, however, proved unsafe for work on cliffs and hillsides, which resulted in deaths and the necessity for guards to deter escapes. The penal experiment lasted only until November of 1903, and the authorities eventually had to acquiesce to assuage laborers' concerns, issuing regular payments directly to the workers, permitting families to accompany their wage-earners, providing better food and entertainment (including cockfights), providing free medical care, improving sanitation in the camps, and even firing supervisors who hit their workers.[34]

Between October of 1903 and June of the following year the Americans hired more than 20,000 workers, although less than half of them were Filipinos. Wages remained higher for skilled labor, as American carpenters earned $2.50–$3.00 per day, while Japanese got $1.50 per day, and native woodwrights received 50¢ daily. General laborers earned $1.00–$1.50 each day if they were Americans, while Japanese made $1.00 and Filipinos had to settle for only 25¢, based upon daily evaluations by the foreman. Such allotments based on race continued to be standard procedures in the next decade as the United States embarked upon the building of the Panama Canal, as did the scientific management strategies designed to produce greater efficiency. Major Lyman Kennon (1858–1918), former military governor of Ilocos Norte in northen Luzon, was assigned to the Corps of Engineers, and brought in to supervise the construction of the Benguet Road (which was later renamed in his honor). By invoking scientific management principles and a good dose of paternalism directed at the workforce he was able to complete the project in 1905, well ahead of schedule. Kennon would later rise to the rank of brigadier general, and American companies adopted industrial relations strategies known as *welfare capitalism*, first employed by George Pullman in 1880 in the construction of a workers' town outside Chicago with better housing, and amenities including outstanding sports facilities that served as a means of socially controlling the workforce during their leisure hours.[35]

In order to facilitate future infrastructure projects the governing body passed a statute in 1906 that required every Filipino male to contribute five days per year to road construction or maintenance or to pay an equivalent fine. When the indigenous officials in the provinces rejected the order, police then coerced residents into "voluntary" servitude. The *Manila Cablenews* backed the proposition by stating that "all of us who have lived in the Far East know that in practice these yellow and brown peoples must be guided and often driven in a forward direction so that they do not obstruct the progress of the world nor infringe on the rights of other nations."[36] Filipinos had begun organizing unions as early as 1899, encouraged by the nationalist media, and by 1910 the US Bureau of Labor reported that the large number of strikes were "the consequence of the unity and solidarity of ideals and sentiments which now reign among the workingmen." Authorities took drastic action, imprisoning the leader of a strike at a tobacco factory, charging him with sedition, and reinstating the law, requiring five days of servitude. Such actions produced massive deaths in the Ifugao community in 1918 when the constabulary forced 1,500 men to labor on a road construction project, and they returned to their village afflicted with the flu and smallpox that quickly spread among the inhabitants.[37]

Francis Harrison inherited a budget deficit upon his ascension to the governor general's office in 1913, and he decided to hire more Filipinos at a lower cost to replace American workers. Dean Worcester protested the decision in a missive to the *New York Times*, to no avail. By the 1920s the Philippine Scouts assumed much of the work of the American military at one-third the salaries.[38]

EXPLOITATION OF THE ISLANDS

The American occupation of the islands brought wholesale change to the culture, as communal property became subject to acquisition by individuals or corporate groups. American lawyers soon arrived in the Philippines to effect the transactions. The Friar Lands Act enabled Americans to buy the property previously controlled by the Catholic Church and both Dean Worcester, as Secretary of the Interior, and W. Cameron Forbes, during his stint as governor general, encouraged Americans to acquire Philippines property as an incentive to investment, despite the apparent conflict of interest.[39]

Both Worcester and Forbes personally benefitted from the land sales. Forbes purchased 15 acres of choice land for his mansion in Baguio for only $43, while Worcester claimed his own 10 acres in the summer capital for only $30. As president of the Baguio Country Club Worcester bought another 88 acres for Americans' recreational purposes at the cost of only $14. E. L. Worcester, a nephew of the administrator, leased another 2,500 acres for his business enterprise at a minimal rate.[40]

Although the colonial lands were intended for purchase by Filipinos and local enterprises, American individuals and corporations found the means to circumvent the statutes. American sugar corporations purchased 55,000 acres of land, and on Negros Island the local producers were no longer able to compete with the operators of the Mindoro Development Company, forcing them into wage labor and a loss of their independent lifestyle.[41]

The colonial administration awarded construction contracts for infrastructure and utilities to Americans and American companies. American mining companies also traveled to the islands in search of riches, but some need not leave American shores to elicit profits. Thomas Edison's (1847–1931) movie company quickly produced a series of supposed battle reenactments from New Jersey, showing heroic American soldiers shooting and chasing Filipino guerrillas, played by African Americans or whites in blackface, through the countryside.[42]

THE BUSINESS AFFAIRS OF DEAN WORCESTER

In 1911 a YMCA report lamented that "a large number of government servants in the Philippines . . . seem to be here chiefly, if not solely, to make all the money they can in a short time, and while they are making it they have very little use for the 'Little Brown Brother.'"[43] The correspondent may have had Dean Worcester, Secretary of the Interior, in mind. Continually criticized for his seeming conflicts of interest, Worcester claimed that he was safeguarding resources from greedy Filipino businessmen. In 1908 Worcester managed to overturn the limitations on land acquisitions by American corporations and increase sales to his acquaintances. He retired in 1913 to become vice president and general manager of the American-Philippines Company, a $5 million corporation with interlocking subsidiary companies intent on large-scale ranching and agricultural operations. The firm had been planned along with Governor General Forbes and John Pershing, then military governor of Moro Province, as early as 1911.[44]

Supported by the company, Worcester returned to the United States to lecture on the inability of Filipinos to govern themselves. Upon his return to Cebu in 1915 he was met by a large protest, but undeterred, he directed the Visayan Refining Company under the guise of welfare capitalism. The company village included a clubhouse, theater, athletic fields, and a majestic house for himself and his family. Employees received free medical care, but the company store charged 20 percent more than others and workers faced higher rents. By 1918 the company had become the largest and most profitable producer of coconut oil, raising its prices to meet the needs of consumers during World War I, as glycerine proved a necessary component for explosives. Worcester's salary rose from $15,000 to $25,000 plus stock in the company. Emilio Aguinaldo, the former leader of the Philippines insurrection, and other political figures were co-opted to meet the company's needs. Aguinaldo raised his economic and political capital as vice president of two American corporations under Worcester's holding company with compensation including a salary of $6,000, a house, and an American education for his son. Worcester led the American domination of the coconut oil industry and installed his son, brother-in-law, and son-in-law as company executives in the 1920s before his untimely death in 1924 at the age of fifty-seven.[45]

THE ROLE OF POPULAR CULTURE

Popular culture posed particular concerns for the American administrators, as they banned nationalist plays that they felt fomented rebellion. Hundreds of black and white American military veterans also chose to remain in the Philippines after their enlistment periods to become entrepreneurs, opening saloons, cabarets, dance halls, pool halls, theaters, and brothels, all of which drew concerns from Protestant missionaries and required scrutiny, regulation, and policing. Licensing of such operations also provided revenue for the government.[46]

One form of popular culture, however, gained nearly universal approval. Missionaries extolled sport as a character-building activity. Military commanders and civic officials espoused it as a means of socially controlling young men during their leisure and colonial administrators invoked it as a primary means of instilling American democratic and capitalist values.

Sport had already proven to be a commercial success in the United States. As early as 1852 the Boston, Concord, and Montreal Railway sponsored the first intercollegiate athletic competition between Harvard and Yale, offering a rowing race on Lake Winnepesaukee in New Hampshire as a marketing device to attract patrons to its resort.[47] The proliferation of baseball teams reached national proportions after the Civil War and culminated in the formation of the National League of Professional Baseball Players in 1876. Albert Spalding, a star pitcher in the league and president of the organization by 1882, parlayed his celebrity into the establishment of a profitable sporting goods company. In search of larger markets Spalding embarked on a global tour from October 1888 to April 1889, introducing baseball to lands throughout the British empire.[48]

Well before the turn of the century baseball had been established as the national game. American soldiers transported their bats and balls to the Philippines with the outset of the Spanish-American War and soon introduced the locals to that sport as well as boxing. Baseball soon achieved local popularity as soldiers contested with marines and the military teams formed a league, dominated by the 24th Infantry Regiment of African Americans from 1899 to 1902. Local fans soon adopted the game. The public schools promoted the American national pastime, and Manila schools began playing interscholastic games in 1903. By 1905 the Southern Luzon Athletic Association offered the first baseball tournament for high school teams. An American all-star team made an Asian tour as a marketing strategy for the Reach Sporting Goods Company and played twelve games in Manila in 1908, only losing two to the military all-stars. In 1910 the University of Chicago sent its team on an Asian tour and won four games in the Philippines. However, three of its players chose to remain in the islands, accepting jobs in Manila. The university received a $1,000 guarantee for its Philippines interlude, a measure of the widespread interest in baseball, and the team returned again for eight games in 1915.[49]

Waseda University in Japan also brought its team to the islands in 1912, which developed into an international rivalry. A thousand Filipino fans backed their team in Cebu, and an American reported that "the rivalry was spirited. Once or twice, it bordered on bitterness. In short, the game was for blood. Having defeated a white foe in war (an allusion to the Japanese victory over Russia), no doubt the Japs could not brook defeat by their neighboring islanders." Cebu triumphed 3–1 as "bedlam broke loose, Japan was whipped, and the Cebu men became heroes." Five thousand spectators showed up for the deciding game in Manila, won by the Filipinos, 3–2.[50] Baseball fever induced the *Manila Times* to declare that it was "more than a game, a regenerating influence and a power for good."[51]

In 1913 the Chicago White Sox and the New York Giants traveled to the Philippines, where they were lavishly fêted, as part of their world tour. Spectators at their Manila game paid an exorbitant $7 for seats.[52] That summer an all Filipino team toured the United States, using their talents to express their nationalist sentiments. A Filipino publication stated that "the Americans who have seen them play with American teams have to acknowledge another proof of the capacity and adaptability of the Filipinos to modern sports. Indeed to those fans who considered Walter Johnson and Ty Cobb the greatest men in the United States, our team will be the strongest argument in favor of Philippine independence." Its dismal record of 16 wins against 38 losses, however, failed to convince Americans.[53]

Sport provided one venue relatively free of the exclusionary practices common in other social events, and competition enabled the Filipinos to test the whites' Social Darwinian presumptions of racial superiority. The Filipino principal of one public school created his own farm system within the institute with intramural games that identified the best players. He sent his pitcher and catcher to an American military base to learn from their athletes, and by 1911 his team defeated the American soldiers of Fort McKinley in a best-of-five series of games.[54]

Even in the more genteel sports, Filipinos began to challenge Americans. Locals beamed when three Filipino doubles teams defeated their American opponents in a tennis match. Such victories provided a sense of empowerment and further enhanced native political beliefs in their abilities to govern themselves.[55]

While the indigenous peoples had their own form of martial arts previous to the American arrival, they learned the gloved form of pugilism from the soldiers. Boxing provided an even more visible test of individual racial comparisons in the ring, and Filipinos willingly paid their hard earned money to witness such encounters. By 1909 American promoters had established the Olympic Stadium and Athletic Club as a commercialized site with 8,500 seats that allowed for integrated crowds, and 3,000 had to be turned away for the first big bout between a British featherweight champion and a local fighter. Frank Churchill (1874–1933) started work in the Philippines as a customs house worker before seeking more lucrative ventures as a fight promoter. He teamed up with brothers Bill and Eddie Tait to produce the Olympic stadium spectacles. Joe Waterman had served as a chief petty officer in the Philippines before turning his interests to boxing as a referee, announcer, and promoter. Waterman believed in the character building capabilities of sport, stating that "the native is manlier, cleaner and healthier because of his interest in boxing. The Filipino as a boxer has done more in two years for Philippine independence and to eradicate the cock fighting evil, than insurrectos and politicians have done in 12 times the length of time." Jack "Kid" Madden, a former boxer in the featherweight and lightweight ranks from 1894 to 1903, later moved from Brooklyn to the Philippines where he served as a prison guard in Manila before becoming an instructor and club manager in the Philippines.[56]

Churchill saw boxing as a means to escape impoverished conditions. "There were a great many ambitious Filipino lads who craved ring glory . . . begging for a chance. . . . Many of them didn't have money enough to buy an outfit of ring togs, so we always kept a supply of trunks, shoes, etc., available for them." The Filipinos, however, refused to wear the athletic cups to protect their vulnerable genitalia, considering it to be an effeminate practice of the Americans.[57]

Amateur bouts took place every Wednesday, enabling aspirants to gain notice and graduate to the professional ranks. The promoters imported both American and Australian fighters to enhance their offerings and Filipinos especially favored black American boxers over white opponents. Although the US military banned bouts with civilian opponents until 1923, clandestine bouts appeared regularly and black American fighters proved among the best. In 1920, Churchill began bringing his Filipino boxers to the United States, where he might earn even larger sums among the many Filipino laborers on the West Coast. He stated that his motives, however, were more than monetary.

> Before I am through here I mean to prove that whatever the Filipinos can do in a prize ring they can do in politics, in commerce, and in finance. I know the Filipino people about as well as anybody knows them. And I know those Filipinos as a hard-working, courageous and intelligent people who not merely are worthy and competent of independence and control of their affairs, but a nation of people which, if given a chance, will rise up within a generation to ranking as one of the most important in any part of the world.[58]

Francisco Guilledo (1901–1925), better known as Pancho Villa, became a world champion in the United States.

Sports required equipment and American firms earned lucrative profits in the islands. The Spalding Company provided the official baseball for leagues in the Philippines as well as assorted other sports supplies, and the Brunswick Balke Collender Company shipped bowling and billiards equipment to increasing numbers of recreational establishments. As early as 1902 the seven-hole Manila Golf Club was established with Governor General Taft, an avid golfer, as president. The Baguio Country Club followed in 1905 with a full eighteen holes and added amenities for tennis, swimming, baseball, cricket, croquet, trap shooting, and polo. A Manila polo club attracted the city's wealthy by 1909.[59]

Field sports also presented opportunities for development. Dean Worcester claimed that "the Philippines offer strong attractions to the devotees of the shotgun and the rifle, and they are a fisherman's paradise." He presented a list of wild game of interest to hunters and extolled the possibilities for deep sea fishing. He recalled that "soon after his arrival, Governor General Forbes began to inquire about the opportunities for sea fishing. . . . The sport is now firmly established on a sound basis." In addition to power boats, fishermen needed rods and reels, tackle, and gaffs for the large tarpon available in the local waters. The colonial administrators were particularly fond of deep sea fishing. Leo J. Grove (1876–?), governor of Nueva Vizcaya Province, landed a fish of nearly 53 pounds, and Forbes captured a 60 pound bonito; both with rod and reel. For those who could not afford their own boats the Coast Guard rented government vessels at $115 per day.[60]

WORLD WAR I

With the American entry into World War I residents of the Philippines raised funds for the war effort. One such fundraiser, a 1917 baseball game between two all-star teams, drew 3,000 spectators and garnered 2,000 pesos for the cause. The Manila Carnival that year featured an army version of Buffalo Bill Cody's Wild West Show and, in keeping with the martial combats of Europe, Filipino boxers contested with American military personnel in the islands.[61]

The war presented a number of economic opportunities for the Filipinos. Despite the opposition of American producers, the United States imported greater quantities of sugar, copra, coconut oil, and cordage from the islands. Filipinos also joined the American navy in increasing numbers: 2,000 in 1917 and 5,700 by the end of the war they would account for 5 percent of all navy personnel over the next decade; although they were limited to the roles of stewards and mess hall attendants.[62]

The influx of Filipino laborers to the United States, however, set off racist backlashes that included violent attacks and antimiscegenation laws directed at young, male Filipinos who frequented the taxi dance halls. White females in such establishments exploited the Filipinos' vulnerability with pretensions of romance while white males attacked the Filipinos for attempting to associate with white women.[63] Carlos Bulosan (1911–1956), one of the Filipino migrants to the United States, expressed his sense of dehumanization in the United States. He worked as an itinerant laborer, earning only $13 for a full season of work in an Alaskan cannery. In Washington he picked apples, but whites set fire to the bunkhouse where he slept. In Los Angeles he was relegated to a ghetto life, stating "I know deep down in my heart that I am an exile in America. I feel like a criminal running away from a crime I didn't commit. And this crime is that I am a Filipino in America."[64]

THE WOOD-FORBES REPORT

In April of 1921 the US government sent General Leonard Wood and former Governor General W. Cameron Forbes back to the Philippines to report on the status of Filipino self-governance. The report proved to be highly critical, claiming that the Filipino government was inefficient and required continued American supervision. While praising the number of schools built in the islands, it stated that the increasing numbers of Filipino teachers were ineffective and lacked proficiency in the teaching of the English language. It praised the strong interest in sports at the university and in the schools as a means to inculcate the desired values, but ultimately recommended the continued retention of the islands under American supervision with greater authority provided to the governor general.[65]

Wood retired from the US Army later that year and was appointed the governor general of the Philippines. Over the next six years his tenure resulted in a tumultuous relationship with Filipino leaders, as he continuously vetoed their legislative efforts and ruled in an auotocratic style. In 1923 he supported an American police officer deemed guilty of corruption by the Filipino officials, which led to the resignation of the Filipino members of the cabinet. The internecine quarrels continued, spurring widespread distrust and anti-Americanism until Wood's death in 1927, while undergoing surgery for a brain tumor in the United States.[66]

Filipino Plutocracy

The American cultivation of elite Filipino families, mostly *mestizos* of Spanish or Chinese descent, during the colonial period had lasting political and economic effects. Historian Stanley Karnow asserted that sixty such families have controlled the economy since 1900, and that 20 percent of the population acquired 50 percent of the national income.[67] In the wake of World War I, Speaker Sergio Osmena called for "economic nationalism" and began establishing government corporations to develop the nation's resources. The Philippines Constitution of 1935 required a minimum of 60 percent equity by Filipino investors in such developments. Few Filipinos other than those already possessing economic, social, and political capital had the means to partake of such ventures, thus reinforcing their hegemony. Such elite families paternalistically assumed that their own interests contributed to the public good.[68]

The Tydings-McDuffie Act of 1935 granted the Philippines commonwealth status and a ten-year timeline for complete independence. The advent of World War II resulted in the Japanese occupation of the islands throughout the hostilities, and the United States granted full independence to the nation in the aftermath of the war on July 4, 1946. The Bell Trade Act of 1946, however, maintained free trade rights for the United

States, as well as access to resources in the Philippines and its public utilities. The United States also retained its large military bases with a rent-free lease for a period of ninety-nine years, despite the protests of Filipinos.[69] The Subic Bay naval installation covered 262 square miles and Clark Air Base occupied another 206 square miles of Filipino territory, employing thousands of Filipinos, but at greatly reduced wages relative to their American coworkers. Fifty thousand squatters at the Clark facility existed nearby in the hopes of some largess. The towns of Angeles and Olongapo adjacent to the military bases consisted largely of bars and brothels that catered to the needs of American military personnel. The social distance that characterized colonial relationships continued during the Cold War era. Americans accounted for the deaths of thirty-one Filipinos from 1952 to 1964, yet none faced a trial. When subsequent deaths occurred in 1965 thousands of Filipinos took matters into their own hands, marching on the US embassy, which resulted in minimal compensation for the bereaved families. An analyst characterized the relationship as one of "mutual suspicion, distrust, contempt, and hostility."[70]

The locals appropriated food from the abundant American warehouses as well as 564 bombs, extracting the dynamite for underwater explosions that changed their fishing strategies and greatly increased their catch. More politically conscious natives formed communist cells that continued to thwart the government in armed insurrection over the remainder of the century. The military bases remained a point of contention for nearly half a century after World War II, and Ferdinand Marcos used the threat of insurrection as an excuse to impose a fifteen-year dictatorship, backed by the US government. With the popular overthrow of Marcos in 1986 the elite Filipino families returned to their customary positions of power.[71]

ECONOMIC LEGACY

The American occupation of the first half of the twentieth century and its economic dominion in its latter half produced mixed blessings for the Philippines. The Filipino legislature finally ousted the US military from its bases in 1991, turning the facilities into tax- and duty-free zones to rival those of Hong Kong and Singapore. Still, the country is one of the largest recipients of US aid and "the US the economic and cultural privileges of neo-colonial domination, and that the Philippine Republic, despite vociferously anti-American nationalism, continues to be culturally and economically subordinate to American interests." The economy has shown consecutive surpluses since 2003, with a 4.5 percent level of growth during the administration of Gloria Macapagal-Arroyo (2001–2010), daughter of the ninth Filipino president (1961–1965) Diosdado Macapagal (1910–1997). In 2012 its stock market registered the second-best gains in Asia. Despite the regular devastations of typhoons and earthquakes the national economy has made great strides and attracting foreign capital after banking reforms were enacted in 2014. Its credit rating has been upgraded and debt levels decreased. Nevertheless, high unemployment rates and nearly a fifth of the country underemployed, with 40 percent engaged in informal rather than acknowledged jobs, pose ongoing concerns. Such conditions force as many as five million Filipinos to seek gainful employment abroad, and they dutifully remit their earnings back home to meet family needs. Such remittances topped $6 billion in 2002. The blight of corruption still haunts the country, fueling popular uprisings, and several senators faced embezzlement charges in 2014 and internecine quarrels among the plutocratic families continue in the quest for power and lucre.[72] Capitalism transformed the economy of the Philippines and the educational system installed by the Americans produced a docile workforce often unable to find employment in their own homeland.

NOTES

1. John A. Garraty, *The American Nation: A History of the United States* (New York: Harper & Row, 1983), 408, 430–59; Zimmerman, *First Great Triumph*, 25.
2. Zimmerman, *First Great Triumph*, 34.
3. Harris, *God's Arbiters*, 15, 17.
4. H. W. Brands, *American Colossus*, 532–36; Millis, *The Martial Spirit*, 3, 20–27, 37–41, 179; Bain, *Sitting in Darkness*, 38–40, 68 (quote).
5. Dirk Bonker, "Social Imperialism Revisited: Navalism, Reform, and Empire in Germany and the United States Around 1900," presentation delivered at the Organization of American Historians Convention, January 3, 2003, Chicago, Illinois; Rasenberger, *America 1908*, 40–48, 55–56, 65–66, 156–57, 242–44.
6. Paul A. Kramer, "Empires, Exceptions, and Anglo-Saxons: Race and Rule between the British and U.S. Empires, 1880–1910," in Julian Go and Anne L. Foster, eds, *The American Colonial State in the Philippines: Global Perspectives* (Durham, NC: Duke University Press, 2003), 43–91; Zimmerman, *First Great Triumph*, 319, 346; Worcester, *The Philippines: Past and Present*, 887; Brands, *The Reckless Decade*, 334 (quote); Delmendo, "The Star Entangled Banner, 238.
7. Zimmerman, *First Great Triumph*, 346–47 (quote); Delmendo, "The Star Entangled Banner," 221; Erlyn Ruth F. Alcantara, "Baguio Between Two Wars: The Creation and Destruction of a Summer Capital," in Angel Velasco Shaw and Luis H. Francia, eds., *Vestiges of War: The Philippine-American War and the Aftermath of an Imperial Dream, 1899–1999* (New York: New York University Press, 2002), 207–23; Jones, *Honor in the Dust*, 169; Tuason, "The Ideology of Empire in National Geographic Magazine's Coverage of the Philippines," 39, 44.
8. Greg Bankoff, Conservation and Colonialism: Gifford Pinchot and the Birth of Tropical Forestry in the Philippines," 479–88; and Patricio N. Abinales, "The U.S. Army as an Occupying force in Muslim Mindanao, 1899–1913," 410–20, both in McCoy and Scarano, eds. *Colonial Crucible*.
9. Stanley, *A Nation in the Making*, 106.
10. Glenn Anthony May, "The Business of Education in the Colonial Philippines, 1909–30," in McCoy and Scarano, eds. *Colonial Crucible*, 151–62 (quote, 152).

11. Kramer, "The Pragmatic Empire," 318–19, 318 (quote); Edward Marshall, "Baseball Helping to Revolutionize the Philippines," *New York Times*, September 22, 1912, n.p.

12. Kramer, "The Pragmatic Empire," 321–26; Worcester, *The Philippines Past and Present*, 508–9; May, "The Business of Education in the Colonial Philippines, 1909–30"; Paulet, "To Change the World," 201 (quote).

13. Paulet, "To Change the World," 198.

14. Ibid., 199; Karnow, *In Our Image*, 212.

15. Torres, *The Americanization of Manila*, 58–64; Brody, "Building Empire," 129; Thomas Hines, "The Imperial Façade: Daniel Burnham and American Architecture in the Philippines," *Pacific Historical Review*, 41:1 (1972), 33–53; Daniel F. Doeppers, "Manila's Imperial Makeover: Security, Health, and Symbolism," in McCoy and Scarano, eds. *Colonial Crucible*, 489–98; Charles Moore, ed., *Plan of Chicago* (Chicago: Commercial Club, 1909), 29 (quote).

16. Brody, "Building Empire," 133; Alcantara, "Baguio Between Two Wars," 221.

17. Doeppers, "Manila's Imperial Makeover," in McCoy and Scarano, eds., *Colonial Crucible*, 489–98; Licuanan, *Filipinos and Americans*, 45–50.

18. Gavin Shatkin, "Colonial Capital, Modernist Capital, Global Capital: The Changing Political Symbolism of Urban Space in Metro Manila, the Philippines," *Pacific Affairs*, 78:4 (Winter 2005–2006), 577–600. (quote, 584).

19. Licuanen, *Filipinos and Americans*, 33–35; Alcantara, "Baguio Between Two Wars," 208–15.

20. Kramer, *The Blood of Government*, 159, 167–68; Stanley, *A Nation in the Making*, 90, 102–6; Torres, *The Americanization of Manila*, 70–81.

21. Report of the Philippine Commission to the Secretary of War, 1900–1915, 21, at books.google.com/books?id=8TLSAAAAMAAJ&pg=PA21&lpg=PA21&dq=Filipino+labor+strike+of+1903&source=bl&ots=j5Vd8lD-YD&sig=WezkBz0c_4Q9rJJk-mKgHDAjdso&hl=en&sa=X&ved=0CDsQ6AEwBWoVChMI8OzDi-S_yAIVTJMNCh1TKwDx#v=onepage&q=Filipino%20labor%20strike%20of%201903&f=false; Pante, "A Collision of Masculinities," 267, 266–67, 268 (quotes respectively).

22. Anderson, "'Where Every Prospect Pleases and Only Man Is Vile,'" 512 (quote).

23. Ibid., 513–26, 506 (quote).

24. Ibid., 526 (quote); Torres, *The Americanization of Manila*, 110–19.

25. Dr. Licien Warner cited in Paulet, "To Change the World,"180.

26. Ibid., 198.

27. Right Rev. Charles H, Brent, "Upbuilding the Wards of the Nation," booklet (New York: Harmony Club of America, n.d.) in University Presidents' Papers, 1889–1925, University of Chicago, Special Collections.

28. Pante, "A Collision of Masculinities," 263.

29. Worcester, "The Non-Christian Peoples of the Philippines," 1189, 1158 (quotes, respectively).

30. Kramer, *The Blood of Government*, 314.

31. Worcester, "The Non-Christian Peoples of the Philippine Islands," 1253.

32. Worcester, *The Philippines Past and Present*, 515, 886 (quote).

33. Greg Bankoff, "'These Brothers of Ours': Poblete's *Obreros* and the Road to Baguio," *Journal of Social History* (Summer 2005), 1047–72 (quotes, 1050).

34. Ibid.

35. Ibid.; Gems, *The Athletic Crusade*, 143–44; Gerald R. Gems, *Windy City Wars: Labor, Leisure, and Sport in the Making of Chicago* (Lanham, MD: Scarecrow Press, 1997), 44–47.

36. Bankoff, "These Brothers of Ours"; Stanley, *A Nation in the Making*, 107 (quote).

37. Bankoff, "These Brothers of Ours," 1063 (quote); Kramer, *The Blood of Government*, 314–17.

38. Torres, *The Americanization of Manila*, 41; Coffman, *The Regulars*, 338.

39. Torres, *The Americanization of Manila*, 35–36; Alcantara, "Baguio Between Two Wars," 217; Jones, *Honor in the Dust*, 284.

40. www.thefilipinomind.com/2012/09/the-friar-land-scandal-how-filipinos.html (October 17, 2015).
41. Ibid.
42. Torres, *The Americanization of Manila*, 212–15; Susan A. Brewer, *Why America Fights: Patriotism and War Propaganda from the Philippines to Iraq* (New York: Oxford, 2009), 32; Nick Deocampo, "Imperialist Fictions: The Filipino in the Imperialist Imaginary," in Shaw and Francia, eds., *Vestiges of War: The Philippine-American War and the Aftermath of an Imperial Dream, 1899–1999* (New York: New York University Press, 2002), 225–36.
43. Clymer, *Protestant Missionaries in the Philippines*, 186.
44. Kramer, *Blood of Government*, 216, 343–44, 366–69; Sullivan, *Exemplar of Americanism*, 127–30, 169; Ronald K. Edgerton, "Dean C. Worcester's Mission Among Philippine Upland Tribes," presented at the Philippine Studies Conference in Athens, Ohio, August 2–4, 1983, in Fred Eggan Papers, University of Chicago, Special Collections. Box 104, folder 19.
45. Sullivan, *Exemplar of Americanism*, 182–235.
46. Gleeck, *The Manila-Americans*, 13–14, 33; Torres, *The Americanization of Manila*, 178, 214–15.
47. Gems, Borish, and Pfister, *Sports in American History*, 133–34.
48. Peter Levine, *A. G. Spalding and the Rise of Baseball: The Promise of American Sport* (New York: Oxford University Press, 1985).
49. Jones, *Honor in the Dust*, 151, 223; Henry Chadwick, ed., *Spalding's Base Ball Guide and Official League Book for 1901* (New York: American Sports Publishing Co., 1901, 76; Joseph A. Reaves, *Taking In a Game: A History of Baseball in Asia* (Lincoln: University of Nebraska Press, 2002), 94–97; Amos Alonzo Stagg to Dear "Stuffy" (Alfred W. Place), July 12, 1910, and January 9, 1911, in Stagg Papers, Box 63, folder 3, University of Chicago Special Collections; Department of Physical Education and Athletics Papers, 1892–1974, Box 27, folder 2, University of Chicago, Special Collections.
50. Frederic S. Marquardt Papers, University of Michigan, Bentley Library; National Baseball Hall of Fame, Philippines file; Monroe Wooley, "'Batter Up' in the Philippines," *Outdoor World and Recreation*, May 1913, 313–14 (quotes).
51. Karnow, *In Our Image*, 18.
52. Elfers, *The Tour to End All Tours*, 138–144; *Chicago Tribune*, August 28, 1913, 16; *Chicago Tribune*, December 18, 1913, 10.
53. *Filipino People*, 1:11 (July 1913), 13, cited in Kramer, *The Blood of Government*, 371; Tom Walsh, "Baseball in the Philippines: A Capsule History," *Bulletin of the American Historical Collection*, 23:3 (July–September 1995), 106–9; Joseph A. Reaves, *Taking In a Game: A History of Baseball in Asia* (Lincoln: University of Nebraska Press, 2002), 102.
54. Gleeck, Jr., *The Manila-Americans*, 240; Luis Santiago, "The Organization of the San Mateo Baseball Team," *The Teachers' Assembly Herald* (Baguio: Dept. of Public Instruction), 5:26 (1912), 142–43, in Geronima T. Pecson and Maria Racelis, eds., *Tales of the American Teachers in the Philippines*, (Manila: Carmelo & Bauermann, 1959), 195–99.
55. Gleeck, Jr., *The Manila-Americans*, 111.
56. Gleeck, Jr., *The Manila-Americans*, 120; Runstedtler, Theresa, "The New Negro's Brown Brother: Black American and Filipino Boxers and the 'Rising Tide of Color,'" in Davarian L. Baldwin and Minkah Makalani, eds., *Escape from New York: The New Negro Renaissance Beyond Harlem* (Minneapolis: University of Minnesota Press, 2013), 105–26, 114 (quote); boxrec.com/media/index.php?title=Human:137869.
57. Ibid., 115 (quote); Gems, *Athletic Crusade*, 56.
58. Runstedtler, "The New Negro's Brown Brother," 115–17, 117 (quote).
59. John B. Foster, ed., *Spalding's Official Base Ball Record, 1909* (New York: American Sports Publishing Co, 1908), 254; Gleeck, Jr., *The Manila Americans*, 47, 66, 68–72; Benitez Licuanen, *Filipinos and Americans*, 68–80.
60. Worcester, *The Philippines Past and Present*, 806–18 (806, 807, quotes, respectively).
61. Gleeck, Jr., *The Manila-Americans*, 116–17.

62. Kramer, *The Blood of Government*, 384–85, 394–95, 398.

63. Kramer, *The Blood of Government*, 401–24; Paul G. Cressey, *The Taxi Dance Hall* (Chicago: University of Chicago Press, 1932); Allen Lumba, "Common Wealth in Precious Times: Militant Politics and Transient Labor across the Global Philippines, 1919–1942," presented at the Organization of American Historians Conference, St. Louis, MO, April 19, 2005.

64. E. San Juan, Jr., ed., *On Becoming Filipino: Selected Writings of Carlos Bulosan* (Philadelphia: Temple University Press, 1995), 4–11; Carlos Bulosan, *America Is in the Heart: A Personal History* (New York: Harcourt, Brace & Co., 1946); www.historylink.org/index.cfm?DisplayPage=output.cfm&file_id=5202 (July 24, 2015, quote).

65. Leonard Wood, *Report of the Special Mission to the Philippine Islands to the Secretary of War* (Washington, DC: Government Printing Office, 1922).

66. Lane, *Armed Progressive*, 250–75.

67. Karnow, *In Our Image*, 22, 40.

68. Anna Leah Fidelis T. Castaneda, "Spanish Structure, American Theory: The Legal Foundations of a Tropical New Deal in the Philippine Islands, 1898–1935," in McCoy and Scarano, eds., *Colonial Crucible*, 365–74.

69. Julian Madison, "American Military Bases in the Philippines, 1945–1965: Neo-Colonialism and Its Demise," in Richard Jensen, Jon Davidann, and Yoneyuki Sugita, eds., *Trans-Pacific Relations: America, Europe, and Asia in the Twentieth Century* (Westport, CT: Praeger, 2003), 125–45.

70. Madison, "American Military Bases in the Philippines," 135.

71. Bocobo-Olivar, *History of Physical Education in the Philippines*, 153–60; Hunt and Levine, *Arc of Empire*, 268–69.

72. Delmendo, "The Star Entangled Banner," 212–16, 216 (quote); www.heritage.org/index/country/philippines (November 7, 2015); www.theodora.com/wfbcurrent/philippines_economy.html (November 7, 2015): Shatkin, "Colonial Capital, Modernist Capital, Global Capital," 591–99; McCoy, "Policing the Imperial Periphery," 106–7.

SEVEN
Education

EDUCATION IN THE PHILIPPINES UNDER THE SPANISH

Religious instruction held a primary importance during the Spanish occupation of the Philippines. The University of Santo Tomas, the oldest in Asia, had been founded in Manila in 1611, a quarter century before Harvard University in America. Priests wielded both ecclesiastical and political power in the towns, where an 1863 decree legislated separate primary schools for boys and girls with instruction in the Catholic faith. The schools lacked grades and any system for advancement or graduation, and girls' education revolved around domestic skills. In the latter nineteenth century local school boards assumed greater control and introduced curricular reforms, but the religious emphasis remained. Few local teachers spoke Spanish and most children continued to be illiterate. The number of children enrolled in the schools increased in the latter decades, with more than 10,000 receiving a secondary education by the 1880s and about 200,000 in the more than 2,000 primary schools during the next decade. Despite the efforts of the priests and the teachers outside of the urban areas few learned to speak the Spanish language and many tribes adhered to their animist beliefs.[1]

SCHOOLING UNDER THE AMERICAN MILITARY

With the American occupation of the Philippines the US army wasted little time in initiating its own educational measures. William D. McKinnon (1858–1902), a Catholic priest and chaplain of the First California Volunteer Regiment, assumed the role of superintendent of Manila schools, and the army established more than 30 schools with 5,000 students enrolled by 1899. The soldier-teachers eliminated religious instruction and introduced English to their students despite the fact that they had no English textbooks. From 1899 to his early death in 1902 McKinnon served as an intermediary between Filipino Catholic clerics and the American administration. While employing American soldiers as teachers in the primary grades, he secured priests from the Catholic teaching orders to instruct in the secondary schools and higher education. In 1900 the Director of Education declared English to be the official language and an expedient lingua franca in lieu of the multitude of tribal dialects. Employing soldiers as teachers, the army had established 39 schools in Manila and about 1,000 throughout the archipelago by 1901, which counted more than 100,000 pupils.[2]

The Americans believed that education would be the most effective means of assimilating and acculturating Filipinos into the American value system. An American officer in Tayabas Province in southern Luzon stated that "the bureau of education in these islands . . . can be more beneficial than troops in preventing future revolutions." An American colonel in Cebu felt that "education would have an excellent political effect, and materially aid in establishing towns under American orders and law." General Arthur MacArthur, who assumed command of the Philippines in May of 1900, recommended that "the archipelago be submerged immediately under a tidal wave of education."[3]

The education of the Filipinos meant more than just the instruction of civics and the English language. Sport played a primary role in the inculcation of the American values of competition, democracy, respect for authority, morality, discipline, and the development of a strong work ethic. Soldiers quickly introduced their students to the American national game of baseball.

American educators likened the Filipinos to American Indian tribes, who were forced to acculturate by removing their children from the reservations to residential boarding schools, where they were taught the English language, vocational industrial skills, white lifestyles, and sports to hasten their assimilation. American educators noted such common characteristics of the Indians and the Filipinos as "lack of thrift, of industry, of foresight, of the habit of saving . . . a lack of self-restraint . . . They have not reached moral manhood."[4] Fred W. Atkinson (1865–1941), the first official Superintendent of Schools in 1901, declared that "The Filipino people, taken as a body, are children, and child-like, do not know what is best for them."[5] Consequently, like the Indians, education would be not only imposed upon, but forced on the Filipinos. Atkinson favored manual training similar to the education of African Americans and Indians at Hampton Institute in Virginia, but such education assumed relegation to the laboring class rather than full inclusion in the polity. Atkinson deemed the Filipinos to be incapable of self-government, and he was soon replaced. David Barrows became Superintendent of Education in 1903, and he initiated village schools which taught American values and

American patriotism. Schools were adorned with American flags and celebrated American holidays. Such festivities aligned well with the Filipinos' love of festivals, music, and pageantry, allowing the competing cultures to find agreement on some measures.[6]

Schooling included lessons in morality as well as civics, and sport provided the means to inculcate both, as students learned to play fairly, respect authority in the person of an umpire or referee, and the democratic principles inherent in teamwork. Before girls gained inclusion in the athletic ventures their education consisted of domestic chores, inculcating an American sense of hygiene and decorum. W. Cameron Forbes praised the efforts of the American teacher who

> brought with him the American spirit. He was the apostle of progress. He gave the children a healthy outlook toward life; he explained to them the principles of hygiene and sanitation. He brought with him the spirit of service. He inculcated into them a realization of the dignity of labor. And the children carried this spirit back into the homes, where it made its impress upon the parents.

One such apostle of progress explained that "the visitor does not so frequently have to gain the goodwill of the two or three bony dogs, fighting cock, or family pig at the entrance of the Filipino home as was formerly the case. These pets are being dispensed with, or being relegated to their proper places."[7]

Filipinos learned to cook with American utensils, adopt western notions of privacy, appreciate western art and culture, and decorate and redesign their homes according to the "civilized" standards of Americans. Much to the delight of American businessmen, such a transition in cultural standards offered an expanding market for their goods.[8]

American Teachers in the Philippines

The US government began recruiting trained American teachers to replace the soldiers in the colonial schools. More than 8,000 applicants sought such positions, which paid a salary of $75 to $125 per month. The teachers worked the five weekdays and half a day on Saturday and also taught adult classes three times per week. The first group of forty-eight pioneers arrived at Manila in June of 1901 on the *Sheridan*. A larger contingent of five hundred arrived in August on the *Thomas*, along with their baseball bats and tennis equipment, and they were deployed to the public schools throughout the islands by October. Philinda Rand (1876–1972), one of the female recruits, expressed her sense of mission. "We are not merely teachers. We are social assets and emissaries of good will."[9] Thereafter known as the *Thomasites*, such teachers were to provide primary instruction to Filipino students for the first two years and train local indigenous teachers to fill positions in the rapidly expanding school network. Another 925 American teachers arrived in 1902. The primary school curriculum initially consisted of four years of English language instruction, two years of math, one year of geography, as well as vocational, moral, and physical training. Intermediate schools, established in the larger communities, offered three years of instruction in English and literature, arithmetic, geography, civil government, history, and sciences, and industrial training or agriculture for boys and housekeeping classes for girls. Each of the thirty-five provinces established a high school, while Manila held three such institutions dedicated to teacher training, arts and trades, and a nautical school, funded by an internal revenue law of 1904.[10]

By 1903 American teachers in the islands numbered more than 1,000, assisted by 3,500 Filipinos, but the latter were not accorded equal measures of respect or authority. Under Spanish rule teachers had absolute rule and carried out their duties in a dictatorial fashion. Under Barrows' leadership elementary education decreased to three years to encourage enrollment and the American teachers assumed a greater role in secondary education. Barrows' initiatives did appeal to the lower classes, who were largely deprived of education during the Spanish regime, but attendance dwindled during harvest time as children's familial obligations superseded American dictates.[11]

Cultural differences contributed to the difficulties of the American teachers. The American work ethic proved foreign to Filipinos, who employed servants to conduct manual labor. Another female teacher, Mary Fee, complained that "Although the Filipinos are eager for education, their ambition is Filipino, not American. . . . They regard it as a means of getting along without work."[12] Mary Cole, among the Thomasites who traveled to the Philippines with her husband Harry, tried to teach proper American manners such as "no whispering, no spitting, no studying out loud, and no animals in the classroom"; Harry complained that he had to "teach 'monkeys' to speak English."[13]

The concept of time proved especially disconcerting to the Americans. Some students came to school at daylight, others at noon time. The Filipino teachers also arrived late for their duties or even took a day off to attend local fiestas. The Americans complained that "Children . . . felt no shame when caught copying. It took time to show them why it was wrong."[14] The American teachers were expected to serve as role models, but some of their practices confounded their pupils. The Spanish segregated boys and girls, while the Americans arranged coed classes. Whereas Filipinos observed more formal social relations, such as kissing the hands when greeting someone, or requiring chaperones during the courtship process; Americans simply shook hands upon greeting and the more independent American women traveled freely without escorts. Students were encouraged to adopt the American customs as more egalitarian, which disrupted family traditions and local culture.[15]

American lifestyles, however, were hardly egalitarian. Despite their long hours at work, and although provincial life lacked typical American amenities, the teachers lived a relatively leisurely existence compared to most Americans back home. Philinda Rand, who taught at Silay on Negros Island, had three servants, including a cook. Benjamin Neal (1879–1966), assigned to Pangasinan Province, found time to peruse the football scores of his alma mater, Syracuse University. For those teachers stationed in Manila the city offered musical concerts, baseball games, horseback riding, golf, tennis, polo, vaudeville shows, movie theaters, cabarets, social clubs, and much more.[16] Service in the Philippines also offered the possibility of social mobility, as teachers earned promotions or returned to more lucrative positions in the United States. Blaine F. Moore began teaching in 1900, but got disgusted with what he perceived as the Filipinos' lack of discipline. He was rewarded with an administrative position and found time to dabble in mining enterprises before returning to university roles in the United States. George A. Malcolm (1881–1961) began as a teacher in 1906, but stayed for decades and rose to the position of Supreme Court justice in the Philippines.[17]

American teachers also brought their racial beliefs to the Philippines. While Harry Cole deemed the Filipinos to be "monkeys" incapable of self-government, many others shared his sense of racial superiority. The teachers were warned not to associate with the townspeople among whom they lived. They declined to enter Filipino homes and generally adhered to the segregation practices of the United States.[18] Prescott F. Jernagan (1866–1942), wrote books for the Philippine schools, in which he asserted that it was "not a nation, but the wandering fragments of many different tribes," which were rated according to racial characteristics.[19] Jernagan's racializing coincided with the claims of the Dillingham Commission, a three-year (1907–1910) congressional study of immigration to the United States, which categorized people into forty-five different races with ascribed characteristics that eventually led to immigration quotas based on desirability for American citizenship.

ENGLISH AS A UNIFYING FORCE

With the polyglot tongues spoken across the disparate islands, the American government quickly settled on English to be "the common medium of communication . . . and [it] will greatly assist in teaching them self-government on Anglo-Saxon lines." Americans believed their English to be the language of modernity, the language of democracy and liberty, and the source of heroic struggles in mind and body derived through the classic literature produced by writers of the English tongue.[20] John B. Devins (1856–1911), a Protestant clergyman in the Philippines, concurred. "Only as English is spoken, enabling the Filipinos to study the literature of America, as well as to read current periodicals, newspapers and other books, will the people understand what is meant by the institutions and the civilization behind them which the Americans in the Philippines represent."[21]

Such intentions had limited success. The Filipino *ilustrados*, who spoke Spanish, objected to the imposition, but were forced to acquiesce if they hoped to partake in the American largesse. The vast majority of Filipinos, however, received only a fraction of the intended education, and that at the elementary level, where they were instructed by indigenous teachers with limited understandings and deficient pronunciation skills.[22]

In 1903 the American government began sending Filipinos to the United States for education, where some of them served as guides at the Philippines exhibit at the 1904 World's Fair in St. Louis. There they were chagrined by Americans who thought they had discovered the islands and asked if they enjoyed wearing clothes. Some of those sent to America developed an interest in the American game of football, and sports had a decidedly greater interest for Filipino youth in the schools as well.[23]

SPORT AS EDUCATION

Sport proved a less onerous means of inculcating the values that Americans deemed important for the Filipinos to adopt. A Filipino diplomat explained that "the American teachers succeeded in teaching the Filipinos to play with sportsmanship and to develop the proper attitude toward work." A Filipino university administrator agreed that through the "popularization of baseball and basketball . . . youngsters' leisure time activities were channeled toward games and away from useless activities like gambling."[24] Dean Worcester, Secretary of the Interior in the Philippines, claimed that "quite as important as the development of the minds of the young is the development of their bodies through the introduction of athletic games and sports, which have incidentally promoted intercommunication and mutual understanding between the several Filipino peoples. In many regions baseball is emptying the cockpits, and thus aiding the cause of good order and morality."[25] Mary Fee, one of the early Thomasites, noted the popularity of baseball among Filipino youth, stating that every green space in Manila was utilized for games and that every secondary school fielded a baseball team. As early as 1903 neighboring towns competed in Capiz in the western Visayan Islands. Girls also played the game, using fruit for a ball and a board for a bat. Fee claimed that "those children got more real Americanism out of that corrupted ball game than they did from singing 'My Country, 'tis of Thee' every morning."[26] The inculcation of American patriotism in the public schools was accompanied by the use of school textbooks that referred to baseball and the prominent display of the American flag.[27] Such devices were meant to promote a respect for and an allegiance to the United States in the ongoing war with the Filipino guerrilla army.

The emphasis on physical education, however, was not an American invention, as it had been suggested by Jose Rizal, the national hero executed by the Spanish authorities in 1896. An all-around athlete and scholar, Rizal participated in weight training, gymnastics, boxing, wrestling, martial arts, fencing, cricket, hiking, mountain climbing, riflery, and chess. He proposed a model school that also included horsemanship and instruction in swimming and dancing, as well as running and jumping. During his exile to Dapitan on the southern island of Mindanao in 1892 he established such a school with an extensive program of physical education and included a swimming pool. The Superior Normal School for Men Teachers also offered gymnastics in its curriculum as early as 1893.[28]

The promotion of the physical education program by the Americans throughout the islands is detailed in the chronicles of Frederic S. Marquardt, born in 1905 to American teachers. His father, Walter. W. Marquardt (1878–1962), served as principal of a provincial high school at Tacloban in the eastern Visayan Islands. His son stated that the high school was established in 1905 and moved to Tacloban the following year.

> Athletics began to receive more attention with baseball as the main and favorite event. All the boys were compelled to take part in military drills.... The girls ... had calisthenics under Mrs. Carpenter. Athletics then, however, was [not] so extensively carried out as the present. Now each student and pupil has one kind of athletics. There is a team of each game; and in each boys' class has a team is [sic] baseball, indoor baseball, volley ball [sic] and basket ball [sic]. Each girls' class has a team in indoor baseball and volleyball. Regular schedule [sic] are followed for each game and there is a close contest on to decide the class championship. The school spirit is excellent

In 1907 "baseball was given more prominence," and the following year

> the baseball team was fully organized and has shown good work while playing against the American soldiers at Camp Bumpers and the Scout team at Tanauan. The team grew stronger every year and to-day [sic] it has made an admirable record in the athletic world of the Philippines. [An athletic meet was added by 1910, and] the athletic field which consists of a quarter mile track with 220 yards straight-a-way [sic], and several baseball and indoor baseball diamonds, basket ball [sic], tennis and volley ball [sic] courts witnessed the East Inter Visayan Meet in December, 1913. The province had spent over P2,000,000 (pesos) putting it in shape and in constructing a grand stand [sic] which seats about 500 persons. The Leyte baseball team celebrated the occasion by winning the Inter-Visayan championship and later the championship of the Philippines.[29]

The athletic competitions helped to produce the desired qualities in the Filipinos, but they might also release nationalist sentiments, particularly in games versus the American military forces. Luis Santiago, principal of the San Mateo intermediate school in Rizal, near Manila, organized teams within the school, managed by the teachers. His interschool tournament of six teams proved insufficient for his competitive zeal. Nor was he satisfied with winning the Rizal city championship in 1911. He took the field as a pitcher for the school team in the Southern Tagalog Interprovincial Championship, and then sent his pitcher and catcher to the American military base at Fort McKinley to learn from the Americans. He then scheduled a five-game series with the American soldiers in which his Filipino team won three matches, an obvious blow to American notions of racial superiority.[30]

Filipino Opposition to American Education

While sport provided one means of more subdued retaliation against the Americans, Filipinos expressed their opposition in more overt fashion as well. In 1901 the Philippines Commission established a public school system that invoked the American principle of separation of church and state, which removed religious instruction from the curriculum, a move that drew the ire of Filipinos. Their protests and a threatened boycott resulted in a compromise that permitted religious education after the normal school hours.[31]

That agreement, however, also provided the opportunity for the American teachers, the vast majority of whom were Protestants, to proselytize as well. Combined with the ardent efforts of the American missionaries such endeavors incurred the wrath of Filipino priests, who opposed any transgressions on their religious monopoly. The Catholic Church responded with the assignment of more Catholic priests to the islands and formation of private schools, more than 1,300 by 1903, which enrolled more than 90,000 students.[32]

The University of Santo Tomas, staffed by Dominican priests, continued to teach in Spanish rather than English, the prescribed language of the American schools. In parts of the Visayan Islands and in Mindanao the American teachers faced opposition, and an education department report in 1903 admitted that "the people have been slow to accept the radical innovations of the American educational system."[33]

The battle over the nature of the schools continued over the next three decades. The Philippine Assembly attempted to substitute local dialects for educational instruction, but their efforts were continually vetoed by the Philippines Commission. In 1921 the Vatican assigned another twenty Jesuit priests from the United States to teach at the Ateneo, a Jesuit university established in 1859. The militant and aggressive Irish-American priests taught in English and managed to elevate the status of the Ateneo to that of the older Santo Tomas, which maintained the prestige of a Catholic education, but also promoted its Americanization. In addition to the use of English, American sports, particularly baseball, augmented the formal instruction. Americans felt that the sports and games taught the order and structure necessary for self-government.[34]

The contested nature of the educational process greatly limited the effect of the democratization of the Philippines. American intentions to liberate Filipinos from the hierarchy of the Spanish imperial administration were subverted by the lack of general access to higher education. Only the wealthy *ilustrado* families had the means to pursue the academic training that would lead to leadership roles in the development of nation building.[35]

Education for Civil Service

In 1908 the American-owned *Manila Times* scolded the school system for providing higher aspirations for Filipino youth, rather than more suitable vocational or educational training, and called for less money to be spent on education and more on public works projects. The more nationalistic *El Ideal* also called for education reform in 1910, but it desired "Filipinized Filipinos" rather than the "Americanized Filipinos" produced by the schools. In response, the wealthy Filipino families founded their own private schools "to keep intact and conserve Filipino ideals . . . against the danger of complete Americanization of the islands." The *Manila Times* carried more weight among the American administration, and by 1913 the number of public schools had decreased to 2,934 from 4,531 in 1910. The 9,086 teachers employed in 1911 numbered only 7,671 in 1913 and student enrollment dropped from 484,689 in 1911 to 349,454 two years later.[36]

For those who stayed in school, education provided the pathway to lucrative civil service jobs within the American administration. In Manila, private English language schools trained their students for the required civil service exams. The students selected for the *pensionado* program, which sent them to colleges in the United States, were required to return to the Philippines as employees in civil service positions for five years after their graduation.[37] Placed in such positions the civil servants not only learned the ways and means of government and politics, but succeeded to positions of power.

PRIVATE EDUCATION

The Philippine Normal School, a teacher training institution for men, was established in 1865, but the colonial administration privatized the facility in 1901. It ceased to function by 1905. The private schools founded by

American missionaries often adopted a curriculum similar to the public schools with industrial education and sports, but also included Protestant religious instruction. Silliman Institute, founded in 1901 in Dumaguete in the Visayan Islands by the Presbyterians originated as an industrial school for boys modeled on the Hampton Institute in the United States. It began accepting females in 1912 and eventually grew to obtain university status by 1938. Likewise, Central Philippine College in Iloilo began as a Baptist industrial school for boys in 1905 in Jaro on the island of Panay, accepted females by 1913, and gradually grew into a high school, junior college, and degree granting college.[38]

In the early years of the American occupation such schools did not meet the needs of aspiring Filipinos, and the extent of private education provided some indication of the Filipino resistance to the American efforts. In Maasin, on the island of Panay, the public school languished while the private school flourished by 1909.[39]

Americans drew clear distinctions in the education of their own children. As early as 1901 they founded the American School for ex-patriate students. Bishop Brent later founded an exclusive boarding school for Americans in Baguio that promoted religious instruction and sports, while segregating its students from socialization with Filipinos. He founded a separate school for Moro boys in Jolo, where baseball and boxing were meant to "civilize" the pupils; although the experiment did not always meet with success. In a 1908 baseball game between a uniformed Filipino provincial school team and the Moro school team that had no uniforms, W. Cameron Forbes offered a 10 peso prize to the winners. A teacher from the provincial school acted as the umpire, but the Moros became disgusted with his officiating and quit after two innings. When they were persuaded to replay the game, they once again quit after disputes with the umpire.[40]

INDUSTRIAL EDUCATION

While the *ilustrados'* children trained for leadership, the overwhelming number of Filipino students engaged in education for roles in the labor force. Under the leadership of Frank White (1875–1913), who assumed the role of Director of Education in 1909, the curriculum in the schools emphasized industrial arts and the production of handicrafts which could be sold. Within a year more than 350,000 students in the primary grades were introduced to vocational skills. Boys engaged in vocational training such as carpentry and gardening, while girls were taught domestic skills such as cooking, housekeeping, childcare, weaving, and sewing. By 1911 the Bureau of Education in Manila established a School of Household Industries and a sales agency to sell the products made by the students, which included baskets, mats, embroidery, hats, lace, slippers, pottery, and handicrafts. The agency was disbanded in 1915 in favor of a general sales department that employed 16,000 embroidery workers with an annual trade of $480,000.[41]

Not only the public schools, but the religious schools founded by missionaries emphasized vocational skills suitable for the labor force. By 1905 the Industrial School for Boys established by the Baptists in Jaro on the island of Panay in the western Visayas, offered classes in tailoring, shoemaking, and tinsmithing. Other schools provided training in blacksmithing and mechanical drawing. By 1913 almost all (93 percent) of the primary grade students were involved in industrial education. By 1924 there were about 900,000 students engaged in such work, a figure that declined precipitously as the Filipinos gained greater leverage in educational matters.[42]

Americans intended such training to wrest the Filipinos from their ascribed lethargy and to induce discipline, a strong work ethic, and respect for the dignity of labor. Such training induced a form of social control, as Americans perceived a moral laxity that revolved around gambling, the cockpits, and too many fiestas. Moreover, the Filipinos trained for the labor force came cheaply, for as little as 6 percent of what the Americans were paid. One historian judged that "the U.S. government's ultimate objective in promoting public education in the Philippines had more to do with developing commerce than with the benevolent goals of freedom and cultural unity."[43]

PHYSICAL EDUCATION

The continued emphasis on physical education ultimately proved of greater value to the American cause than that of industrial training, for it instilled the same values without the overt taint of exploitation. Required physical education for both boys and girls became a part of the schools' curriculum by 1905 and interscholastic teams competed in a variety of sports, including baseball, indoor baseball, basketball, and volleyball. Tennis courts and running tracks were added to the school facilities by 1910. The competition that ensued taught the basis for the capitalist economic system, while team games fostered democracy in the leadership and communal efforts needed for team success. Umpires and referees fostered a respect for authority, and success required the discipline and work ethic the administrators had hoped to achieve in their manual training efforts.[44]

Americans believed that physical education would contribute to the health and growth of the Filipinos. Particular exercises were directed at correcting perceived physical deficiencies. Students were required to achieve a grade of 75 percent in their physical education classes in order to gain promotion to the next grade. The curriculum included daily hygiene inspections, marching, calisthenics, military drills, dances, and games, as well as sports. Students could earn ribbons, buttons, or badges for participation in athletic contests, similar to the program offered in the New York public schools under Luther Gulick (1865–1918). Bonus points for participation in athletics could be applied to students' grade point averages or other academic deficiencies. The authorities believed that athletic contests served as surrogate means of warfare among the rival tribes, and that the games developed the character of the participants. By 1917 the Director of Education reported a decrease in tuberculosis cases due to athletics, and the medical director of the Philippine Constabulary claimed that his survey of 1,000 recruits showed that they were physically larger than those of eight or nine years previous, "due no doubt to athletic training the younger generation has been and is receiving in the primary, intermediate, and high schools of the islands."[45] By 1919, in his address to the national convention, William H. Burdick (1871–1935), President of the American Physical Education Association, wondered at the extent of the Philippines program (4,500 of the 4,702 schools) and the importance placed on the subject, and hoped that the United States might fare as well.[46]

The physical education program achieved even greater prominence with the arrival of Elwood S. Brown in Manila as the YMCA director in 1910. Brown worked closely with the Philippines Commission and the YMCA soon assumed a primary role in the organization of athletic contests and the formation of interscholastic leagues. A member of the YMCA staff served as the acting director of public education, and the YMCA produced a handbook for the control and conduct of games. Brown also trained the playground directors and served on the initial Playground Committee in 1913. Playgrounds served as a further means of social control by occupying children's time during their nonschool hours and provided playground directors to reinforce the sports and games taught in the schools with their inherent value systems. A 1913 survey indicated the value of the playgrounds, where 105 games of indoor baseball or volleyball were counted in the three original playgrounds in only one day. The YMCA, as an overtly Protestant organization, presented an apparent conflict between the American constitutional separation of church and state; yet the civil government of the Philippines offered ardent support for its efforts.[47]

The students in the primary schools engaged in calisthenics and drills, but sports and games proved to be most popular among boys and girls. By 1915 the YMCA counted 29,000 girls playing indoor baseball on uniformed teams and claimed that volleyball was equally popular. More than 90 percent of the 450,000 registered students participated in some form of athletics. The work of the YMCA also extended beyond the schools and playgrounds, as it included games among the Philippines Scouts and the Constabulary, who trained as an indigenous police force under American direction. Volleyball games were played on large spaces and might include as many as thirty players per side. Street children, such as shoe shine boys and newspaper vendors, were also enticed into the YMCA facilities with a dinner, a field day, and an aquatics meet, that rewarded all with prizes.[48]

As in the United States, the increased participation of females in the sporting culture fostered social change. Active sport required dress reform and some Filipino parents objected to the introduction of blouses and bloomers in lieu of traditional Filipino skirts and long-sleeved blouses. The 1911 Annual Report of the Director of Education stated that "a departure from former precedents in the Philippines appears in the development of basketball as a sport for girls. During the past year this game has received some attention in school divisions. From the beginning the experiment has had satisfying results. The girls have entered into the contests with enthusiasm. A certain conservative element in the population looks with some disapproval upon the introduction of his sport, but the game may now be considered as well established." Both basketball and volleyball were sports invented by the YMCA personnel in the United States during the 1890s, and the global missionaries of the YMCA promoted them around the world thereafter. In the ensuing years Filipino girls' teams traveled to Shanghai and Tokyo to introduce indoor baseball to those nations (although the Japanese had adopted American baseball as early as the 1870s).[49]

HIGHER EDUCATION

Colonial administrators favored the employment of alumni from their own American institutions, such as Harvard and Yale, for civil service positions in the Philippines, but the University of Michigan graduates perhaps effected the greatest influence on the educational system. Dean Worcester, a Michigan graduate who had a long tenure as Secretary of the Interior—a position that covered responsibilities for health and science issues—employed a number of alumni for important roles. The Philippine Medical School opened in 1907 under Worcester's auspices rather than the Department of Education. Paul Freer (1862–1912), a professor at the University of Michigan and Worcester's brother-in-law, served as the first dean from 1907 until his death in 1912. It became the College of Medicine and Surgery of the University of the Philippines in 1910. The Philippine General Hospital opened that same year under Worcester's supervision. It included a nursing school staffed by American teachers.[50]

Worcester also served on the board of regents of the University of the Philippines, established in 1908, and modeled after Harvard University in the United States. By 1911, it included a College of Agriculture, a College of Engineering, a College of Liberal Arts, a College of Law, the aforementioned College of Medicine and Surgery, a College of Veterinary Medicine, and a School of Fine Arts. Women were admitted to the university in 1916, six years after Filipino families established the Philippines Women's University for the education of their daughters. George Malcolm, another graduate of the University of Michigan, proved instrumental in the founding of the College of Law, serving as its first dean. Malcolm arrived in the Philippines as a teacher in 1906 and stayed for forty years, eventually serving as the presiding judge on the Philippines Supreme Court, where Elias Finley Johnson (1861–1933), another Michigan graduate, also held a position. Clarence G. Wrentmore (1867–1934), yet another Michigan alum, assumed the role of dean of the College of Engineering.[51]

Higher education sometimes augmented the sense of Filipino nationalism, supported by some sympathetic American teachers, but it did not affect the entrenched Filipino class system, which only reinforced the plutocracy. Filipinos might choose to send their offspring to the University of Santo Tomas, the remnant of the Spanish empire, or the American-dominated University of the Philippines, but it was a choice reserved for the wealthy. Part of that choice revolved around religious practices, as the Santo Tomas faculty consisted of Jesuit priests, while the first president of the University of the Philippines, Murray Bartlett, was an Episcopalian clergyman.[52]

Under the Americans, the University of the Philippines did greatly advance research into health issues and tropical diseases. The Medical School under Paul Freer addressed cholera, dysentery, and smallpox, while research on climate and environment concentrated on their debilitating effect on white bodies. While early studies offered rationalizations for the moral lapses of Americans in the islands, later research overturned such faulty science. Ethnographic anthropological studies, however, continued to reinforce Social Darwinian attitudes of racial superiority. The Panama-Pacific Exposition of 1915 in the United States continued to portray Filipinos as savage dog eaters, and Worcester's similar publications and presentations persisted for decades, denying complete equality, and Filipino independence.[53]

FILIPINIZATION

The number of American teachers in the Filipino schools continually decreased after 1902 with a consequent increase in indigenous faculty. The use of English soon declined outside of Manila. In 1915 Ignacio Villamor (1863–1933) became the first Filipino president of the University of the Philippines. Despite the increasing Filipinization of the educational system, the Central High School of Manila did not admit Filipino students until 1932, when ordered to do so by Governor General Theodore Roosevelt, Jr. (1887–1944); the private American schools which did not fall under his jurisdiction continued to maintain their segregation practices.[54]

While the American educational efforts greatly benefitted the children of the *ilustrados*, the masses fared considerably worse: 38 percent of Filipinos never reached the third grade and less than 50 percent reached the fourth grade. After four decades of US rule only 26 percent could speak the English language. In 1934 a Filipino House of Delegates speech was presented in Tagalog (the language of northern Luzon, which was adopted as the national language) rather than English for the first time, a clear reversal of the American objective. In 1953 at least eighty-seven dialects were still spoken in the islands.[55]

The American educational system was judged a failure by 1940, with 90 percent of Filipinos still considered to be uneducated (although the 49 percent literacy rate in 1939 was the highest in Asia). In the aftermath of World War II (1948) the nation still registered only a 60 percent literacy rate. The rising literacy rate actually had a detrimental effect on the national economy, as more educated Filipinos and an aspiring middle class could not find suitable employment and began migrating abroad in quest of a better life. The English language, the elements of a democratic form of government, and American sport forms are still prominent features of the American educational efforts. One lasting effect of the American curriculum is most noticeable in the adoption of basketball, which became and remains the national sport of the Philippines.[56]

NOTES

1. Salamanca, *The Filipino Reaction to American Rule*, 10; Stanley, *A Nation in the Making*, 31–32; May, *Social Engineering in the Philippines*, 78; Le Roy, *Philippine Life in Town and Country*, 216–19; Fred W. Atkinson, *The Present Educational Movement in the Philippine Islands* at quod.lib.umich.edu/p/philamer/AHK8492.0001.001?rgn=main;view=fulltext (November 24, 2015).

2. John N. Schumacher, "Father McKinnon: The First California's Chaplain: The Story of the Heroic Chaplain," *Philippine Studies*, 9:1 (1961), 194–97; Gates, *Schoolbooks and Krags*, 61, 137; Salamanca, *The Filipino Reaction to American Rule*, 82–83; Eric Gamalinda, "English Is Your Mother Tongue/Ang Ingles Ay ang Tongue ng Ina Mo," in Shaw and Francia, eds., *Vestiges of War*, 247–59, Stanley, *A Nation in the Making*, 83, Le Roy, *Philippine Life in Town and Country*, 214–19.

3. Gates, *Schoolbooks and Krags*, 138, 138–39, 143 (quotes, respectively).

4. Anne Paulet, "To Change the World," 180–81, cites Dr. Lucien Warner in the *Proceedings of the 18th Annual Meeting of the Lake Mohonk Conference of the Friends of the Indian in 1900*. On American Indian Schools see Adams, *Education for Extinction: American Indians and the Boarding School Experience*; and Hoxie, *A Final Promise: The Campaign to Assimilate the Indians*.

5. Paulet, "To Change the World," 181.

6. Ibid., 186–94; May, *Social Engineering in the Philippines*, 77–81, 88–92. Elmer Bryan served briefly as superintendent from 1902–1903.

7. Paulet, "To Change the World," both quotes on 197.

8. Ibid., 197–98; Guerrero, *Philippine Society and Revolution*, 39–43.

9. May, *Social Engineering in the Philippines*, 85; Torres, *The Americanization of Manila*, 138; Taft, *Civil Government in the Philippines*, 44; Rand cited in Karnow, *In Our Image*, 196 (quote).

10. Le Roy, *Philippine Life in Town and Country*, 219–28, May, *Social Engineering in the Philippines*, 88–92; Salamanca, *The Filipino Reaction to American Rule*, 76; Clymer, *Protestant Missionaries in the Philippines*, 189; Pecson and Racelis, eds., *Tales of the American Teachers in the Philippines*, 35; W. T. Ross, "Education in the Philippines," in Fred Eggan Papers, University of Chicago, Special Collections.

11. Rawlein G. Soberano, *The Politics of Independence: The American Colonial Experiment in the Philippines* (New Orleans: Alive Associates, 1983), 60; Fred W. Atkinson, *The Present Educational Movement in the Philippine Islands*, at quod.lib.umich.edu/p/philamer/AHK8492.0001.001?rgn=main;view=fulltext (November 24, 2015); May, *Social Engineering in the Philippines*, 93, 97–112; Salamanca, *The Filipino Reaction to American Rule*, 81–82; Torres, *The Americanization of Manila*, 159.

12. Gleeck, Jr., *American Institutions in the Philippines*, 105.

13. Alidio, "When I Get Home, I Want to Forget," 111, 117 (quotes, respectively).

14. Amparo Santamaria Lardizabal, "Pioneer America Teachers and Philippine Education," in Pecson and Racelis, eds., *Tales of the American Teachers in the Philippines*, 85–118 (92, quote).

15. Ibid.; Torres, *The Americanization of Manila*, 159.

16. Karnow, *In Our Image*, 203–11.

17. May, *Social Engineering in the Philippines*, 95; Torres, *The Americanization of Manila*, 156.

18. Alidio, "When I Get Home, I Want to Forget," 117; Paul A. Kramer, "Jim Crow Science and the 'Negro Problem' in the Philippines," in Judith Fossett, Ed Jackson, and Jeffrey A. Tucker, eds., *Race Consciousness: African American Studies for the New Century* (New York: New York University Press, 1997), 231.

19. Harris, *God's Arbiters*, 98. See Jackson Murphy, "Prescott Jernagan and the Gold from Seawater Swindle," for the story of Jernegan, a former minister who perpetrated a ruse to swindle investors by claiming that he could extract gold from seawater. He fled to Europe and then the Philippines, where he lived from 1900 to 1910.

20. Taft, *Civil Government In the Philippines*, 49–50 (quote); Paulet "To Change the World," 199–201.

21. Paulet, "To Change the World," 200.

22. Stanley, *A Nation in the Making*, 315; May, *Social Engineering in the Philippines*, 83.

23. Guerrero, *Philippine Society and Revolution*, 43; Karnow, *In Our Image*, 206–7; Kramer, *The Blood of Government*, 274; Pecson and Racelis, eds., *Tales of the American Teachers in the Philippines*, 112.

24. Pecson and Racelis, eds., *Tales of the American Teachers in the Philippines*, 113 (quotes).

25. Worcester, *The Philippines Past and Present*, 928.

26. Fee, *A Woman's Impressions of the Philippines*, 283–86, 286 (quote).

27. Gleeck, Jr., *American Institutions in the Philippines*, 110.

28. Bocobo-Olivar, *History of Physical Education in the Philippines*, 27–33; slideshare.net/rovelynbasilad/historical-development-of-physical-education-in-the-philippines? (December 1, 2015).

29. Frederic S. Marquardt Papers, Bentley Historical Library, University of Michigan, 1936 folder.

30. Luis Santiago, "The Organization of the San Mateo Baseball Team," The Teachers' Assembly Herald (Baguio: Department of Public Instruction), 5:26 (1912), 142–43, in Pecson and Racelis, eds., *Tales of the American Teachers in the Philippines*, 195–99.

31. May, *Social Engineering in the Philippines*, 82; Karnow, *In Our Image*, 201.

32. May, *Social Engineering in the Philippines*, 87, 96; Gleeck, Jr., *The Manila-Americans*, 48–49; Salamanca, *The Filipino Reaction to American Rule*, 71–83; Le Roy, *Philippine Life in Town and Country*, 224.

33. Salamanca, *The Filipino Reaction to American Rule*, 71–93, 82 (quote).

34. Salamanca, *The Filipino Reaction to American Rule*, 87; Gleeck, Jr., *American Institutions in the Philippines*, 81–83; Beran, "Americans in the Philippines," 82.

35. Salamanca, *The Filipino Reaction to American Rule*, 92.

36. Stanley, *A Nation in the Making*, 162, 194–95; Gleeck, Jr., *American Institutions in the Philippines*, 104 (quote).

37. Pecson and Racelis, eds., *Tales of the American Teachers in the Philippines*, 40; Kramer, *The Blood of Government*, 201–5; Guerrero, *Philippine Society and Revolution*, 43; Salamanca, *The Filipino Reaction to American Rule*, 76–77.

38. Torres, *The Americanization of Manila*, 141: su.edu.ph/page/10–History (December 23, 2015); cpu.edu.ph/about/history1.php (December 23, 2015). May, *Social Engineering in the Philippines*, 107.

39. May, *Social Engineering in the Philippines*, 107.

40. Gleeck, Jr., *The Manila Americans*, 32; Bishop Charles H. Brent Papers, Library of Congress, Box 47, Philippine Islands folder; Zabriskie, *Bishop Brent*, 56, 70–72; Karnow, *In Our Image*, 215; Frederick Starr Papers, University of Chicago Special Collections, Box 11, notebook 7, p. 15.

41. Kramer, "The Pragmatic Empire," 319–25; May, "The Business of Education," Torres, *The Americanization of Manila*, 143, 214.

42. Clymer, *Protestant Missionaries in the Philippines*, 87; Gleeck, Jr., *American Institutions in the Philippines*, 61–63; May, "The Business of Colonial Education in the Philippines"; Tuason, "The Ideology of Empire in National Geographic Magazine's Coverage of the Philippines," 43.

43. Tuason, "The Ideology of Empire in National Geographic Magazine's Coverage of the Philippines," 40–43 (quote, 43).

44. Frederic S. Marquardt papers; Wooley, "'Batter Up'"; Lucrezia T. Calo, *Organization and Management of Athletic Meets* (Manila: Rex Book Store, 1984), 2–3.

45. Bocobo-Olivar, *History of Physical Education in the Philippines*, 47–48; Antolihao, *Playing with the Big Boys*, 39–40; Bocobo-Olivar, *History of Physical Education in the Philippines*, 40–50. See Robert Pruter, *Rise of American High School Sports and the Search for Control, 1880–1930* (Syracuse, NY: Syracuse University Press, 2013) for the best account of high school programs in the United States.

46. Bocobo-Olivar, *History of Physical Education in the Philippines*, 50.

47. Elwood S. Brown, *Annual Report, October 1, 1912–October, 1, 1913*; Philippines Correspondence Reports, 1911–1968, Administrative Reports, 1912–1917 file, YMCA Archives.

48. Elwood S. Brown, *Annual Report, October 1, 1914–October 1, 1915*. Antolihao, *Playing with the Big Boys*, 38, cites a figure of 95 percent of 700,000 in physical education classes in 1911. That figure did not include non-students.

49. Bocobo-Olivar, *History of Physical Education in the Philippines*, 43–44 (quote).

50. Torres, *The Americanization of Manila*, 110, 112, 119–20, 125–27; Sullivan, *Exemplar of Americanism*, 106, 117; Kirkwood, "'Michigan Men' in the Philippines and the Limits of Self Determination in the Progressive Era."

51. Eric Gamalinda, "English Is Your Mother Tongue/Ang Ingles Ay ang Tongue ng Ina Mo," in Shaw and Francia, eds., *Vestiges of War*, 247–59; Torres, *The Americanization of Manila*, 144–49, 156; Gleeck, Jr., *American Institutions in the Philippines*, 48; *The Michigan Chime*, 1:1 (November 1919), 26; *The Michigan Alumnus*, 15 (1909), 250.

52. Kramer, "The Pragmatic Empire," 345; Salamanca, *The Filipino Reaction to American Rule*, 92–95; Guerrero, *Philippine Society and Revolution*, 43; Gleeck, Jr., *American Institutions in the Philippines*, 52–53, 81–83.

53. Torres, *The Americanization of Manila*, 112, Anderson, "'Where Every Prospect Pleases and Only Man is Vile'"; Kramer, "The Pragmatic Empire," 317, 328, 336–45.

54. Pecson and Racelis, eds., *Tales of the American Teachers in the Philippines*, 8; Salamanca, *The Filipino Reaction to American Rule*, 87; Torres, *The Americanization of Manila*, 141, 145, 153; Gleeck, Jr., *The Manila-Americans*, 157, 194–95.

55. Stanley, *A Nation in the Making*, 315; *School News Review*, September, 1, 1934, 8, in US National Archives, RG 350, Box 1187; W. T. Ross, "Education in the Philippines," in Fred Eggan Papers, Box 142, folder 13, University of Chicago Special Collections.

56. Gleeck, Jr., *American Institutions in the Philippines*, 301–2; Anderson, "Cacique Democracy in the Philippines"; Torres, *The Americanization of Manila*, 164–66. Americans judged literacy by the ability to read and write the English language.

EIGHT
Sport

As late as 1914, Dean Worcester, former Secretary of the Interior in the islands, claimed that, "Before the American occupation of the Philippines the Filipinos had not learned to play. There were no athletics worthy of the name."[1] Such statements belied the cultural complexity of Filipino popular culture.

INDIGENOUS SPORTS AND GAMES

In the mountains of northern Luzon Igorot children played marbles with round fruits, spun tops, and played stick games not unlike American youths. As they grew older, gender identity was expressed through masculine physicality to prove bravery and one's stoicism in the face of pain. The Igorot dead were buried in coffins hung from the sides of cliffs, and boys showed their disdain for fear by visits to burial caves. In the game of *dang pil* they had to bear the pain of crossing one's legs while the knees were forced backward. Boys also engaged in various forms of martial arts, graduating from wrestling with the middle finger (*tolsi*) to arm wrestling (*sangdol*) to a form of boxing known as *sinoto*. They also engaged in a slapping game that only ended when a blow sufficient to produce a bruise was dealt.[2]

In the Visayan Islands children played leap frog and kicked a rattan ball around a circle similar to modern hacky sack. That diversion eventually transformed into the game of *sipa*, similar to volleyball, in which the ball is propelled over a net by using the feet. In other areas they flew kites, pitched coins, played jack straws, threw stones at targets, swung on ropes, played hopscotch (*piko*), chased each other in games of tag and hide-and-seek, and jumped rope (*luksong lubid*). Some engaged in a local form of football, while others ran, jumped, swam, sang, and danced in pursuit of pleasure; children even gambled on games.[3]

SPANISH PASTIMES

The Spanish overlords introduced traditional sports from their homeland, including jai alai and bullfighting, although few Filipinos were attracted to either activity, and Americans considered the latter to be barbaric. The Manila Jockey Club offered horse racing as early as 1867. Card games, lotteries, and cockfighting insured that gambling became endemic among the Filipinos. Cockfighting became a national obsession, and continual American attempts to ban the practice proved ephemeral, despite the threat of six months imprisonment and fines up to $500.[4]

The adherence to cockfighting exhibited a sense of both nationalism and resistance to American dictates and the maintenance of a residual culture in the face of change dictated by the American occupiers. American missionaries and administrators tied the activity to Catholicism and a general moral laxity. They decried the Spanish values inherent in the Filipino *ilustrados*, who favored leisure over the Protestant work ethic and cherished their ascribed social status over the benefits of democracy. Despite their pretensions of machismo, Americans considered the Spanish to be somewhat effeminate, and their empire, especially in their treatment of Cubans, to be immoral. They considered the Spanish Catholic faith to be a degenerate religion and their Filipino subordinates to be primitive and ignorant.[5]

Worcester described an Ilongot festival in which carabaos were hacked to death for consumption. "Terrific scrimmages result, in the course of which men are badly cut, but the injuries received on such occasions must be taken in good part. A man who complains over having a few fingers chopped off would lose caste as completely as would a football player who objected to being tackled hard." Among the savage tribes of northern Luzon successful headhunting served as a prelude to marriageability and proof of masculinity.[6] Worcester opined that "we have tried, with a good deal of success, to direct them into less turbulent channels by teaching them American athletic games and by encouraging their fondness for dancing."[7]

The Americans embarked on a program of education through sport to attain the desired values of honesty, industry, thrift, patriotism, and sportsmanship, and they placed an abiding faith in the ability of their national game, baseball, to achieve the desired ends. "The game which seems to breathe the restless spirit of American life, that calls for quick action and quicker thinking, that seems characteristic of a great nation itself, is baseball."[8] Consequent tribal festivals approximated an American country fair with wrestling, a variety of foot races, a greased pole climb, a tug-of-war, and dancing, but "baseball is one of the really important things which the Bureau of Education has taught the boys ... it brightens them up and increases their activity and alertness. Keen interest is taken not only by the boys themselves, but by their fathers and mothers, in competitive games between different settlements." Thus baseball replaced headhunting in the civilizing process.[9] Despite widespread adoption, however, baseball failed to suppress cockfighting, which continued unabated throughout the American occupation.[10]

Military Sport

Sport has served as a means of social control for American military forces since the Civil War when soldiers played baseball, boxed, and wrestled during their leisure hours to amuse themselves and confront boredom. Even before the Spanish-American War naval all-star teams battled Japanese teams in decidedly racial confrontations that persisted until superseded by the real conflict of World War II.[11]

Sailors and marines engaged in the first baseball game in Manila as early as May of 1898, and the baseball team from Admiral George Dewey's flagship, *Olympia*, played five games at the Cavite naval base from May to October that year, defeating an army team from the 25th Infantry Regiment, and another navy team from the *USS Utah*, but losing to the contingent from the *USS Colorado*. Dewey's athletes also challenged the local population to boxing, rowing, and soccer contests in the aftermath of the Battle of Manila Bay.[12]

The military squads soon formed a Manila Baseball League, which featured the African American 25th Infantry Regiment team, considered to be the island champions each year between 1899 and 1902. The team was undefeated in 1899, and won a $500 wager on the championship game against the 6th Artillery team in 1900. One of its members lost his life as a result of a baseball game in which he slid into a base with a dagger on his belt, which caused a self-inflicted abdominal wound that caused his demise. Games were played three times per week and by 1901 the Manila League contests were reported in *Spalding's Baseball Guide and Official League Book* back in America, noting that "it was an auspicious opening of our national game in the 'expanded' territory of Uncle Sam." Six players from the league played in the professional ranks in the United States. Major Arlington Pond (1873–1930) of the Medical Corps, had pitched for Baltimore in the National League from 1895 to 1898 and managed the 25th Infantry team in 1902.[13] The league expanded to include a team of colonial personnel and Sunday doubleheaders drew thousands of spectators by the end of the decade, decreasing church attendance to the consternation of the Catholic priests. The first all-Filipino team joined the league in 1912, only adding to the interest among native fans.[14] The league achieved such prominence by 1913 that the best players in the army were assigned to Manila as clerks. A reporter charged that "It is easy to have the men detailed on duty at the various headquarters, ostensibly as clerks and messengers, but really as professional ball players."[15]

The African American 25th Regiment was reassigned to the United States after 1902, where it continued to beat white teams in Kansas, but when stationed in Texas and Oklahoma they were subjected to segregation and racism that resulted in a riot. In 1907 the regiment returned to the Philippines. Stationed in Mindanao it formed another baseball league, winning the island championship over the next three years with only two losses during that time. In 1913 it was reassigned to Hawaii, where it also dominated the Honolulu league.[16]

American military bases throughout the main island of Luzon included facilities for leisure activities. Fort Mills was constructed on the island of Corregidor in Manila Bay in 1908, and provided tennis courts, a bowling facility, a movie theater, a nine-hole golf course, swimming beaches, clubs, fishing, and the all-important baseball field. Fort Stotsenburg, located in Angeles, would evolve into the Clark Air Base after 1912, but its parade ground provided ample space for polo matches among officers and baseball games for all.[17]

The baseball fever, especially when introduced to the schools, soon engaged Filipino youth. Major Arlington Pond, who served on the Manila Board of Health in 1902, was transferred to Cebu in the Visayan Islands in 1908, where he founded a hospital for lepers, but also found time to promote his beloved baseball among high school students. Between Pond and George Dunlap, a Presbyterian missionary who had played catcher at Princeton University and cultivated the game at the Silliman Institute in Dumaguete in the Visayan Islands, the region became a center of baseball in the Philippines. Cebu won the interscholastic championship in 1910, 1912, and 1913.[18]

The Philippine Scouts and the Constabulary, indigenous personnel trained by the US Army in Manila starting in 1901, were also taught American sports and sent into the provinces to instruct the local populace in the values of athletics. Baseball became a mainstay in the Filipino sporting culture and by 1917 when the United States entered World War I, a contest between an army team and an all-star contingent drew thousands of fans and raised 2,000 pesos for the war effort.[19]

While baseball assumed centrality in the American military efforts, boxing held particular interest as a martial art. General Leonard Wood stated that "Boxing develops every muscle in the human body, quickens the brain, sharpens the wits, imparts force, and, above all, it teaches self-control."[20] Boxing soon became popular in Manila, where theaters featured American soldiers in tournaments for a prize of $60 in 1900. Within the decade American entrepreneurs became the major promoters of the sport. Frank Churchill, a customs house worker, opened a Manila gym and along with brothers Bill and Eddie Tait established the Olympic

Stadium with seating for 5,000 for weekly bouts. Three thousand fans had to be turned away for the first fight which featured a local boxer against the British featherweight champion.[21]

Joe Waterman quit the US navy to seek his fortune as a boxing promoter in the Philippines. Jack "Kid" Madden, a Brooklyn bantamweight, left the United States in the wake of World War I to become a boxing instructor and club manager in the Philippines. In the ensuing years Filipino boxers would move beyond the islands to seek world championships in the United States.[22]

With the waning of the guerrilla war in the Philippines the American military enjoyed a comparatively casual lifestyle. In 1910, an officer at Fort McKinley in Manila wrote, "This post is like a big country club. A little work in the morning. Golf, polo, tennis, riding in the hills in the afternoon. The Club at sunset. Dinner in the evening. A lazy man's paradise."[23]

AMERICAN LEISURE IN THE PHILIPPINES

The Burnham architectural plan for Manila included the development of parks, the waterfront, and boulevards, which offered pleasant carriage rides. The moat surrounding the Intramuros fortress was filled in as a sunken garden and for use as play fields. The bayfront provided stunning views for the governor general's residence, military headquarters, and clubs. The Manila Hotel offered a casino and boat club. The array of clubs included the Army and Navy Club (originally established by Admiral Dewey in 1898), the University Club (organized by William Howard Taft), the Columbia Club, the Masons Club, the Elks Club, the Knights of Pythias, the Odd Fellows, the boat club, a golf club, a polo club, fencing clubs, and a host of other fellowship associations, open solely to white patrons. Several of the clubs offered swimming pools, gyms, libraries, and rooms for social events. By 1931 the exclusive Army and Navy club boasted a bar, a barber shop, a swimming pool, tennis and squash courts, a bowling alley, a dining room, card rooms, a library, a ladies' room with a beauty specialist, an equipped gymnasium, and regular dances. It also had branch club in Baguio. Membership required endorsements by at least two of the directors.[24]

Major Pond helped to reorganize the Army and Navy club in Cebu. An all-around athlete, Pond had played and coached baseball at Indiana University before coming to the Philippines. He also played cricket, golf, and polo, and excelled at billiards and pool. His talent as a tennis player was evident by his winning of the national singles title in the Philippines, to which he added the doubles title along with his partner Barney Clark, a civil engineer. After brief service in World War I, Pond returned to the Philippines as a lieutenant colonel to continue his medical practice, but he also acquired a coconut plantation and a cattle ranch that made him a millionaire.[25]

Even in distant Mindanao, Americans enjoyed swimming at sandy beaches, sailing, fishing, and the La Loma Gun Club for trap shooting. In Zamboanga military wives and families enjoyed such activities and children roller skated on sidewalks. With the area secured, they rode horses through the plantations of the countryside and delighted in the concerts at the bandstand in the public square. The local Army and Navy Club and regular dinner parties offered convivial friendships. Similar to the Manila Carnival, Zamboanga hosted a business and agricultural exhibit at its local fairgrounds. Many families considered it to be a tropical paradise.[26]

As in Manila and Cebu, the Americans introduced baseball to the Moro population of the southern archipelago. Similar to the tribes of northern Luzon, the games assumed a less violent means of settling internecine quarrels. When the elementary school team from Jolo defeated the team from Zamboanga they were fêted and feasted upon their return, and the sultan of Jolo conferred an honorary chiefdom on the American teacher who coached the team.[27]

Manila schools began interscholastic baseball play as early as 1903, and the Southern Luzon Athletic Association was formed in 1904 with the first interscholastic baseball tournament held in April of that year. George W. Moore, a former coach at the University of Indiana and school superintendent of Masbate Province, an island southeast of Manila, promoted the game in that area. Crowds of 5,000 fans turned out for the competition and Moore noted that "Everybody in town turns out for the games and there is a spirit of rivalry that reminds one of the league games in the United States. . . . The umpire's decisions are always received without kicking, and the official is accorded a respect that would seem impossible to the men who decide the game in the United States." In 1908 the Reach Company all-star team included Manila on its Asian tour to Japan, playing twelve games in the city and losing two to military all-star teams. That same year a national interscholastic baseball championship was introduced.[28]

Americans, however, continued to separate themselves from the Filipino masses in cloistered clubs, the Manila Polo Club considered to be the most important of their segregated enclaves. The club was constructed in 1909 with money from William Cameron Forbes' own fortune, and included bowling alleys, tennis and badminton courts, and a swimming pool. Civilian teams competed against the military squads, but the highlight of the social season was a polo match in which the Americans defeated a British team from Hong Kong in 1911. Polo remained a mainstay of the social elite throughout the American occupation. By the 1930s female socialites began gathering in the Escolta shopping district and christened themselves the Escolta Walking Society, a reference to their ambles within the air-conditioned Crystal Palace Arcade, an enclosed structure that housed upscale shops.[29]

Merv Simpson attended the American School in Manila during the interwar years and spent much of his time at the Polo Club. At home he had Filipino servants, a cook, a nanny, and a personal driver, with whom he did not converse. "Before the war we didn't play with Filipino kids or associate with them very much. . . . We didn't have any Filipino friends — all expats." Simpson spent enough time on the golf course to win the 1939 amateur championship of the Philippines before heading off to college in the United States.[30]

After World War II a new polo club was constructed in the wealthy suburb of Makati, near Fort McKinley, but by that time most of the Americans preferred other pastimes such as bowling, badminton, tennis, and softball. Filipinos gained admittance to the club in the postwar years, but they comprised only 17 percent of the membership by 1953. The club did not have a Filipino president until 1964.[31]

Golf became an earlier engine of integration, as profit trumped race. William Howard Taft served as president of the first Manila golf club in 1902, a seven-hole layout that served as a male preserve. It moved to Caloocan in 1906. Although initially excluded, white women gained entry when a female proved she could play the game by beating a male patron, opening the doors to other women. Filipinos of some wealth were permitted to join the country club at the Baguio mountain resort as early as 1910 due to the need to cover the expenses of construction rather than any sense of fraternity. While Filipinos might play at a municipal course in the capital they were not members of the Manila Golf Club. Bill Shaw (1877–1939), an American outraged at white racist attitudes that affected his Filipino golfing partners and whose *mestizo* children were not allowed at whites-only establishments, began construction of the Wack Wack Club as an integrated facility in 1931.[32]

Americans played tennis throughout the archipelago, and the game became popular among Filipinos as well, taught in the schools and at the YMCA. Such sports fostered a transition in gender roles among the indigenous population as females emulated the "new women" of the United States, whose independence, vitality, and athleticism began to challenge the prescribed gender order by the late nineteenth century. In the aftermath of World War I, a reporter stated that "ten years ago the ladies who played or attempted to play tennis or basketball would be ridiculed by her people. Today they are admired, and those who were strongest in their criticism are now loudest in their praise."[33]

Americans enjoyed a host of cultural activities, particularly in Manila, where theaters, music halls, and cabarets offered entertainment. Some of the latter, established by discharged American soldiers who remained in the Philippines as entrepreneurs, catered to the wants of lonely, young men. The bachelor subculture could find such reverie and company at the

Santa Ana Cabaret, considered to be the largest of its kind in the world, where they paid a peso for admission, 25 centavos for a beer, a peso per hour to dance with the female employees, and 5 pesos to spend the night with her. The charge included breakfast and a massage the next morning. The proprietor of the club, John Canson, became a wealthy investor in the Philippine Racing Club, a member of the Manila Yacht Club (formed in 1927), a member of the prestigious Army and Navy Club, and a close friend of Manuel Quezon, who became the first president of the commonwealth. Both Quezon and Governor General Francis Harrison patronized the club.[34]

The club catered to wealthy clientele as well as military personnel and represented a more fashionable establishment than the lowly brothels. Prostitution had been a perennial problem for the American military. Among the first contingent of troops sent to the Philippines 25 percent reported to sick bay with venereal diseases. The YMCA offered dances as a moral alternative with little attraction to the ribald soldiers. Continual morality crusades were easily circumvented and by the 1920s the brothels were simply designated as "dancing schools" and the female "teachers" required to submit to testing for venereal diseases.[35]

By then, Americans paraded to such establishments in their cars, but they also had the choice of more wholesome vaudeville theaters and movie houses. Two radio stations provided domestic entertainment at home, and sports still served as a healthy alternative. Outside of the capital, hunting, fishing, sailing, trap shooting, and horseback riding could be found in more rural settings.[36]

AMERICAN EXCURSIONS TO THE PHILIPPINES

Intrepid American tourists traveled to the islands in search of exotic and erotic pleasures unavailable at home. There, wily Filipinos dressed in tribal garb and loincloths and some native women worked the fields naked, subjects of prurient American photographers, who were surprised that some of the male tricksters spoke perfect English and had lived for several years in the United States.[37]

The Americans living in Manila were thrilled by the global baseball excursions of American teams that included stops in the islands. The universities of Chicago and Wisconsin had already been traveling to Japan for baseball games with their counterparts there; in 1910 Chicago included the Philippines in its itinerary, invited by Frank White, an alumnus of the school then serving as director of education in the islands. The college squad played four games against military teams and one against a Filipino contingent, losing only one to the marines, winners of the Manila professional league. The university repeated the trip in 1915, playing eight games and winning six.[38]

In December of 1913 John McGraw (1873–1934) the pugnacious manager of the New York Giants, and Charles Comiskey (1859–1931), the parsimonious owner of the Chicago White Sox, arrived in the city as part of their worldwide tour in the off-season. Both teams were elaborately fêted by the Americans, though they played only two games in the capital. The American owned *Manila Times* declared that baseball "is more than a game, a regenerating influence, or power for good."[39] Filipinos had sent their own all-star team to the United States that year, hoping to garner sentiment for their independence movement, but its dismal record only made the case for further American tutelage.[40]

The success of the joint venture by the American teams earned substantial profits and encouraged other teams to make the long Pacific voyage. American barnstorming teams, often consisting of professional all-stars, continued to thrill the Manila fans thereafter. A 1934 contingent included hall of famers Babe Ruth, Lou Gehrig, and Jimmie Foxx.[41]

Interscholastic Sports

Americans considered sports to be integral in the training of Filipino youth. Informal instruction began even before a formal school system was established and selected soldiers acted as teachers even before educators arrived from the United States. Schools fielded competitive baseball teams by 1903 and a formal interscholastic league followed in 1905, which eventually included district, provincial, and national championships featured in the Manila Carnival starting in 1908. The *Athletic Handbook* of 1911 stipulated that only American games were to be taught in the schools. The Director of Education reported that "It is believed that no county in the world, certainly no State [sic] in the American Union [sic], has such a carefully worked out plan to make athletics national in scope and determine who are the athletic champions." Not only the public schools, but the private ones also offered competition in basketball, soccer, and volleyball. By 1916 the Bureau of Education policies allowed students to earn bonus points as athletes, which could be applied to deficiencies in other subjects. Given such regulations, it is not surprising that 95 percent of the students were engaged in sports that year, with 1,555 completely equipped and uniformed baseball teams alone. The following year the Director of Education even claimed that sports participation had reduced the number of tuberculosis cases, and officials even maintained that such physical activities produced larger and healthier bodies "due no doubt to athletic training the younger generation has been and is receiving in the primary, intermediate, and high schools of the islands."[42] In 1919 the president of the American Physical Education Association exclaimed that the Philippine schools "show a progress and a conception of physical training that do not seem to exist here in America."[43] The following year the authorities required students to achieve a grade of 75 percent in physical education in order to earn promotion beyond fourth grade.[44]

Competition ensued at all levels from intermediate school to the universities and included both male and female teams. The introduction of basketball for girls fostered a dress reform as they eschewed traditional, more formal clothing for blouses and bloomers that allowed for greater freedom of movement. Girls took to the game readily, practicing nightly in Zambales province by 1910. Their teacher claimed that the athletic activity cured their physical ailments. Within two years more than forty girls joined the team, and they proved to be the healthiest of students who also earned the highest grades. In 1911, eleven girls' teams engaged in provincial play and five competed at the Manila Carnival for a national championship. In 1912 the Director of Education asserted that "the development of the girls has been quite marvelous, which is partly due to the fact that the Filipino female . . . has a far more satisfactory status than is given to women in any Oriental country." By 1913 1,200 boys' baseball teams with 10,000 players contested for provincial laurels, and the Director of Education even claimed that baseball in the islands was "nearer to being the national sport of the Philippines than of the United States." An American newspaper reporter stated that the game was played in every vacant lot and games with rivals drew thousands of fans who were as raucous as any at New York's Polo Grounds. He opined that the discipline and character learned via the game supplanted the lessons learned in books.[45]

Governor General William Cameron Forbes ardently promoted sport throughout the islands. He presided over the Manila Carnival and its athletic events, personally attended the provincial championships, and offered uniforms to winning teams in the 1910 tournament, in which 483 squads competed. Forbes not only watched, but actively played the game. He set aside a portion of the Manila Polo Club for baseball, and in Baguio his team went undefeated in winning the local league championship.[46]

YMCA

The YMCA proved to be one of the primary promoters of sport in the Philippines, especially after the arrival of Elwood S. Brown as director in 1910. Brown worked closely with Governor General Forbes to establish the Philippines Amateur Athletic Federation (PAAF), transform the Manila Carnival, previously a business exposition, into an athletic spectacle, and establish more widespread sports competitions. The Manila Carnival included more than twenty sports and served as both the Philippines national championships (male and female) and the Far Eastern regional championships with the addition of Japanese and Chinese teams. Competition ensued in track and field, swimming, baseball, basketball, bowling, boxing, wrestling, tennis, rowing, golf, polo, soccer, football, volleyball, cycling, and handball. With Forbes serving as president of the PAAF and Brown as its secretary, professional athletes, such as the boxers and ballplayers in the military, were banned from amateur competition. The close relationship between the two sponsors carried over into the educational sphere as Brown served on the playground board and a YMCA member filled the role of acting director of physical education in the schools, providing a pulpit to spread the YMCA's particular version of morality. Brown had originally dubbed the biennial athletic spectacle the Far Eastern Olympics, which drew the ire of Pierre de Coubertin (1863–1937), founder of the modern Olympic Games. Brown soon relented, but the regional contests served as a surrogate form of warfare and transferred a measure of Filipino nationalism away from the American occupiers and toward regional rivalries.[47]

Governor General Forbes opened the first such Games in 1913 with an avuncular speech. "I hope that all your contests will be carried on in the spirit of fair play, which in after years may govern your conduct in business and other vocations of grown-ups."[48] The first such Games featured more than 130 athletes from the Philippines, China, and Japan, and attracted more than 150,000 spectators. Frank L. Crone (1875–1960), Director of Education, claimed American credit for bringing the Asian entrants into the modern world. "Nothing previous to this meeting has shown so clearly the departure of the Oriental nations from the old conservative standards, for the interest of the East in organized sports is only recent."[49] During Crone's tenure in office, even interscholastic teams in track and field, baseball, and basketball, and, later, swimming were sent to Japan for regional competition at a cost of $10,000 to the government.[50]

The Filipinos not only won the initial Far Eastern Games, but continued to excel in subsequent encounters. Such accomplishments boosted national pride and produced native heroes and a sense of progress. One of the first such victors, Regino R. Ylanan (1889–1963), exemplified Filipino progress, presumably under American tutelage. At the first Far Eastern Games in 1913 he won the pentathlon, shot put, and discus events, and earned two more medals at the next Games in Shanghai in 1915, and then captained the national baseball team as a catcher at the 1917 Games in Tokyo. Ylanan was one of the *pensionados* then sent to study in the United States. He earned his medical degree and became a doctor for the national team and coach of the baseball and track teams during the 1920s, including its Olympic contingents in 1924, 1928, and 1936. In 1925 he organized the Philippines version of the NCAA to govern collegiate athletics and became the national physical director from 1927 to 1960.[51]

National and international competition continued despite the debilitating onset of the Depression in the 1930s. In 1933 the interscholastic championships were held outside of Manila for the first time, drawing large crowds in Cebu in the Visayan Islands. One baseball game held in Negros Occidental drew 16,000 fans. Two years later the Philippines defeated Formosa (Taiwan) at a swim meet in Manila, but the more important Far Eastern Games had already begun to disintegrate over political differences and Japanese incursions in mainland China.[52]

The Games were one of the few events that allowed for interracial competition, though the YMCA maintained separate buildings for whites, Filipinos, and Chinese. Sport thus provided an opportunity for people of color to challenge the Social Darwinian presumptions of white superiority. In the 1914 volleyball competition, Brown remarked that "these American business men, who have nothing to do with the Filipino people socially and who actually employed some of the boys against whom they played" were defeated in the semifinal round by their supposed inferior subordinates.[53]

Gender roles, too, transformed as the YMCA encouraged girls to play basketball and volleyball, and offered gym classes for women. A local sporting goods dealer sold 11,000 volleyballs by 1921, almost all of them to Filipinos. A national tennis tournament for women originated in 1923. The first interscholastic gymnastics meet and a track meet for girls appeared in 1925, the same year that female students at the University of the Philippines established a swimming club. National championships followed only two years later. In 1926 a YWCA was established for women, which offered a wide variety of sports, including: tennis, bowling, volleyball, basketball, badminton, table tennis, swimming, gymnastics, indoor baseball, dancing, and camping. While such social change persisted for women, the segregation practices of the organization coupled with the colonial government's slow pace toward independence only intensified Filipino resentment and resulted in increased anti-Americanism by the 1920s. By 1922 a YMCA officer admitted to Brown that much of his labor was for naught "as for the work that we came out here to do, there seems little likelihood of its immediate accomplishment."[54]

Despite the Filipinization of the government under Governor General Harrison, Americans resumed greater control with the appointment of Leonard Wood to that role in 1921. In 1926 the PAAF, of which Wood was the honorary president, gained a charter that gave it legal authority to "conduct, supervise, and administer athletics in the Islands." Extensive competition and municipal leagues ensued that pitted American military teams, teachers, administrators, and college students against each other in integrated play that included baseball, basketball, swimming, football, track and field, bowling, cycling, handball, and tennis. In the latter sport women joined the men in mixed doubles competition. Girls vied for championships in volleyball and indoor baseball and the traditional Filipino game of *sipa* featured singles, doubles, and team contests. The inclusion of *sipa* indicates a measure of Filipino influence in the American athletic efforts, but other Filipinos found the means to physically challenge Americans at their own games. Some teams utilized professional athletes in the volleyball matches, while other minimally skilled players entered the tennis competition simply to avoid the cost of admission to the facility.[55]

The American national game of baseball began to wane in the 1930s as urbanization appropriated the vacant lots where the sport had been played in Manila. Among college students basketball gained ascendancy in the 1920s as teams vied for the national championship. By 1935 a writer for *The Filipino Athlete* stated that "perhaps no other game is as widely played today as basketball. No school is so small or obscure that it does not have a team that aspires to local championship at least." The game created and promoted by the YMCA had certainly taken hold, but had been claimed as the Filipinos own, particularly after a strong showing in the 1936 Olympic Games, in which the Philippines lost only to the United States, but had to settle for fifth place even though it had defeated Mexico, which won the bronze medal.[56]

In addition to its athletic enterprises the YMCA offered boys' clubs, camping, excursions, and scouting activities aimed at community service. Such efforts, however, met with resistance from the Catholic hierarchy, who feared Protestant proselytism to the point of threatening youth with excommunication for participation in YMCA programs.[57]

Playgrounds

The YMCA also had a hand in the development of playgrounds in the Philippines. The playground movement originated in Boston in the 1880s as a means to provide a safe environment for young children who might be injured playing in the city streets. The creation of small sand boxes soon grew to larger areas to accommodate older youth. The idea spread to Chicago, where Jane Addams (1860-1935) incorporated such a play area into her Hull House Settlement in an immigrant neighborhood. By 1906 a national Playground Association of America was organized at a YMCA in Washington, DC, utilizing play under the direction of trained supervisors as a means to Americanize ethnic immigrant youths. The concept soon found its way to the Philippines and the ubiquitous Elwood Brown served on the playground committee and trained the playground directors. In addition to the implementation of sports and games, the playgrounds contained swings, horizontal climbing ladders, slides, and teeter-totters, all under the auspices of adult supervisors, who also aspired to Americanize the Filipinos through play.[58]

RESIDUAL CULTURE

Despite the mammoth efforts of the American organizers to supplant traditional Filipino culture, elements of the indigenous lifestyle persisted. American educators not only accepted the traditional crafts of the indigenous peoples, but incorporated them into the industrial education curriculum as commercial products. With the exception of *sipa*, a traditional Filipino game included in the acceptable athletic activities, the Americans sought to eradicate Filipino sports and their accompanying gambling without success. The Filipinos continued to gamble on cards, dominoes, billiards, horse races, and cockfights. One American commentator stated that "gambling is a national vice." Both men and women played the card games, and even the children gambled in their games.[59]

The cockpit most disturbed the American missionaries. Town fiestas included three days of cockfights, and despite repeated efforts and a failed national crusade by American moralists to condemn the activity the pastime prevailed. The American government relented as early as 1902. Unable to ban the sport, it decided to license and tax it, which drew the ire of the Protestant ministers. Nevertheless, even the 1908 Manila Carnival included sanctioned cockfights, and even American military personnel became avid participants in the gory spectacle. By the 1930s Filipino migrant workers to California brought the pastime with them.[60]

Under the Spanish, Filipinos engaged in a form of fencing with wooden bolos, known as *armis*. In 1925 the women at the University of the Philippines resurrected fencing as part of the curriculum.[61] Francisca Reyes Aquino (1899–1983), a teacher at the university, labored throughout her career to revive the traditional folk dances of the country. She authored ten books and made musical recordings of traditional songs to sustain the native culture, receiving top awards from national and international associations for her work. In 1937 a Folk Song and Dance Club, which served as a performance troupe, was established, and folk dance became part of the required curriculum. In an example of reverse cultural flow in the era of globalization, the tinikling folk dance is now taught to children in many American schools.[62]

THE RISE OF FILIPINO BOXERS

The cockfighting that the clergy tried to eradicate found an equally rabid following when the battles transferred to human practitioners. Public exhibitions with professional boxers began in Manila in 1910 at Frank Churchill's Olympic Club. The US War Department officially banned bouts between military personnel and civilians until 1923, so promoters imported American and Australian boxers, as Filipinos preferred interracial confrontations and thousands willingly paid admission fees to witness such Social Darwinian encounters. Despite the ban on military involvement, boxing matches at Corregidor and Subic Bay proved to be most popular, including clandestine bouts with local fighters.[63]

The popularity and increasing number of bouts resulted in additional regulation by the authorities. By 1918 bouts were limited to only ten rounds (later rescinded) and participants were required to undergo medical examinations. In 1920 boxing clubs were required to pay quarterly taxes. Two years later bouts between female boxers were banned, and by 1928 boys less than sixteen years of age were prohibited from appearing in the stadium bouts. The latter restriction affected the weekday schedule of bouts that included amateurs and provided a means for promoters to identify emerging talent for the professional ranks.[64]

Such prohibitions had little effect on the popularity of the sport and the Philippines became a hotbed of boxing talent in the 1920s. Francisco Guilledo, born to a peasant family in 1901, emerged as the first and greatest star in Churchill's stable of fighters, which he brought to the United States in search of even bigger paydays starting in 1920. Under Churchill's guidance Guilledo adopted the pseudonym of Pancho Villa, the Mexican bandit who terrorized the American Southwest during the early years of World War I. The Filipino pugilist precipitated his own version of terror in the boxing ring. He fought Mike Ballerino, the US Army champion and a future American national champion, thirteen times and never lost (11–0–2). He allegedly suffered only three losses in the Philippines, all to bigger men. In 1922 he traveled to America with Churchill to seek the flyweight championship, a title he captured a year later.[65]

Villa became a boxing sensation, attracting record crowds and grossing nearly $300,000 in two years. White American sportswriters—in disbelief at his speed in the ring and his ability to dismantle the belief in white racial superiority—characterized him as a monkey and a demon, somewhat less than human. Despite his gentlemanly manners in the ring, Villa antagonized whites in his emulation of Jack Johnson, the first African American champion who thwarted social convention by his profligate spending, marrying white women, and disdaining segregation norms of the era. Villa, too, dressed lavishly, spent his money extravagantly, and had a coterie of white women. In so doing he became a heroic idol in the Philippines, whose populace had chafed under the American pretensions of racial hegemony. Villa died abruptly in 1925 from complications in a surgery for an infected tooth while in San Francisco. His Filipina wife contended that he was murdered by an overdose of anesthetic at the behest of gamblers who had lost a large sum on his last fight. While the allegation of an overdose is a certainty, the contention of criminal intent has never been substantiated.[66]

His body was returned to Manila for burial and 100,000 mourners turned out to bid him goodbye.

> Into his person he collected all the swank and swagger of the period and the whole country felt a vicarious pride in his rise from rags to riches—and in his magnificent wardrobe, his collection of silk shirts and natty hats, his pearl buttons and gold cufflinks, and his princely retinue. He had a valet to massage him, another valet to towel him, another valet to put on his shoes, another valet to help him in his trousers, and still other valets to comb his hair, powder his cheeks, and spray him with perfume. He was, perhaps, more idolized as a magnifico rather than as a boxer, and when he died the nation's heart broke.[67]

A belated recognition of his greatness occurred in 1999 when the Associated Press named Villa the "flyweight of the century."[68]

A host of Filipino fighters followed Villa to make their mark in the United States. By the 1930s at least a dozen Filipinos boxed in America, with a large following among the itinerant Filipino laborers in California. Frank Churchill's next find, Speedy Dado (Diosdado Posadas, 1906–1990), proved to be a durable bantamweight, who fought from 1925 to 1940. Dado lost two bouts for the world featherweight title in 1928 and 1933, but fought repeatedly for the California state bantamweight crown, which he won in 1931 and 1933. He earned as much as $4,000 a month in the United States, a king's ransom in the Philippines. After Churchill's untimely death in 1933, Dado continued to gain notoriety as a chauffeur and bodyguard for the actress Mae West (1893–1980), who sponsored the careers of several boxers who filled her retinue.[69]

Small Montana (Benjamin Gan, 1913–1976), a contemporary of Dado, fought from 1930 to 1941 as another flyweight contender, winning the New York State version of the world championship in 1935, a year in which he fought a dozen times. He lost world championship bouts for the flyweight title in 1937 and 1938, and a bantamweight championship bout in 1940, but proved to be a perennial contender.[70]

Ceferino Garcia (1906–1981) began boxing in the Philippines in 1923 and traveled to the United States in 1930. He became a favorite of the Filipino laborers there, who would travel hundreds of miles to see him fight as a middleweight among the usually heavier American boxers. Garcia perfected a bolo punch, an upper cut supposedly derived from cutting sugar cane, symbolic of the poverty shared by his itinerant followers. "A Garcia fight scheduled anywhere on the Pacific Coast is a signal for a cavalcade of motor cars of various vintages to converge on the scene of action."[71]

Garcia generally did not disappoint his fans, knocking out almost half of his opponents, a symbolic retribution for destitute Filipinos at home and abroad. A Filipino sportswriter declared that "very few fighters dare risk their chins against Garcia's bolo punch, which is usually deadly."[72] He first won the middleweight championship of the Orient in Manila in 1928, and then captured the California state championship in 1933. From 1934 to 1939 he fought in four world championship bouts, bringing even greater prestige to the Philippines. Like Speedy Dado, he gained additional renown as a member of Mae West's entourage. Though he lost the 1937 title bout to Barney Ross (1909–1967), the sports editor of the *Los Angeles Times* admitted that "the bolo punching Filipino, hitting one punch to the champion's two but carrying more real murder in one of his lethal wallop [sic] than Ross had in a dozen, came from behind in the last four rounds with an exhibition in gameness that forced a highly partisan audience to forget their prejudice in appreciation of the Filipino's courageous comeback."[73] Garcia won the New York version of the world middleweight championship in Madison Square Garden in 1939, then successfully defended his title in the first title fight held in Manila later that year. The occasion justified a national holiday. The *New York Times* admitted that "Garcia embodies everything that goes to make a titleholder. . . . He is strong. He can box. He can punch. He can absorb punishment. He can adjust himself to ring situations as they develop, is resourceful, alert, cool under fire, a perfect fury when the tide swings his way." Such a recognition represented a significant change of opinion relative to the earlier colonial administrators who judged the Filipinos unable to care for themselves, but racist sentiments still lingered. When another Filipino fighter, Little Dempsey (Roberto Hilado, 1913–2004), fought a white opponent, a female fan encouraged the American to "c'mon, kill that monkey."[74]

Boxing waned thereafter in the Philippines as World War II and the Japanese occupation of the islands disrupted the flow of fighters to the United States. In the aftermath of the conflict Gabriel "Flash" Elorde (1935–1985) emerged as a prominent contender, winning the junior lightweight championship by knockout in 1960, a title he held for seven years. He began fighting at the age of seventeen, progressing through the Asian bantamweight, featherweight, and lightweight divisions. Elorde honored the Filipino tradition of patronage, using his wealth to build a chapel, an orphanage, and school buildings in his hometown of Paranaque.[75] After nearly half a century of American rule, Filipinos had clearly adopted American sports, but maintained the residual cultural characteristics that marked their difference.

ATHLETIC LEGACY

A quarter century after the Filipinos received formal independence a historian of sports in the Philippines stated that "from 1946 to the present the Philippines has tried to continue the policies initiated by Americans . . . [but there is a] trend to return to native games and recreational activities of old."[76] That process has resulted in mixed results. Seven countries sent their soccer teams to the Philippines in 1951, which generated some popular interest in the sport, but that has not been sustained. Sport officials, imbued with the American need to win, refused to fund international trips due to the lack of success (as measured by wins) after 2010. University of Santo Thomas also decided to provide greater support for basketball and volleyball teams rather than soccer because the latter had not yet produced sufficient star players.[77]

Other American sports continued to thrive. Following World War II the San Francisco Lions, a successful African-American baseball team, traveled to the Philippines in 1948, but lost to the locals. The following spring the Filipino teams consistently defeated the American military teams. The Philippines captured the Asian baseball championship in 1954. While baseball lost its prominence in the Manila area, which finally disbanded its municipal league in 1979, the game continued to enjoy a substantial following in the outer islands. In 1992 the Little League team from Zamboanga in Mindanao won the World Championship, but was later forced to surrender the title for using ineligible players.[78]

By that time basketball had clearly superseded baseball as the national sport in the Philippines. The performance of the Filipino basketball players in the international tournaments during the 1950s had created a new set of heroes and fostered national pride. Despite a distinct disadvantage in height the Filipinos adapted a strategy previously employed by African-American teams in the United States, employing a fast pace, crisp passing, and a high-scoring offense to overcome any physical deficiencies. The Filipinos captured the Asian championship in 1960, 1963, and 1967. In the process "basketball not only afforded the Filipinos the chance to play with modernity but it also expanded this opportunity to transcend various, class, ethnic, religious, linguistic, and geographical divisions that kept the nation under a constant threat of disintegration." The national unity that the Americans had hoped to achieve moved closer to reality after they had left. In 1975 Filipinos established a professional league, the first in Asia, modeled after the American National Basketball Association, with teams sponsored by corporations. Players have obtained such celebrity status that they have copied their American counterparts by extending their brands to acting and political office.[79]

Nowhere is that more evident than in the emergence of Manny Pacquiao (1978–) as a global icon. Once considered the best pound-for-pound boxer in the world, Pacquiao held championships in eight different weight classes. Named Fighter of the Year three times, the Boxing Writers Association also honored him as the Fighter of the Decade after 2010. He parlayed that celebrity into entrepreneurship as a promoter, and alternative careers as a singer and television and movie actor. In 2009 Filipinos elected him to Congress and he embarked on a war against poverty, establishing a foundation to address such problems in the Philippines. The initial American administrators of the country had achieved their idealistic dream of creating well rounded and self-governing individuals through the power of sport, but they could not have imagined the circuitous route that the process would travel over the following century.[80]

NOTES

1. Worcester, *The Philippines Past and Present*, vol. 2:514.

2. Fred Eggan Papers, Box 134, folder 31; Dean C. Worcester, "Field Sports Among the Wild Men of Luzon," *National Geographic*, 22:3 (March 1911), 215–67.

3. Fee, *A Woman's Impression of the Philippines*, 280–82; Beran,"Americans in the Philippines," 69; Bocobo-Olivar, *History of Physical Education in the Philippines*, 22–23; kulturapilipinas.webs.com/about-magna-kultura (January 13, 2016).

4. Beran,"Americans in the Philippines," 69; Torres, *The Americanization of Manila*, 177; Best of Philippines, "Games" at www.marimari.com/content/philippines/best_of/games.html (January 13, 2016); Davis, "Cockfight Nationalism," 549, 552 asserts that cockfighting in the islands predated the arrival of the Spanish.

5. Davis, "Cockfight Nationalism"; Gleeck, Jr., *American Institutions in the Philippines*, 21–29.

6. Worcester, "Field Sports Among the Wild Men of Luzon,"82–90; Worcester, "The Non-Christian Peoples of the Philippine Islands," 1197 (quote), 1199.

7. Worcester, "Field Sports Among the Wild Men of Luzon," 221.

8. Gleeck, Jr., *American Institutions in the Philippines*, 29, Charles Conlon cited in Neal McCabe and Constance McCabe, *Baseball's Golden Age* (New York: Harry N. Abrams, 1993), 9.

9. Worcester, "Field Sports Among the Wild Men of Luzon," 228–59; Worcester Papers, University of Michigan, Box 5; Worcester, "The Non-Christian Peoples of the Philippine Islands,"1253 (quote).

10. Pecson and Racelis, eds, *Tales of the American Teachers in the Philippines*, 161; Fee, *A Woman's Impression of the Philippines*, 270.

11. Gems, *The Athletic Crusade*, 30–44.

12. Reaves, *Taking In a Game*, 91–92.

13. Ibid., 94; John H. Nankville, ed., *The History of the Twenty-Fifth Regiment of the United States Infantry, 1896–1926* (Ft. Collins, CO: The Old Army Press, 1927 [1971]), 163–69; Tom Simon, "Arlie Pond," sabr.org/bioproj/person/2d68aec2 (January 16, 2016); Beran, "Americans in the Philippines," 71; Henry Chadwick, ed., *Spalding's Baseball Guide and Official League Book for 1901* (New York: American Sports Publishing Co., 1901), 76, 77 (quote).

14. Antilohao, *Playing with the Big Boys*, 69.

15. Wooley, "'Batter Up' in the Philippines,"313.

16. Coffman, *The Regulars*, 111, 128–33; Nankville, *The History of the Twenty-Fifth Regiment of the United States Infantry*, 169–71, 211–12.

17. Joseph P. McCallus, *The MacArthur Highway & Other Relics of American Empire in the Philippines* (Washington, DC: Potomac Books, 2010), 202, 282.

18. Reaves, *Taking In a Game*, 97; Simon, "Arlie Pond."

19. Antilohao, *Playing With the Big Boys*, 37; Gleeck, Jr., *The Manila-Americans*, 116.

20. Joseph R. Svinth, "The Origins of Filipino Boxing, 1899–1926," *Journal of Combative Sport* (July 2001) at http.//ejmas.com/jcs/jcsart_svinth_0701.htm (July 8, 2011).

21. Torres, *The Americanization of Manila*, 174; Gleeck, Jr., *The Manila-Americans*, 119–20.

22. Runstedtler, "The New Negro's Brown Brother"; boxrec.com/media/index.php?title=Human:137869 (October 20, 2015).

23. Arnold, *The Moro War*, 191.

24. Torres, *The Americanization of Manila*, 60–64; Benitez Licuanan, *Filipinos and Americans*, 65–66; Karnow, *In Our Image*, 212–13; Gleeck, Jr., *The Manila-Americans*, 32, 64–67; Le Roy, *Philippine Life in Town and Country*, 112; Wolff, *Little Brown Brother*, 254;

Army and Navy Club Annual Report, December 31, 1931, National Archives, RG 350, Box 1074; McCallus, *The MacArthur Highway & Other Relics of American Empire in the Philippines*, 274.

25. Simon, "Arlie Pond." Clark spent many years in the islands, aiding defense efforts in the prelude to World War II.

26. Arnold, *The Moro War*, 173, 198–99.

27. Antilohao, *Playing With the Big Boys*, 42.

28. Reaves, *Taking In a Game*, 95–96, Henry Chadwick, ed., *Spalding's Official Base Ball Guide for 1907* (New York: American Sports Publishing Co., 1907), 25 (quote); Antilohao, "From Baseball Colony to Basketball Republic," 1399.

29. Kirkwood, "'Michigan Men' in the Philippines and the Limits of Self-Determination in the Progressive Era," 67; Coffman, *The Regulars*, 87; Hedman and Sidel, *Philippine Politics and Society in the Twentieth Century*, 122–23.

30. McCallus, *The MacArthur Highway & Other Relics of American Empire in the Philippines*, 16–19 (quotes, 17–18).

31. Gleeck, Jr., *The Manila-Americans*, 11, 68–72, 286, 325–27.

32. Gleeck, Jr., *The Manila-Americans*, 11, 66, 72–73; Benitez Licuanen, *Filipinos and Americans*, 44–92, 136; www.philstar.com/sports/613932/wack-wacks-bill-shaw-and-social-responsibility (January 23, 2016).

33. Cited in Antilohao, *Playing with the Big Boys*, 53.

34. Gleeck, Jr., *The Manila-Americans*, 100–101, 176; Thomas P. Walsh, *Tin Pan Alley and the Philippines: American Songs of War and Love, 1898–1946, A Resource Guide* (Lanham, MD: Scarecrow Press, 2013), 241; Torres, *The Americanization of Manila*, 178–79.

35. Wolff, *Little Brown Brother*, 178; Clymer, *Protestant Missionaries in the Philippines*, 38; Karnow, *In Our Image*, 214.

36. Torres, *The Americanization of Manila*, 179; Pante, "A Collision of Masculinities."

37. Coffman, *The Regulars*, 66; Bulosan, *America Is in the Heart*, 66–67; San Juan, *On Becoming Filipino*, 62.

38. Stagg Papers, University of Chicago, Special Collections, Box 27, folder 2.

39. *Chicago Tribune*, December 18, 1913, 10; Elfers, *The Tour to End All Tours*, xxii, 114, 135–44; Gleeck, Jr. *American Institutions in the Philippines*, 39 (quote).

40. Kramer, *The Blood of Government*, 371; Gleeck, Jr. *American Institutions in the Philippines*, 40.

41. Antolihao, *Playing With the Big Boys*, 71.

42. Marquardt Papers, "History of Leyte High School," 1936 folder; Pecon and Racelis, eds., *Tales of the American Teachers in the Philippines*, 191; Beran, "Americans in the Philippines,"73; Bocobo-Olivar, *History of Physical Education in the Philippines*, 47–50, 47, 50 (quotes, respectively). The positive effect of physical activity on academic performance has since been ratified by Harvard professor John Ratey in *Spark: The Revolutionary New Science of Exercise and the Brain* (New York: Little, Brown & Co., 2007).

43. Ibid., 50.

44. Beran, "Americans in the Philippines," 78.

45. Ibid., 74–75; quotes in Edward Marshall, "Baseball Helping to Revolutionize the Philippines," *New York Times*, September 22, 1912, n.p.

46. Reaves, *Taking In a Game*, 97–100.

47. Elwood S. Brown, Annual Reports, 1911–1914, in YMCA Archives, Box Philippines, NP, Correspondence Reports, 1911–1968, administrative reports file.

48. Elwood S. Brown, *Annual Report, October 1, 1912–October 1, 1913*, n.p., YMCA Archives, Administrative reports file, 1912–1917.

49. Ibid., n.p (quote); Antolihao, *Playing with the Big Boys*, 59.

50. Elwood S. Brown, *Annual Report, October 1, 1916–October 1917*, n.p., YMCA Archives; www.indiana.edu/~liblilly/digital/exhibitions/exhibits/show/crone/intro (January 26, 2016). Interscholastic teams sent to China included two girls' indoor baseball (softball) squads that played an exhibition match in Shanghai (Bocobo-Olivar, *History of Physical Education in the Philippines*, 44, 63).

51. Bocobo-Olivar, *History of Physical Education in the Philippines*, 103–4.

52. *School News Review*, February 15, 1933, 1; February 1, 1934; July 1, 1934, 8; July 15, 1934, 8; September 15, 1935, 8; all in National Archives, RG 350, Box 1187.

53. YMCA Archives, Philippines Box, Manila file, 1906–1907, William H. Taft to James F. Smith, Governor General of the Philippines, December 31, 1906; Chengting T. Wang to My dear [sic] Fletcher, February 19, 1915; "Report on the Chinese in the Philippines"; Elwood S. Brown, *Annual Report, October 1, 1914–October 1, 1915*, n.p. (quote).

54. E. J. Mazurkiewicz, *Annual Report of the Physical Department*, American Branch YMCA, Manila, Philippine Islands, September 30, 1917, YMCA Archives; Joel S. Franks, *Crossing Sidelines, Crossing Cultures: Sport and Asian Pacific American Cultural Citizenship* (Lanham, MD: University Press of America, 2000), xiii; Bocobo-Olivar, *History of Physical Education in the Philippines*, 44, 75–76; Beran, "Americans in the Philippines," 79; J. Truitt Maxwell, Manila YMCA Executive Secretary, to Elwood S. Brown, April 18, 1922, YMCA Archives, Correspondence and reports file, 1920–1923.

55. *Annual Report*, Philippine Amateur Athletic Federation, 1926, in YMCA Aexhives, Philippines, miscellaneous reports, n.p.

56. Antilohao, *Playing With the Big Boys*, 76–77, 76 (quote).

57. Gleeck, Jr., *American Institutions in the Philippines*, 77–80.

58. Gems, Borish, and Pfister, *Sports in American History*, 185–86; Philippines Correspondence Reports, 1911–1968, YMCA Archives, n.p.; W. W. Marquardt, Director of Education, October 25, 1916, and Governor General Harrison, Executive Orders #78 (September 16, 1914) and #30, (April 4, 1917) in National Archives, RG 350, Box 931; Bocobo-Olivar, *History of Physical Education in the Philippines*, 54, 71.

59. Worcester, *The Philippines Past and Present*, 508; Bocobo-Olivar, *History of Physical Education in the Philippines*, 24; Freer, *The Philippine Experiences of an American Teacher*, 7, 286; Fee, *A Woman's Impression of the Philippines*, 270 (quote), 280–81.

60. Freer, *The Philippine Experiences of an American Teacher*, 76, 83, 320–21; Circular letter #562, January 23, 1916, and *Philippines Herald* clipping, September 30, 1933, n.p., both in National Archives, RG 350, Box 656; Davis, "Cockfight Nationalism," 559–61; Espana-Maram, *Creating Masculinity in Los Angeles in Little Manila*, 64–65.

61. Bocobo-Olivar, *History of Physical Education in the Philippines*, 22, 44.

62. Ibid., 108–10, 112–17.

63. Bocobo-Olivar, *History of Physical Education in the Philippines*, 55, 66–67; Runstedtler, "The New Negro's Brown Brother," 114–15.

64. Runstedtler, "The New Negro's Brown Brother," 114–17; National Archives, RG 350, Box 691, boxing proclamations.

65. Gems, *Boxing*, 38–39, 98–99.

66. Ibid., 100; boxrec.com/media/index.php?title=Human:9433 (January 30, 2016).

67. Torres, *The Americanization of Manila*, 176.

68. boxrec.com/media/index.php?title=Human:9433 (January 30, 2016).

69. Franks, *Crossing Sidelines, Crossing Cultures*, 32–37; Runstedtler, "The New Negro's Brown Brother," 120–21; Espana-Maram, *Creating Masculinity in Los Angeles in Little Manila*, 77–78; boxrec.com/boxer/9907 (January 21, 2016); Gems, *Boxing*, 225.

70. boxrec.com/boxer/12 (January 30, 2016).

71. boxrec.com/media/index.php?title=Human:9601 (January 30, 2016); Espana-Maram, *Creating Masculinity in Los Angeles in Little Manila*, 70–82, 79 (quote).

72. Ibid., 78.

73. Ibid., 78; boxrec.com/media/index.php?title=Human:9601 (January 30, 2016).

74. boxrec.com/media/index.php?title=Human:9601 (January 30, 2016); Roger Mooney, "Going Home a Hero: How Ceferino Garcia Finally Realizes His Dream," *Ring*, April 1994, 26–28, 60, clipping in Garcia file, Intrnational Boxing Hall of Fame; Espana-Maram, *Creating Masculinity in Los Angeles in Little Manila*, 94, 101 (quotes, respectively).

75. Bocobo-Olivar, *History of Physical Education in the Philippines*, 166; Elorde file, International Boxing Hall of Fame.

76. Bocobo-Olivar, *History of Physical Education in the Philippines*, 200.

77. Satwinder Rehal, "In the Quest for Recognition: A Critical Sociological Reflection on Football's 'Resistance' in the Philippines," presented at the International Sport Sociology Association World Congress for the Sociology of Sport, Malmo, Sweden, June 10, 2015.

78. Reaves, *Taking In a Game*, 105–6; Antilohao, *Playing with the Big Boys*, 79–91.

79. Antolihao, *Playing with the Big Boys*, 23, (quote), 61, 75, 103–48.

80. Gems, *Boxing*, 187–88.

NINE

The Legacy of the American Occupation

Nearly a half century of American preeminence in the Philippines left an indelible impression on the emergence of the country as a nation-state, with lasting effects on its political framework, its economy, its educational system, and its national identity. Despite seven decades of independence the process of nation building remains an ongoing issue both promoted and inhibited by the past and continuing American influences in several respects.

MILITARY

From 1898 until World War I the Philippines served as the major training ground for American military officers. Lessons learned there were later applied in Vietnam and again in the American wars in the Mideast. Much of that training revolves around the leadership of General Arthur MacArthur, commander of American forces during the early part of the war against the Filipinos, and his son, Douglas MacArthur (1880-1964). After his own combat experiences in World War I, Douglas MacArthur returned to the Philippines as a garrison commander in 1922, and assumed leadership of all American forces in the islands in 1928. He once again returned to the Philippines in 1935 to assist commonwealth president Manuel Quezon (1871-1944) in the establishment of a national army. As commander in chief of the Pacific forces, MacArthur was forced to abandon the Philippines with the invasion of the Japanese at the outbreak of World War II. While American narratives and some Filipinos revere General Douglas MacArthur's "liberation" of the Philippines from Japanese occupation as a heroic promise fulfilled, other Filipinos view it as an unnecessary invasion that destroyed the city of Manila and cost 100,000 lives, mostly to enhance MacArthur's quest for legendary status.[1]

With the rise of Japanese power in the Pacific at the turn of the twentieth century American officers saw a need for military installations in the Philippines, which resulted in the construction of the largest bases in the region, the Subic Bay naval station and Clark Air Base. The Philippines and the United States agreed to a mutual defense treaty after the war and the Military Bases Agreement of 1947 allowed the United States to retain control of such bases with a ninety-nine-year lease. The bases proved instrumental in the conduct of the Vietnam War, supplying transport, armaments, hospitalization, and even leisure for American troops. Clark offered a golf course, and the Philippines proved an enticing location for combat veterans' R&R (one week leave for rest and recreation). Such developments enhanced the weak Filipino economy, but raised the ire of Filipino nationalists. In 1966 the Rusk-Ramos Agreement altered the lease terms to expire in 1991 and the vast majority of the Clark Air Base acreage was returned to the Philippines by 1979. Still, Filipinos decried the damage to their national dignity. Filipino workers at the US bases received only one-eighth the salary of their American coworkers and more than 50,000 squatters inhabited the environs of the Clark Air Base. The towns of Olongapo, outside Subic, and Angeles, outside Clark, had become open brothels catering to the lust of American servicemen. Drugs, gambling, corruption, and smuggling were widespread. Rapes and murders by American personnel resulted in minimal punishment. Thirty-one Filipinos died at the hands of Americans between 1952 and 1962, and yet none of the cases reached trial. Filipinos retaliated with a march on the US embassy in 1965, but took more immediate measures by smuggling food and bombs from the American installations. The extracted dynamite from the bombs was used in underwater fishing, resulting in larger catches and meeting immediate nutritional needs.[2]

The Philippines also needed American assistance in combatting a communist insurgency in the post-WWII years. During the war the communist resistance movement known as the Huks (Hukbalahap movement) collaborated with the United States in conducting a guerrilla war against the Japanese occupiers. In 1946 six communists were elected to Congress, but banned from taking their seats. The communist victory in the Chinese civil war in 1949 raised additional concerns for their expansion in Asia. By the 1960s, political and doctrinal differences led to clandestine warfare and attacks in the Philippines, where the New Peoples Army (NPA) operated in an estimated 20 percent of the villages and had alliances in Manila. By 1981, US military aid amounted to $83 million annually, and the Philippines would remain dependent on such assistance thereafter.[3]

The guerrilla warfare tactics and pacification programs developed in the Philippines would be utilized in American incursions in Vietnam,

Iraq, and Afghanistan with equally limited levels of success. Despite the closing of the US bases in 1991 the rising influence of communist China brought a return of American forces to the Philippines in 1998 and 1999. The discovery of oil in the Spratly Islands of the South China Sea, jointly claimed by China, Vietnam, and the Philippines, brought the threat of military intervention.[4]

Despite the reliance on American military might nationalist tensions continued to threaten American-Filipino relations throughout the latter twentieth century. Over the past three decades the Filipino government and Catholic Church officials have made repeated requests for the United States to return the bells confiscated from the Balangiga church after the massacre of American troops there in 1901. The United States military and the government consider the bells to be trophies of war, memorialized at American bases in the United States and Korea, and refuse to accommodate such a request. Even intercession by the pope has not resolved the impasse. The history of the Philippines and the United States remains inextricably intertwined however. The former Fort McKinley was converted into the Manila American Cemetery for the 17,000 servicemen killed in the region during World War II. It remains the largest cemetery in the Pacific, but unlike the American segregation practices of the original occupation, it also includes the graves of the brave Philippine Scouts, an everlasting tribute to shared heroism and brotherhood.[5]

POLITICS

The American authorities instituted a democratic framework for government patterned after their own political system in the United States. A distinct difference, however, rested in the suffrage rights of the citizenry. Although all American women did not possess universal suffrage at the time of the initial American invasion of the Philippines, they did obtain voting rights by 1920. Filipinas did not gain that right until 1937. Not only gender, but social class distinctions greatly colored power and leadership in the Philippines. While American cultural values fostered individualism, Filipinos adhered to communalism, a feature of tribal and familial life under the Spanish rule and the Catholic Church. The American commissions which governed the early occupation of the islands also courted and mentored the *ilustrado* and *mestizo* elites, who gradually assumed leadership roles within the government. That oligarchy has resulted in a very limited form of democracy with cacique families ruling their territorial domains, often through the use of private armies and violent means, and dispensing patronage positions as well as social and economic capital to maintain their hold on power and enrich their extended families in the process. When the United States relinquished oversight in 1946, nepotism and patronage only increased. By

1953, 42 percent of farm land was owned by 0.4 percent of families. Of the twenty-eight families represented in the 1903 Chamber of Commerce rolls at least fourteen still number among the powerful elites, with an estimated sixty families throughout the islands who maintain the vast majority of the wealth and power.[6] In that sense one might say that the United States has emulated the Philippines with families such as the Kennedys, Bushes, and Clintons extending their political and economic capital and political elections reliant on the large sums of money provided by political action committees (PACS).

Manuel Roxas (1892–1948), the first president of the independent Philippines, catered to his American supporters by extending military and trade rights, and died in office in 1948. His successor, Elpidio Quirino (1890–1956), engaged in graft, corruption, and a fraudulent election in 1949, and his administration faced a resurgence of the communist Huk movement. Ramon Magsaysay (1907–1957), the Secretary of Defense who curtailed the Huks, defeated Qurino in the 1953 presidential election. Known for his honesty, Magsaysay intended to bring land reform and aid to the peasantry, but was frustrated by a recalcitrant Congress of elites, who felt their wealth and power threatened by such changes. When he died in a plane crash in 1957 he was succeeded by Vice President Carlos Garcia (1896–1971), who took a more nationalist approach in deliberations with the United States and was defeated by Diosdado Macapagal (1910–1997) in the 1961 election. Macapagal tried to address the ongoing corruption in the government, bring about land reform laws, and require the income tax payments generally flaunted by the wealthy. Predictably, the elitist members of the Congress failed to pass such measures and he lost the 1965 election to Ferdinand Marcos (1917–1989).[7]

The Marcos regime marked the installation of his dictatorship with the tacit acceptance of the US government. Marcos pillaged government funds to insure his reelection in 1969, then declared martial law in 1972, presumably to counter a communist insurgency. He used the excuse to arrest and imprison his political rivals, and extend the political, economic, and military powers of the presidency. He abolished Congress, appointed his hand-picked officials to government posts, and expropriated the businesses of his wealthy rivals to enhance his own wealth and power. Despite the opposition of the former oligarchy and the Catholic Church, multiple United States presidents acquiesced in his rule while they conducted the Vietnam War and were in need of favorable arrangements for the numerous American military bases in the islands.[8]

Marcos faced several crises: a resurgence of the Huks and the communist party in 1969, increased immigration of Christian settlers to Mindanao that fostered conflict with Muslim residents, student activism in Manila, and the oil production decline in the 1970 that increased foreign debt. In 1983 Marcos declared a moratorium on repayment of the debt. Nevertheless, his wife, Imelda Marcos (1929–), continued to spend lavishly on her shoe collection and other ostentatious displays of wealth. In that same year Benigno Aquino, Jr. (1932–1983), an opposition leader whom he had imprisoned for seven years, returned from his exile in the United States after a surgery to once again challenge Marcos. He never got the chance, as he was assassinated as he got off the plane in Manila. The resultant outrage of the populace, the Catholic Church, and even the clandestine support of the United States finally resulted in the "people power" revolution that finally overthrew Marcos, and brought Corazon Aquino (1933–), widow of the slain challenger, to office as the first female president of the Philippines. Marcos retired in exile to Hawaii with the aid of the US government until his death in 1989.[9]

Cory Aquino passed a new constitution in 1987, reestablishing the two houses of Congress, and limiting the president to one term of six years, and elected members of the legislature to four years. Still, by 2004 an estimated 50 percent of the House of Representatives were kin of former Congressmen, as the new laws did not ban spouses or children from running for office, which resulted in the elite families maintaining their power. Even Imelda Marcos returned to the Philippines and won multiple elections to Congress. Cory Aquino, from an elite family herself, eschewed labor reform and concentrated on the perennial battle against the communists. Multiple coup attempts by Marcos loyalists failed to dislodge her from the presidency, and political violence continued unabated as seven public officials, including five mayors were killed in Cavite alone from 1986 to 2000. Aquino was replaced by her Secretary of Defense, Fidel Ramos (1928–), who managed to quell some of the Muslim opposition in Mindanao and address the economic issues of the country. A movie star, Joseph Estrada (1937–) gained the presidency in 1998, but he was impeached for corruption in 2001. Gloria Macapagal-Arroyo (1947–), daughter of the earlier president succeeded to the office, which she held until she yielded to Benigno Aquino III (1960–), son of Cory Aquino, in 2010. Despite the election of Cory Aquino and Gloria Macapagal-Arroyo, Filipino women held only 15 percent of elected offices by the turn of the century. In 2013 women held only five of the twenty-four senatorial seats and virtually all political power continued to rest in the hands of the elite families, a strategy promoted by the US administrators a century earlier.[10]

The new constitution gives an inordinate amount of power to the president, who may appoint all of the fifteen judges of the Supreme Court without Congressional approval. The president also appoints all military personnel at the rank of colonel or higher. At the local levels mayors and other officials make the appointments to government positions, which promotes patronage and nepotism. Bribery and corruption are widespread. Gregorio Honasan (1948–), leader of a 1987 coup to depose Cory Aquino that resulted in about one hundred deaths, won amnesty under President Ramos, and was elected to the Senate three times thereafter. Likewise, Antonio Trillanes IV (1971–), who led a coup against President Arroyo in 2006, was elected to the Senate a year later and again in 2013. Although Arroyo was charged with nepotism, embezzlement, and widespread corruption and even arrested, she relinquished her presidency for a seat in the Congress. Joseph Estrada, too, lost his presidency due to corruption, but was elected mayor of Manila in 1913. Such cases are indicative of the local power retained by the elites despite national scandals and disgrace. Scholar Lynn White has described the situation as "many local polities . . . in conflict with each other and with 'the state.'"[11]

RELIGION

The ardent efforts of Protestant missionaries at the turn of the twentieth century had little success, but lasting influence in the Philippines, leading to a resurgence of proselytism at the onset of the twenty-first century. Moros in the southern islands historically had been tied more closely to the Muslim culture of Indonesia, and ongoing efforts to settle Christian Filipinos in Mindanao inevitably resulted in religious and social clashes.[12]

After World War II, Protestant efforts in the Philippines declined, only to be reasserted in the 1980s. Protestant preachers focused on the widespread poverty of the populace and offered evangelical promises of hope in religion. Whereas only 3 percent of Filipinos had converted to Protestantism by 1980, in the last two decades of the century 13,600 fundamentalist churches were counted in the islands. Less than 300 Christian groups operated in the Philippines in 1980, but that number multiplied more than fivefold to 1,676 by 1988. Jerry Falwell (1933–2007), one of the most prominent Protestant evangelists in the United States and head of the Moral Majority organization, traveled to the Philippines in 1985, in support of Ferdinand Marcos and to denounce the perceived evils of communism. Fundamentalists, such as Falwell and others, convinced that they had a universal message to deliver, expanded their global reach as the millennium approached.[13]

The encroachment of Protestantism in previously Catholic domains such as the Philippines brought concern from Pope John Paul II (Karol Wojtyla, 1920–2005), who traveled to more than a hundred countries to also preach against communism and call for peace and greater attention to human rights. The last issue differed with Falwell, as the Catholic Church in the Philippines joined the growing opposition to the dictatorial rule of Ferdinand Marcos. Cardinal Jaime Sin (1928–2005) emerged as one of the leaders of the People Power Movement that overthrew Ferdinand Marcos in 1986 and Joseph Estrada in 2001. Pope John Paul II made two trips to the Philippines, in 1981 and again in 1995. During the latter, an estimated four million followers filled the Luneta (Rizal Park) to participate in a papal mass, the largest papal gathering in history.[14]

One area of agreement between the Catholics and evangelical Protestants is the issue of abortion and the Catholic opposition to birth control has resulted in a high birth rate. The population growth provides employers with an overabundant labor force, allowing them to keep wages low and adding to the widespread poverty.[15]

One of the lasting influences of the original Protestant missionaries has been in the field of education. The schools founded by a variety of Christian churches have not only endured, but grown into universities, such as: Silliman University founded by Presbyterians in 1901, the Central Philippines University established in 1905 by Baptists, and the Seventh Day Adventist University instituted in 1917. After World War II Filipino Methodists, Baptists, and Episcopalians each organized their own universities. Still, the Aeta tribe (Negritos) of central Luzon clung to their animist beliefs and ostracized by the mainstream Filipino community, remained a challenge for Pentecostal preachers even after 2000. The Church of Christ, however, had made a considerable number of conversions by 2016, claiming two million members throughout the nation. Despite such inroads 83 percent of Filipinos still adhere to Catholicism, 8 percent subscribe to some form of Protestantism, 2 percent follow the nationalist Iglessia ng Kristo church, and another 2 percent cling to animism.[16]

The religious competition for hearts, minds, and souls continues after a century of proselytism in the Philippines, but a secular form of religion brought by the early American occupiers largely unites Filipinos in a common interest. Sociologists, psychologists, and anthropologists now contend that sport provides characteristics similar to religion in its idealistic beliefs, role models and heroic figures, rituals, shrines, potentially character-building qualities, and the passion and intensity of its followers. In that sense Filipinos have adopted basketball as a national secular religion.[17]

Modeled after the American NBA, the Philippines' professional basketball league has its own athletic stars, idolized by millions of fans, who worship fervently and raucously in packed arenas, not unlike the megachurches in the United States. The game has become a ritual fiesta, in which fans express their gaiety in singing and revelry, and even pray for the success of their teams. A Filipino journalist claims that "Today's Filipino is basically a man of two religions. He is a god-fearing Christian and an irrepressible basketball devotee."[18]

Economy

The early US administration undertook the transformation of the Philippines' economy, providing the infrastructure such as roads, railroads, and ports necessary for modern trade. In 1902, 55 percent of the population was engaged in agriculture, 13 percent in industry, and another 32 percent in service occupations. With the appointment of Francis Harrison as governor general from 1913 to 1921 Filipinos gained greater control over their own affairs, but a loss of $35 million in gold from the national bank during that era led Leonard Wood to charge that the Filipinos were still in need of American guidance. The US government appointed Wood as governor general, which resulted in continual conflict with the indigenous leadership during his tenure. Under the commonwealth Filipinos made more headway in running their own affairs, but the economy was still largely dependent on the United States. In 1900 exports to the United States amounted to 13 percent and imports at 9 percent. By 1940 those figures reached 83 percent in exports and 78 percent of Filipino imports. The Philippines became the world's largest exporter of coconut products and hemp by 1934. Sugar also dominated the economy until the 1970s, accounting for 43 percent of its revenue. By 2000 coconut plantations still accounted for 25 percent of the land.[19]

In the aftermath of World War II, the Philippines' economy made considerable strides, although still closely tied to and dominated by the United States. The Bell Trade Act of 1946 provided American companies with easy access to the Philippines, while Filipinos could only trade with the United States if there were no American competitors for their products. By 1960 its manufacturing and exports exceeded those of Taiwan and Korea. Economic crises, natural disasters, and politics would hinder growth thereafter, causing the country to fall behind other emerging national economies in Southeast Asia. The political and economic power of the elite families in particular resulted in an uneven development, with wealth and production in the hands of a few, and the vast majority relegated to roles as poor sharecroppers or underpaid industrial employees. Between 1950 and 1967 the elite families established banks and insurance companies that provided capital for their own increasing entrepreneurial activities, centered in the greater Manila area. By the 1980s, 44 percent of the Manila population resided in poverty, while the destitute in the Visayan Islands reached more than 70 percent. The economy experienced further decline due to a failure to innovate and the collapse of the logging, coconut, and sugar industries by 2000. The refusal of the wealthy families to agree to agrarian reforms and land ownership left many mired in poverty.[20]

By the turn of the twenty-first century the inefficient operation of the ports, and failure to upgrade roads also hampered development. Only 17 percent of roads consisted of asphalt or concrete, most of those in the Manila area. The wealthy families, however, found new means to increase their own economic capital by providing financial services (banks and insurance companies) to themselves or foreign investors, who developed squatters' lands with shopping malls, real estate ventures, and tourist attractions. The wealthy entrepreneurs invested in fleets of jeepneys (military jeeps converted to public taxis that could transport multiple passengers at once) that they rented to daily drivers. The drivers managed a subsistence living. By 2012 a quarter of the population over the age of 18 remained unemployed.[21]

Some poor families resorted to the sale of their daughters to avoid starvation. Prostitution was widespread, particularly in Manila, Olongapo, and Angeles, the latter two towns serving the American military during the Vietnam War era. After 1990 Subic Bay and Clark Air Base were turned into economic trade zones with hotels, casinos, a golf course, duty-free goods, and the international airport at Angeles to serve tourists, many of whom were participants in the globalized sex trade. Although prostitution is technically illegal in the Philippines, customers simply pay their "fine" at the bar of the nightclub or to the brothel owner. Graft and corruption of police and public officials assure that such establishments are not too troubled in their business.[22]

Poverty continues to be an endemic problem in the Philippines. Tondo, a district in Manila, is one of the largest slums in all of Asia. Minimum wage laws have been disregarded with impunity, the few labor unions have little power, and overpopulation provides a pliable labor force. With limited health care, the average life expectancy was 64.79 for men and 71.64 for women in 2016.[23]

Since the 1990s the increasing numbers of educated Filipinos, as well as the poverty-stricken laborers have sought a better life abroad. By 2000 at least five million Filipinos, 18 percent of its labor force, sought overseas employment. Their remittances to family in the Philippines amounted to $6.8 billion in 1999. That figure reached $10.6 billion by 2005. The thousands that migrate daily represent a considerable brain drain on the nation as doctors, engineers, nurses, teachers, and other professionals leave for the United States or other relatively wealthy countries. The less educated females find positions as nannies, maids, or sex workers. Such women are often subjected to overwork, abuse, and rape. Millions of Filipinos work in the countries of the Mideast, where males provide the labor for construction projects, most notably in Saudi Arabia, the United Arab Emirates, and Qatar. In the latter, Filipinos are among the laborers constructing multiple stadiums in anticipation of the 2022 soccer World Cup to be hosted by Qatar, and an Olympic bid. There they live in deplorable conditions that have drawn the ire of human rights organizations. Nevertheless, migrant labor continues to be a large part of the Filipino economy, with only China and India supplying more than the ten million Filipinos now working abroad. In 2013 their remittances amounted to $1.8 billion a month, more than 40 percent of it from the United States, which enables the Philippines to repay its international debts.[24]

The socioeconomic gap, however, continues to grow. In 1956 the richest 10 percent of Filipinos possessed 27 percent of the national income, and 37 percent by 1985. The fifty richest families controlled more than a quarter of the gross national product in 2013, while a third of all Filipinos were still mired below the poverty line. Twenty percent of Filipinos still own 80 percent of the land, much of it possessed by members of Congress, who rent it out to tenants.[25]

Tax evasion continues to limit the government's ability to pay its bills and promote economic development. Only 22 percent of professionals pay their taxes, and bribes account for untold amounts of lost income. Even lowly street vendors make bribes to local police in order to maintain their meager businesses. A Congress member admitted that businessmen "are so used to the corruption. . . . they have already set aside ten percent or twenty percent of the project price for the guy who signs the papers. To them, it is no longer whether it is corrupt or not—it is part of the business." Officials even pay journalists for positive coverage in the media.[26]

On a brighter note, the Philippines' economy has shown considerable improvement since 2003 with annual surpluses. The banking system has stabilized, international reserves are at a record high, the credit rating has been upgraded, and foreign investment has increased, despite limitations imposed on foreign ownership by the Philippines' constitution. The biggest benefactors, however, remain the elite families, many of Chinese ancestry, that dominate the social, political, and economic culture of the nation. "Chinese-Filipinos have long played a key (and today dominant) role in the domestic tobacco (cigar and cigarette) industry, just as they have figured prominently as sawmill owners, lumber dealers, furniture makers, and in competition or combination with politicians as logging concessionaires." As a result, unemployment remains at 7 percent, underemployment at nearly 20 percent, and 40 percent of people are engaged in informal work, i.e. street vendors, etc.[27]

EDUCATION

Despite the early American administrators' hopes for the power of education, it has produced limited results after a century of institutionalization. At the turn of the twenty-first century 30 percent of Filipino did not complete their elementary education, largely due to the need for their labor among agricultural families. The average Filipino completed seven years of schooling and 93 percent were literate. Secondary education has been free since 1988, yet only 14 percent completed that level and only 7 percent finished with a college degree, which is no guarantee of employment. Thirty-nine percent of college graduates have no job.[28]

There is a dearth of teachers, as wages are low, similar to that of factory workers. College graduates can earn considerably more in the United States and other more affluent nations. While English remains the language of instruction, teachers are not always fluent and those in the provinces may not comply with the directive. Few college grads can pass the licensing exams and some simply offer bribes to obtain the position. One-third of students have no textbooks, and teachers face large class sizes with a ratio of 50:1.[29]

A lasting influence of the American occupation remains in the emphasis on physical education and sport. The curriculum requires physical education with instruction in indigenous games and dances, health and fitness, and sports. Secondary students also take a class in American literature. The sports programs follow the American model and competition ranges from interscholastic and intercollegiate contests to professional leagues. American sport forms, particularly basketball and baseball, remain popular.[30]

CONFLICTED NATIONAL IDENTITY

The geographic, religious, and tribal cultures that beset both the Spanish and the American colonialists continue to vex the Philippine sense of nationhood. The archipelago of more than seven thousand islands is regularly plagued by earthquakes, volcanic eruptions, typhoons, and floods that decimate the populace and strain economic and financial resources. The American imposition of the English language remains the means of communication in schools, the government, and the media. The major newspapers are printed in English, but television shows are broadcast in both English and Tagalog, the official languages of the nation. Tagalog, however, is the language of the dominant tribes of Luzon and Manila, which was adopted due to the political dominance of that region. It is a secondary language for most Filipinos, who adhere to their local or tribal dialects. Nationalists continue to promote Tagalog literature as a means of achieving greater cultural unification in the islands.[31]

The glaring gap between social classes and the widespread poverty continues to foment a communist insurgency movement. The Hukbalahap opposition to the Japanese occupation carried over after independence in a failed campaign for land reform. Although largely subdued under Marcos and his successors, the communist party remains and fields its own National Peoples' Army in a protracted guerrilla war against the government. The communist infrastructure exacts its own taxes, and exerts power and influence over certain regions.[32]

In the southern islands religious differences continue to fuel a Muslim independence movement. The government granted Mindanao autonomy in 1996, but that did not quell the unrest. The Abu Sayyaf Islamist group has been responsible for bombings, kidnappings, ransom demands, and beheadings that have reached beyond their main base in the southern islands in their quest to establish an independent state.[33]

Such separatist movements, combined with the geographical and ethnic diversity of the islands, and the vast migration of its population to a multitude of foreign lands contributes to a fractured and conflicted national identity. Ben Carrington has noted that "'diaspora' provides a framework to think about social movements, relations and politics in a way that does not automatically defer to the nation state as either the primary or only unit of analysis." The American occupation and its continued influence continue to hinder the attempt to stabilize a national identity.[34]

As in other countries, social media and its effects on popular culture also inhibit the sense of nationalism. Despite the widespread poverty, 85 percent of the households had television sets by 2001. American culture represents the aspirations of many. John Hay Air Base near Baguio became the playground of the Filipino wealthy in the 1980s with its swimming pools, golf courses, tennis courts, bowling alleys, movies, restaurants, and dancing facilities. Golf courses and tourist resorts now proliferate throughout the islands. Filipinos not only adopted American sports, but American fast foods restaurants, movies, and shopping malls form a major part of Filipino social life.[35]

Despite the emphasis on Americanism, many Filipinos retain their interest in cockfighting, which persists in Cebu and elsewhere. Despite the retention of such residual culture, basketball has largely replaced cockfighting, and offers a much greater opportunity for the display of nationalism. It not only provides for even greater possibilities for gambling, but a Filipino journalist has noted that "there is deep within the Pinoy (Filipino) cager . . . the heart of a rebel. And nothing could be sweeter, blood-pumping [sic] than to see our cager sneaking up and gracefully propelling himself in the air and scoring a basket against a tall, hulking foreign foe." For some, such symbolism reenacts the guerrilla warfare of the early American occupation by more peaceful means.[36]

While basketball courts are conspicuous in urban neighborhoods, and impoverished youth find solace in the game, not unlike in the United States, it is boxing that continues to play the greatest role in the quest for national identity and cohesion. Filipino boxers are still rated among the best in the world in the lighter weight divisions, and Manny Pacquiao (1978–), champion in eight different weight classes, has been considered to be the best pound-for-pound boxer in the world during the first decade of the twenty-first century. Pacquiao's dominance in the ring led to other ventures and branding opportunities outside of it. Similar to western athletes, he expanded into singing and acting roles, and the national mania over his popularity led to the founding of his own political party and election to Congress in 2009. He stated that "I believe this world needs new heroes. The biggest fight in my life is not boxing but it is now to end poverty in my country."[37]

Pacquiao is projected to become a future presidential candidate, with his political machine focused on patriotism, devout Catholicism, and a crusade against poverty. With a campaign slogan of "For God and Country" he was reelected in 2013, drawing thousands to his political rallies, and providing 20,000 hamburgers and chicken and rice meals for his hungry followers. To many, Pacquiao represents the American dream, the accumulation of political, economic, and social capital through his talent, work ethic, and the perceived meritocracy of sport. In that sense, he learned the lessons envisioned by the early American administration and its hopes for the power of sport.[38]

CONCLUSIONS

The Italian philosopher Antonio Gramsci expressed the concept of hegemony theory in which a dominant group establishes the norms, values, and standards for a society. All subordinate groups have the choice of acceptance, rejection, adoption, or adaptation of such principles. One might trace elements of that process throughout the Americans' dominant role in the Philippines, as the early American administration established governance, a capitalist economy, public education, and sport forms based on American values. Filipinos largely rejected the racial attitudes and religious proselytism of the Americans, while both adopting and adapting other impositions to fit their own historical and cultural traditions.[39]

The Philippines served as a borderlands where Americans might test their notions of American exceptionalism and their ability to influence others to accept and follow their culture. Such missionary zeal would propel the United States into additional wars and "police actions" over the next century, in which they employed strategies and tactics learned in the Philippines. The cultivation of elites, the attempts to impose democratic forms of governance and capitalist economies, the use of local constabularies to enforce American dictates, the establishment of global military bases to thwart the rising power of alternative groups, the use of English as the lingua franca of business, commerce, and education, and the increasing use of soft power, such as music, sport, and popular culture to attract youth to American culture, continue to be evident in the global politics of the twenty-first century.[40]

Despite their efforts the Filipinos would retain elements of their historic Malay culture in their respect for authority and the tradition of "strong man" leadership, particularly at the local level. Their adoption and adaptation of American political, economic, educational, and sport systems eventually resulted in a "hybrid culture that is similar to, yet distinct from that of the United States," and still in search of a true national identity and a complete sense of nationhood.[41]

NOTES

1. McCallus, *The MacArthur Highway & Other Relics of American Empire in the Philippines*, x, 6, 38–40. Some Filipino strategists maintain that the Philippines might have been bypassed and Manila and its citizens spared as the American forces island hopped toward Japan to end the war.

2. W. M. Hoeger to Leonard Wood, November 7, 1904, in Wood Papers, Library of Congress, Philippines box, miscellaneous materials; Leonard Wood to Dear Bishop Brent, March 24, 1910, in Bishop Charles H. Brent Papers, Library of Congress, Box 9; McCallus, *The MacArthur Highway & Other Relics of American Empire in the Philippines*, 157, 196–200; Krinks, *The Economy of the Philippines*, 34; Julian Madison, "American Military Bases in the Philippines, 1945–1965: Neo-Colonialism and Its Demise," in Richard Jensen, Jon Davidaan, and Yoneyuki Sugita, eds., *Trans-Pacific Relations: America, Europe, and Asia in the Twentieth Century* (Westport, CT: Praeger, 2003), 125–45.

3. Krinks, *The Economy of the Philippines*, 33; McCallus, *The MacArthur Highway & Other Relics of American Empire in the Philippines*, 155; Hedman and Sidel, *Philippine Politics and Society in the Twentieth Century*, 1, 41–42, 47.

4. McCallus, *The MacArthur Highway & Other Relics of American Empire in the Philippines*, 157, 207.

5. Ibid., 88–89, 311.

6. Krinks, *The Economy of the Philippines*, 28, 30–31, 40, 49, 52; Rupert Hodder, *Between Two Worlds: Society, Politics, and Business in the Philippines* (London: Routledge Curzon, 2002); White, *Philippine Politics*, 4, 20–29, 30–56. 72. White, 37, measured 107 private armies still existent in 2010.

7. Hedman and Sidel, *Philippine Politics and Society in the Twentieth Century*, 18–23; www.britannica.com/biography/Elpidio-Quirino (February 6, 2016); www.browsebiography.com/bio-carlos_p_garcia.html (February 6, 2016); www.britannica.com/biography/Diosdado-Macapagal (February 6, 2016).

8. Krinks, *The Economy of the Philippines*, 41; Hedman and Sidel, *Philippine Politics and Society in the Twentieth Century*, 22–23.

9. Krinks, *The Economy of the Philippines*, 38, 42, 44; Hedman and Sidel, *Politics and Society in the Twentieth Century Philippines*, 157.

10. Anderson, "Cacique Democracy in the Philippines"; Krinks, *The Economy of the Philippines*, 44–49, 88; White, *Philippine Politics*, 33, 165; Hedman and Sidel, *Politics and Society in the Twentieth Century Philippines*, 36–37, 91: McCallus, *The MacArthur Highway & Other Relics of American Empire in the Philippines*, 10–11, 164–65.

11. White, *Philippine Politics*, 119–26, 176–78, 217–18, 2 (quote).

12. Hedman and Sidel, *Politics and Society in the Twentieth Century Philippines*, 8.

13. McCallus, *The MacArthur Highway & Other Relics of American Empire in the Philippines*, 77–83; www.nytimes.com/1985/11/13/world/falwell-on-visit-acclaims-marcos.html (February 7, 2016).

14. www.biography.com/people/john-paul-ii-9355652#legacy (February 7, 2016); McCallus, *The MacArthur Highway & Other Relics of American Empire in the Philippines*, 80.

15. White, *Philippine Politics*, 3, 84, 211–13.

16. rlp.hds.harvard.edu/faq/protestant-christianity-philippines (February 7, 2016); McCallus, *The MacArthur Highway & Other Relics of American Empire in the Philippines*, 187–90; White, *Philippine Politics*, 213.

17. Among the growing number of scholarly studies examining the relationship between sport and religion, see William J. Baker, *Playing with God: Religion and Modern Sport* (Cambridge, MA: Harvard University Press, 2007); and Rebecca T. Alpert, *Relig-*

ion and Sports: An Introduction and Case Studies (New York: Columbia University Press, 2015).

18. Antilohao, *Playing with the Big Boys*, 121–35, 134 (quote).
19. Typescript of Wood interview, Wood Papers, Library of Congress, Philippines box, miscellaneous material; Krinks, *The Economy of the Philippines*, 11–30; Hedman and Sidel, *Philippine Politics and Society in the Twentieth Century*, 8.
20. Krinks, *The Economy of the Philippines*, 1–9, 35–36, 44, 141–44; McCallus, *The MacArthur Highway & Other Relics of American Empire in the Philippines*, 159–60; White, *Philippine Politics*, 62–66.
21. Krinks, *The Economy of the Philippines*, 188–209; McCallus, *The MacArthur Highway & Other Relics of American Empire in the Philippines*, 312; White, *Philippine Politics*, 82.
22. McCallus, *The MacArthur Highway & Other Relics of American Empire in the Philippines*, 96–103, 200, 218–21.
23. Hedman and Sidel, *Philippine Politics and Society in the Twentieth Century*, 156; Krinks, *The Economy of the Philippines*, 39, 84, 86, 220; White, *Philippine Politics*, 82–83; countryeconomy.com/demography/life-expectancy/philippines (February 13, 2016).
24. Krinks, *The Economy of the Philippines*, 215–17; McCallus, *The MacArthur Highway & Other Relics of American Empire in the Philippines*, 92–93; AsiaNews.it, "Saudi Arabia, 70% of Filipino workers suffer physical and psychological violence," at www.asianews.it/news-en/Saudi-Arabia,-70-of-Filipino-domestic-workers-suffer-physical-and-psychological-violence-24260.html (February 13, 2016); White, *Philippine Politics*, 85–86. Philippines Economy 2015 at www.theodora.com/wfbcurrent/philippines/philippines_economy.html (November 7, 2015), claims that 4 to 5 million Filipinos remit wages from overseas jobs; although Philippines law requires a portion of all foreign contract labor be remitted.
25. White, *Philippine Politics*, 84, 91, 100, 111.
26. White, *Philippine Politics*, 191–97, 192 (quote); Krinks, *The Economy of the Philippines*, 67.
27. www.theodora.com/wfbcurrent/philippines/philippines_economy.html (November 7, 2015); Krinks, *The Economy of the Philippines*, 26, 227–28; White, *Philippine Politics*, 62, 66, 69, 72–73; Hedman and Sidel, *Philippine Politics and Society in the Twentieth Century*, 66–84 (quote, 76).
28. Krinks, *The Economy of the Philippines*, 32, 60, 88; McCallus, *The MacArthur Highway & Other Relics of American Empire in the Philippines*, 151.
29. Krinks, *The Economy of the Philippines*, 89; White, *Philippine Politics*, 156; McCallus, *The MacArthur Highway & Other Relics of American Empire in the Philippines*, 93, 114, 150–52.
30. Bocobo-Olivar, *History of Physical Education in the Philippines*, 172–79.
31. White, *Philippine Politics*, 156, 161; Hedman and Sidel, *Philippine Politics and Society in the Twentieth Century*, 156.
32. McCallus, *The MacArthur Highway & Other Relics of American Empire in the Philippines*, 155, 157; White, *Philippine Politics*, 34, 36.
33. uca.edu/politicalscience/dadm-project/asiapacific-region/philippinesmoro-national-liberation-front-1968-present/ (February 18, 2016); McCallus, *The MacArthur Highway & Other Relics of American Empire in the Philippine*, 210–13.
34. Ben Carrington, "Assessing the Sociology of Sport: On Race and Diaspora," *International Review for the Sociology of Sport*, 50:4–5 (June–August, 2015), 391–96, (quote, 394).
35. White, *Philippine Politics*, 162; Anderson, "Cacique Democracy in the Philippines," 21; McCallus, *The MacArthur Highway & Other Relics of American Empire in the Philippines*, 3–4. 94; Hedman and Sidel, *Philippine Politics and Society in the Twentieth Century*, 118–19, 133–35.

36. McCallus, *The MacArthur Highway & Other Relics of American Empire in the Philippines*, 94; Hedman and Sidel, *Philippine Politics and Society in the Twentieth Century*, 100; Antilohao, *Playing with the Big Boys*, 125 (quote).

37. Hedman and Sidel, *Philippine Politics and Society in the Twentieth Century*, 135; Gems, *Boxing*, 187–88 (quote, 188).

38. White, *Philippine Politics*, 164, 216.

39. Quintin Hoare and Geoffrey N. Smith, eds., *Selections from the Prison Notebooks of Antonio Gramsci* (New York: International Publishers, 1971).

40. Samuel P. Huntington, *The Clash of Civilizations and the Remaking of World Order* (New York: Simon & Schuster, 1996); Michael Hardt and Antonio Negri, *Empire* (Cambridge, MA: Harvard University Press, 2000); Hunt and Levine, *Arc of Empire*; Christopher Capozzola, Andrew Huebner, Julia Irwin, Jennifer D. Keene, Ross Kennedy, Michael Neiberg, Stephen R. Ortiz, Chad Williams, and Jay Winter, "Interchange: World War I," *Journal of American History*, 102:2 (September 2015), 463–99; White, *Philippine Politics*, 28–29; McCallus, *The MacArthur Highway & Other Relics of American Empire in the Philippines*, 312; McCoy, "Policing the Imperial Periphery," 12–13; Antolihao, *Playing with the Big Boys*, 154–59.

41. Gems, *Athletic Crusade*, 150.

Bibliography

———, *The Greatest of Expositions: Completely Illustrated*, official publication (St. Louis: Samuel F. Myerson, 1904).

———, "Baseball in the Islands," *New York Times*, May 11, 1913, part 5:1, in Dean C. Worcester Papers, Box 3, folder 8, newspaper clippings, in the Bentley Historical Library, University of Michigan.

Adams, David Wallace, *Education for Extinction: American Indians and the Boarding School Experience, 1875–1928* (Lawrence: University Press of Kansas, 1995).

Addams, Jane, *Twenty Years at Hull House* (New York: Macmillan, 1930).

Alcantara, Erlyn Ruth E., "Baguio Between Two Wars: The Creation and Destruction of a Summer Capital," in Angel Velasco Shaw and Luis H. Francia, eds., *Vestiges of War: The Philippine-American War and the Aftermath of an Imperial Dream, 1899–1999* (New York: New York University Press, 2002), 201–23.

Alidio, Kimberley, "'When I Get Home I Want to Forget': Memory and Amnesia in the Occupied Philippines, 1901–1904," *Social Text*, 59 (Summer 1999), 105–22.

Allen, Theodore W., *The Invention of the White Race: Racial Oppression and Social Control* (London: Verso, 1998).

Alpert, Rebecca T., *Religion and Sports: An Introduction and Case Studies* (New York: Columbia University Press, 2015).

Anderson, Benedict, "Cacique Democracy in the Philippines: Origins and Dreams," *New Left Review*, 88 (1988), 3–31.

Anderson, Fred, and Andrew Cayton, *The Dominion of War: Empire and Liberty in North America, 1500–2000* (New York: Viking, 2005).

Anderson, Warwick, "'Where Every Prospect Pleases and Only Man Is Vile': Laboratory Medicine as Colonial Discourse," *Critical Inquiry*, 18:3 (Spring 1992), 506–29.

Antolihao, Lou, "From Baseball Colony to Basketball Republic: Post-Colonial Transition and the Making of a National Sport in the Philippines," *Sport in Society*, 15:10 (2012), 1396–412.

———, *Playing with the Big Boys: Basketball, American Imperialism, and Subaltern Discourse in the Philippines* (Lincoln: University of Nebraska Press, 2015).

Arnesen, Eric, "Whiteness and the Historians' Imagination," *International Labor and Working Class History*, 60 (Fall 2001), 3–32.

Arnold, James R., *The Moro War: How America Battled a Muslim Insurgency in the Philippine Jungle, 1902–1913* (New York: Bloomsbury Press, 2011).

Atkinson, Fred W., *The Present Educational Movement in the Philippine Islands*, at quod.lib.umich.edu/p/philamer/AHK8492.0001.001?rgn=main;view=fulltext (November 24, 2015).

Aycock, Colleen, and Mark Scott, eds., *The First Black Boxing Champions* (Jefferson, NC: McFarland, 2011).

Badger, R. Reid, *The Great American Fair: The World's Columbian Exposition and American Culture* (Chicago: Nelson Hall, 1979).

Bain, David Haward, *Sitting in Darkness: Americans in the Philippines* (Boston: Houghton Mifflin, 1984).

Baker, Lee D., *From Savage to Negro: Anthropology and the Construction of Race, 1896–1954* (Berkeley: University of California Press, 1998).

Baker, William J. *Playing with God: Religion and Modern Sport* (Cambridge, MA: Harvard University Press, 2007).

Bibliography

Bankoff, Greg, "'These Brothers of Ours': Poblete's *Obreros* and the Road to Baguio," *Journal of Social History* (Summer 2005), 1047–72.

Barrows, David P., "The Ilongot or Ibilao of Luzon," ms. for *Popular Science Monthly* (December 1910), in Fred Eggan Papers, University of Chicago, Special Collections.

Baylen, Joseph O., and Jack Hammond Moore, "Senator John Tyler Morgan and Negro Colonization in the Philippines, 1901 to 1902," *Phylon*, 29:1 (1968), 65–75.

Bean, Robert Bennett, *The Racial Anatomy of the Philippine Islanders* (Philadelphia: J. B. Lippincott, 1910).

Benitez Licuanen, Virginia, *Filipinos and Americans: A Love-Hate Relationship* (Manila: Baguio Country Club, 1982).

Beran, Janice A., "Americans in the Philippines: Imperialism or Progress Through Sport?," *International Journal of the History of Sport*, 6 (May 1989), 62–87.

Besnier, Niko, and Susan Brownell, "Sport, Modernity, and the Body," *Annual Review of Anthropology*, 41 (2012), 443–59.

Best of Philippines, "Games," at www.marimari.com/content/philippines/best_of/games.html (January 13, 2016).

Bieder, Robert E., *Science Encounters the Indian, 1820–1880: The Early Years of American Ethnology* (Norman: University of Oklahoma Press, 1986).

Bloom, John, *To Show What an Indian Can Do: Sports at Native American Boarding Schools* (Minneapolis: University of Minnesota Press, 2000).

Blum, John M., and Edmund S. Morgan, Willie Lee Rose, Arthur M. Schlesinger, Jr., Kenneth M. Stampp, and C. Vann Woodward, *The National Experience: A History of the United States* (New York: Harcourt, Brace, Jovanovich, 1981).

Bocobo-Olivar, Celia, *History of Physical Education in the Philippines* (Quezon City: University of the Philippines Press, 1972).

Bogue, Allan G., *Frederick Jackson Turner: Strange Roads Going Down* (Norman: University of Oklahoma Press, 1998).

Bonker, Dirk, "Social Imperialism Revisited: Navalism, Reform, and Empire in Germany and the United States Around 1900," presentation delivered at the Organization of American Historians Convention, January 3, 2003, Chicago, Illinois.

Boudreau, Vince, "Methods of Domination and Modes of Resistance: The U.S. Colonial State and Philippine Mobilization in Comparative Perspective," in Julian Go and Anne L. Foster, eds., *The American Colonial State in the Philippines: Global Perspectives* (Durham, NC: Duke University Press, 2003), 256–90.

Bourdieu, Pierre, *Outline of a Theory of Practice* (Cambridge, UK: Cambridge University Press, 1972).

Bradley, James, *The Imperial Crusade: A Secret History of Empire and War* (New York: Little, Brown & Co., 2009).

Brands, H. W., *The Reckless Decade: America in the 1890s* (New York: St. Martin's Press, 1995).

Brands, H. W., *American Colossus: The Triumph of Capitalism 1865–1900* (New York: Doubleday, 2010).

Brent, Rt. Rev. Charles H., *Religious Conditions in the Philippines*, 1904 pamphlet, Library of Congress.

Brewer, Susan A., *Why America Fights: Patriotism and War Propaganda from the Philippines to Iraq* (New York: Oxford, 2009).

Brody, David, "Building Empire: Architecture and American Imperialism in the Philippines," *Journal of Asian American Studies*, 4:2 (June 2001), 123–45.

Bulosan, Carlos, *America Is in the Heart: A Personal History* (New York: Harcourt, Brace & Co., 1946).

Calo, Lucrezia T., *Organization and Management of Athletic Meets* (Manila: Rex Book Store, 1984), 2–3.

Capozzola, Christopher, and Andrew Huebner, Julia Irwin, Jennifer D. Keene, Ross Kennedy, Michael Neiberg, Stephen R. Ortiz, Chad Williams, and Jay Winter, "Interchange: World War I," *Journal of American History*, 102:2 (September 2015), 463–99.

Carnes, Mark C., and Clyde Griffen, eds., *Meanings for Manhood: Constructions of Masculinity in Victorian America* (Chicago: University of Chicago Press, 1990).

Carrington, Ben, "Assessing the Sociology of Sport: On Race and Diaspora," *International Review for the Sociology of Sport*, 50:4–5 (June–August, 2015), 391–96.

Chadwick, Henry, ed., *Spalding's Base Ball Guide and Official League Book for 1901* (New York: American Sports Publishing Co., 1901).

Chadwick, Henry, ed., *Spalding's Official Base Ball Guide for 1907* (New York: American Sports Publishing Co., 1907).

Chaput, Donald, "Private William W. Grayson's War in the Philippines, 1899," *Nebraska History*, 61 (1980), 355–66.

Chavez-Garcia, Miroslava, "Youth of Color and California's Carceral State: The Fred C. Nelles Youth Correctional Facility," *Journal of American History*, 102:1 (June 2015), 47–60.

Chiang, Ying, and Tzu-hsuan Chen, "Adopting the diasporic son: Jeremy Lin and Taiwan sport nationalism," *International Review for the Sociology of Sport*, 50:6 (September 2015), 705–21.

Clymer, Kenton J., "The Methodist Response to Philippine Nationalism, 1899–1916" *Church History* (December 1, 1978), 421–33.

———, *Protestant Missionaries in the Philippines, 1898–1916: An Inquiry into the Colonial Mentality* (Urbana: University of Illinois Press, 1986).

Coffman, Edward M., *The Regulars: The American Army, 1898–1941* (Cambridge, MA: Belknap Press, 2004).

Collier, Price, "Sport's Place in the Nation's Well-Being," *Outing* (July 1898), 302–08.

Courtwright, David T., "The Cycles of American Drug Policy," *The American Historian* (August 2015), 24–29.

Cressey, Paul G., *The Taxi Dance Hall* (Chicago: University of Chicago Press, 1932).

Crunden, Robert M., *Ministers of Reform: The Progressive Achievement in American Civilization, 1889–1920* (New York: Basic Books, 1982).

Dauncey, Mrs. Campbell, *The Philippines: An Account of Their People, Progress, and Condition* (Boston: J. B. Millet Co., 1910).

Davis, Allen F., *Spearheads for Reform: The Social Settlements and the Progressive Era, 1890–1914* (New York: Oxford University Press, 1967).

Davis, Janet M., "Cockfight Nationalism: Blood Sport and the Moral Politics of American Empire and Nation Building," *American Quarterly*, 65:3 (September 2013), 549–74.

Delmendo, Sharon, "The Star Entangled Banner: Commemorating 100 Years of Philippine (In)dependence and Philippine-American Relations," *Journal of Asian American Studies*, 1:3 (1998), 211–44.

Douglas, Ann, *The Feminization of American Culture* (New York: Anchor Books, 1977).

Du Bois, W. E. B., *The Souls of Black Folk* (New York: Random House, 1990).

Dyreson, Mark, "The Physical Value of Races and Nations: Anthropology and Athletics at the Louisiana Purchase Exposition," in Brownell, ed., *The 1904 Anthropology Days and Olympic Games*, 127–55.

Eichberg, Henning, "Forward Race and the Laughter of Pygmies: On Olympic Sport," in Mikulas Teich and Roy Porter, eds., *Fin de Siecle and Its Legacy* (Cambridge, UK: Cambridge University Press, 1990), 115–31.

Elfers, James E., *The Tour to End All Tours: The Story of Major League Baseball's 1913–1914 World Tour* (Lincoln: University of Nebraska Press, 2003).

Elias, Robert, *The Empire Strikes Out: How Baseball Sold U.S. Foreign Policy and Promoted the American Way Abroad* (New York: The New Press, 2010).

Espana-Maram, Linda, *Creating Masculinity in Los Angeles's Little Manila: Working-Class Filipinos and Popular Culture, 1920s-1950s* (New York: Columbia University Press, 2006).

Fee, Mary H., *A Woman's Impression of the Philippines* (Chicago: A. C. McClurg & Co., 1910).

Forbes, W. Cameron, *Football Notebook*, 1901, in Harvard Archives, HUD 10897.24.

Foster, John B., ed., *Spalding's Official Base Ball Record, 1909* (New York: American Sports Publishing Co, 1908).
Franks, Joel S., *Crossing Sidelines, Crossing Cultures: Sport and Asian Pacific American Cultural Citizenship* (Lanham, MD: University Press of America, 2000).
Garraty, John A., *The American Nation: A History of the United States* (New York: Harper & Row, 1983).
Gates, John M., *Schoolbooks and Krags: The United States Army in the Philippines, 1898–1902* (Westport, CT: Greenwood Press, 1973).
Gatewood, Willard B., Jr., *"Smoked Yankees" and the Struggle for Empire: Letters from Negro Soldiers, 1898–1902* (Fayetteville: University of Arkansas Press, 1987).
Geertz, Clifford, "Deep Play: Notes on the Balinese Cockfight," *Daedalus* 101 (Winter 1972), 1–38.
Gems, Gerald, R., "Sport, Religion, and Americanization: Bishop Sheil and the Catholic Youth Organization," *International Journal of the History of Sport* (August 1993), 233–41.
———, *Windy City Wars: Labor, Leisure, and Sport in the Making of Chicago* (Lanham, MD: Scarecrow Press, 1997).
———, "Sports, War, and Ideological Imperialism," *Peace Review*, 11:4 (Winter 1999), 573–78.
———, *For Pride, Profit, and Patriarchy: Football and the Incorporation of American Cultural Values* (Lanham, MD: Scarecrow Press, 2000).
———, "Anthropology Days, the Construction of Whiteness, and American Imperialism in the Philippines," in Brownell, *The 1904 Anthropology Days and Olympic Games*, 189–216.
———, "Jack Johnson and the Quest for Racial Respect," in David K. Wiggins, ed. *Out of the Shadows: A Biographical History of African American Athletes* (Fayetteville: University of Arkansas Press, 2006), 59–77.
———, *The Athletic Crusade: Sport and American Cultural Imperialism* (Lincoln: University of Nebraska Press, 2006).
———, "Whiteness, Sport, and American Imperialism in the Pacific," *Sportwissenschaft*, 2 (2006), 171–92.
———, *Sport and the Shaping of Italian American Culture* (Syracuse, NY: Syracuse University Press, 2013).
———, *Boxing: A Concise History of the Sweet Science* (Lanham, MD: Rowman & Littlefield, 2014).
Gems, Gerald R., Linda J. Borish, and Gertrud Pfister, *Sports in American History: From Colonization to Globalization* (Champaign, IL: Human Kinetics, 2008).
Gleeck, Lewis E., Jr., *American Institutions in the Philippines (1898–1941)* (Manila: Manila Historical Conservation Society, 1976).
———, *The Manila-Americans (1901–1964)* (Manila: Carmelo & Bauermann, 1977).
Go, Julian, and Anne L. Foster, eds., *The American Colonial State in the Philippines: Global Perspectives* (Durham, NC: Duke University Press, 2003).
Go, Julian, *American Empire and the Politics of Meaning* (Durham, NC: Duke University Press, 2008).
Gordon, Lynn D., *Gender and Higher Education in the Progressive Era* (New Haven, CT: Yale University Press, 1990).
Gould, Stephen Jay, *The Mismeasure of Man* (New York: W. W. Norton, 1996 [1981]).
Grant, Madison, *The Passing of the Great Race or the Racial Basis of European History* (New York: Charles Scribner's Sons, 1916).
Gray, J. A. C., *Amerika Samoa: A History of American Samoa and Its United States Naval Administration* (Annapolis: United States Naval Institute, 1960).
Guerrero, Amado, *Philippine Society and Revolution* (Hong Kong: Ta Kung Pao Press, 1971).
Hardt, Michael, and Antonio Negri, *Empire* (Cambridge, MA: Harvard University Press, 2000).

Harris, Susan K., *God's Arbiters: Americans and the Philippines, 1898–1902* (New York: Oxford University Press, 2011).
Hedman, Eva-Lotta E, and John Thayer Sidel, *Philippine Politics and Society in the Twentieth Century* (London: Routledge, 2000).
Hines, Thomas, "The Imperial Façade: Daniel Burnham and American Architecture in the Philippines," *Pacific Historical Review*, 41:1 (1972), 33–53.
———, *Burnham of Chicago: Architect and Planner* (Chicago: University of Chicago Press, 1979).
Hixson, Walter, L., *American Settler Colonialism: A History* (New York: Palgrave Macmillan, 2013).
Hoare, Quintin, and Geoffrey N. Smith, eds., *Selections from the Prison Notebooks of Antonio Gramsci* (New York: International Publishers, 1971).
Hodder, Rupert, *Between Two Worlds: Society, Politics, and Business in the Philippines* (London: Routledge Curzon, 2001).
Hoffman, Shirl J., *Sport and Religion* (Champaign IL: Human Kinetics, 1992).
Hoganson, Kristin L., *Fighting for American Manhood: How Gender Politics Provoked the Spanish-American War and Philippine-American Wars* (New Haven, CT: Yale University Press, 1998).
Hoganson, Kristin, "Buying into Empire: American Consumption at the Turn of the Twentieth Century," in Alfred W. McCoy and Francisco Scarano, eds., *Colonial Crucible: Empire in the Making of the Modern American State* (Madison: University of Wisconsin Press, 2009), 248–59.
Horsman, Reginald, *Race and Manifest Destiny: The Origins of American Racial Anglo Saxonism* (Cambridge, MA: Harvard University Press, 1981).
Hoxie, Frederick E., *A Final Promise: The Campaign to Assimilate the Indians, 1880–1920* (New York: Cambridge University Press, 1989).
Hunt, Michael H., and Steven I. Levine, *Arc of Empire: America's Wars in Asia from the Philippines to Vietnam* (Chapel Hill: University of North Carolina Press, 2012).
Huntington, Samuel P., *The Clash of Civilizations and the Remaking of World Order* (New York: Simon & Schuster, 1996).
Jacobson, Matthew Frye, *Whiteness of a Different Color: European Immigrants and the Alchemy of Race* (Cambridge, MA: Harvard University Press, 1998).
———, *Barbarian Virtues: The United States Encounters Foreign Peoples at Home and Abroad, 1876–1917* (New York: Hill & Wang, 2000).
Jarvis, Christina S., *The Male Body at War: American Masculinity during World War II* (DeKalb: Northern Illinois University Press, 2004).
Jeffers, H. Paul, *Colonel Roosevelt: Theodore Roosevelt Goes to War, 1897–1898* (New York: John Wiley & Sons, 1996).
Jones, Gregg, *Honor in the Dust: Theodore Roosevelt, War in the Philippines, and the Rise and Fall of America's Imperial Dream* (New York: New American Library, 2013).
Karnow, Stanley, *In Our Image: America's Empire in the Philippines* (New York: Random House, 1989).
Kasson, Joy S., *Buffalo Bill's Wild West: Celebrity, Memory, and Popular History* (New York: Hill and & Wang, 2000), 83–88, 90–121.
Kimmel, Michael S., "Men's Response to Feminism at the Turn of the Century," *Gender and Society*, 1–3 (September 1987), 261–83.
King, C. Richard, "Cautionary Notes on Whiteness and Sport Studies," *Sociology of Sport Journal*, 22:3 (2005), 397–408.
Kirkwood, Patrick M., "'Michigan Men' in the Philippines and the Limits of Self-Determination in the Progressive Era," *Michigan Historical Review*, 40:2 (Fall 2014), 63–86.
Kolchin, Peter, "Whiteness Studies: The New History of Race in America," *Journal of American History*, 89:1 (June 2002), 154–73.
Kramer, Paul A., "Jim Crow Science and the 'Negro Problem' in the Philippines," in Judith Fossett, Ed Jackson, and Jeffrey A. Tucker, eds., *Race Consciousness: African*

American Studies for the New Century (New York: New York University Press, 1997), 227–46.

———, "The Pragmatic Empire: U.S. Anthropology and Colonial Politics in the Occupied Philippines, 1898–1916," PhD Dissertation, Princeton University, 1998.

———, "Empires, Exceptions, and Anglo-Saxons: Race and Rule between the British and United States Empires, 1880–1910," *Journal of American History*, 88:4 (March 2002), 1315–353.

———, *The Blood of Government: Race, Empire, the United States & the Philippines* (Chapel Hill: University of North Carolina Press, 2006).

Krinks, Peter, *The Economy of the Philippines: Elites, Inequalities and Economic Restructuring* (London: Routledge, 2002).

Kuo, Lenore, *Prostitution Policy: Revolutionizing Practice through a Gendered Perspective* (New York: New York University Press, 2001).

Lane, Jack C., *Armed Progressive: General Leonard Wood* (Lincoln: University of Nebraska Press, 2009 [1978]).

Lasch, Christopher, "The Anti-Imperialists, the Philippines, and the Inequality of Man," *The Journal of Southern History*, 24:3 (August 1958), 319–31.

Latourette, Kenneth L., *World Service: A History of the Foreign Work and World Service of the Young Men's Christian Association of the United States and Canada* (New York: Association Press, 1957).

Le Roy, James A., *Philippine Life in Town and Country* (New York: G. P. Putnam's Sons, 1905).

Levine, Peter, *A. G. Spalding and the Rise of Baseball: The Promise of American Sport* (New York: Oxford University Press, 1985).

Love, Eric T., *Race Over Empire: Racism and U.S. Imperialism, 1865–1900* (Chapel Hill: University of North Carolina Press, 2004).

Lubinskas, James B., "A Warning From the Past: Lothrop Stoddard and the Rising Tide of Color," *American Renaissance* (January 2000), www.toqonline.com/blog/lothrop-stoddard-and-the-rising-tide-of-color/ (July 22, 2015).

Lumba, Allen, "Common Wealth in Precious Times: Militant Politics and Transient Labor across the Global Philippines, 1919–1942," presented at the Organization of American Historians Conference, St. Louis, MO, April 19, 2005.

M'Adams, Clark, "Cheer Up, Mere Man! You Are the Real–Real Beauty," *St. Louis Post-Dispatch*, October 23, 1904, Section 3:1.

Madison, Julian, "American Military Bases in the Philippines, 1945–1965: Neo-Colonialism and Its Demise," in Richard Jensen, Jon Davidann, and Yoneyuki Sugitaa, eds., *Trans-Pacific Relations: America, Europe, and Asia in the Twentieth Century* (Westport, CT; Praeger Press, 2003), 125–45.

Marks, Patricia, *Bicycles, Bangs, and Bloomers: The New Woman in the Popular Press* (Lexington: University Press of Kentucky, 1990).

Marshall, Edward, "Baseball Helping to Revolutionize the Philippines," *New York Times*, September 22, 1912, n.p.

Martinez, Anne M., *Catholic Borderlands: Mapping Catholicism onto American Empire, 1905–1935* (Lincoln: University of Nebraska Press, 2014).

May, Glenn, *Social Engineering in the Philippines: The Aims, Execution, and Impact of American Colonial Policy, 1900–1913* (Westport, CT: Greenwood Press, 1980).

McCabe, Neal, and Constance McCabe, *Baseball's Golden Age* (New York: Harry N. Abrams, 1993).

McCallus, Joseph P., *The MacArthur Highway & Other Relics of American Empire in the Philippines* (Washington, DC: Potomac Books, 2010).

McCormick, Thomas, "From Old Empire to New: The Changing Dynamics and Tactics of American Empire," in Alfred W. McCoy and Francisco Scarano, eds., *Colonial Crucible: Empire in the Making of the Modern American State* (Madison: University of Wisconsin Press, 2009), 63–79.

McCoy, Alfred, "Philippine Commonwealth and Cult of Masculinity," *Philippine Studies*, 48:3 (2000), 315–46.

McCoy, Alfred W., and Francisco Scarano, eds., *Colonial Crucible: Empire in the Making of the Modern American State* (Madison: University of Wisconsin Press, 2009).
The Michigan Alumnus, 15 (1909).
The Michigan Chime, 1:1 (November 1919).
Miller, Karen R., "'Thin, Wistful, and White': James Fugate and the Disavowal of Muscularity in the Colonial Philippines," paper presented at the Organization of American Historians Convention (April 2015).
Miller, Stuart Creighton, *"Benevolent Assimilation:" The American Conquest of the Philippines, 1899–1903* (New Haven, CT: Yale University Press, 1982).
Millis, Walter, *The Martial Spirit* (Chicago: Ivan R. Dee, 1989).
Mooney, Roger, "Going Home a Hero: How Ceferino Garcia Finally Realizes His Dream," *Ring*, April 1994.
Moore, Charles, ed., *Plan of Chicago* (Chicago: Commercial Club, 1909).
Murphy, Jackson, "Prescott Jernagan and the Gold from Seawater Swindle," at www.mvtimes.com/2012/07/25/prescott-jernegan-gold-from-seawater-swindle-11663/ (June 15, 2016).
Naismith, James, *Basketball: Its Origin and Development* (New York: Association Press, 1941).
Nankville, John H., ed., *The History of the Twenty-Fifth Regiment of the United States Infantry, 1896–1926* (Ft. Collins, CO: The Old Army Press, 1927 [1971]).
Newcombe, Jack, *The Best of the Athletic Boys: The White Man's Impact on Jim Thorpe* (Garden City, NJ: Doubleday, 1975).
O'Bonsawin, Christine, "From Black Power to Indigenous Activism: The Olympic Movement and the Marginilization of Oppressed Peoples," *Journal of Sport History*, 42:1 (Summer 2015), 200–19.
Official Gazette, Vol. 11 (1913).
Oriard, Michael, *Reading Football: How the Popular Press Created an American Spectacle* (Chapel Hill: University of North Carolina Press. 1993).
Pakenham, Thomas, *The Scramble for Africa: The White Man's Conquest of the Dark Continent from 1876 to 1912* (New York: Random House, 1991).
Pante, Michael D., "A Collision of Masculinities: Men, Modernity and Urban Transportation in American-Colonial Manila," *Asian Studies Review*, 38:2 (May 2014), 253–73.
Parezo, Nancy J., "A 'Special Olympics': Testing Racial Strength and Endurance at the 1904 Louisiana Purchase Exposition" in Susan Brownell, ed., *The 1904 Anthropology Days and Olympic Games: Sport, Race, and American Imperialism* (Lincoln: University of Nebraska Press, 2008), 59–126.
Paulet, Anne, "To Change the World: The Use of American Indian Education in the Philippines," *History of Education Quarterly*, 47:2 (May 2007).
Paxson, Frederic L., "The Rise of Sport," *Mississippi Valley Historical Review*, 4 (1917), 143–68.
Pecson, Geronima T., and Maria Racelis, eds., *Tales of the American Teachers in the Philippines* (Manila: Carmelo & Bauermann, 1959).
Pease, Donald E., "New Perspectives on U.S. Culture and Imperialism," in Amy Kaplan and Donald E. Pease, eds., *Cultures of United States Imperialism* (Durham, NC: Duke University Press, 1993), 22–37.
Pier, Arthur S., *American Apostles to the Philippines* (Boston: Beacon Press, 1950).
Pratt, Julius W., *Expansionists of 1898: Acquisition of Hawaii and the Spanish Islands* (Gloucester, MA: Peter Smith, 1959).
Prebish, Charles S., "'Heavenly Father, Divine Goalie': Sport and Religion," *The Antioch Review*, 42:3 (Summer 1984), 306–18.
Pruter, Robert, *Rise of American High School Sports and the Search for Control, 1880–1930* (Syracuse, NY: Syracuse University Press, 2013).
Przybyszewski, Linda, "Judicial Conservatism and Protestant Faith: The Case of Justice David J. Brewer," *Journal of American History*, 91:2 (September 2004), 471–96.

Putney, Clifford, *Muscular Christianity: Manhood and Sports in Protestant America, 1880–1920* (Cambridge, MA: Harvard University Press, 2001).

Rader, Benjamin G., *American Sports: From the Age of Folk Games to the Age of Televised Sports* (Englewood Cliffs, NJ: Prentice Hall, 1990).

Rafael, Vicente, L., "'White Love': Surveillance and Nationalist Resistance in the Colonization of the Philippines," in Kaplan and Pease, eds., *Cultures of United States Imperialism*, 185–218.

———, "The War of Translation: Colonial Education, American English, and Tagalog Slang in the Philippines," *Journal of Asian Studies*, 74:2 (May 2015), 283–302.

Rasenberger, Jim, *America, 1908: The Dawn of Flight, the Race to the Pole, the Invention of the Model T, and the Making of a Modern Nation* (New York: Scribner, 2007).

Ratey, John *Spark: The Revolutionary New Science of Exercise and the Brain* (New York: Little, Brown & Co., 2007).

Reaves, Joseph A., *Taking In a Game: A History of Baseball in Asia* (Lincoln: University of Nebraska Press, 2002).

Reese, William J., *Power and the Promise of School Reform: Grassroots Movement During the Progressive Era* (Boston: Routledge & Kegan Paul, 1986).

Rehal, Satwinder, "In the Quest for Recognition: A Critical Sociological Reflection on Football's 'Resistance' in the Philippines," presented at the International Sport Sociology Association World Congress for the Sociology of Sport, Malmo, Sweden, June 10, 2015.

Roberts, Mary Louise, *What Soldiers Do: Sex and the American GI in World War II* (Chicago: University of Chicago Press, 2013).

Roberts, Randy, *Papa Jack: Jack Johnson and the Era of White Hopes* (New York: Free Press, 1983).

Robinson, Michael C., and Frank N. Schubert, "David Fagen: An Afro-American Rebel in the Philippines, 1899–1901," *Pacific Historical Review*, 44:1 (February 1975), 68–83.

Roediger, David R., *The Wages of Whiteness: Race and the Making of the American Working Class* (London: Verso, 1999 [1991]).

———, *Working Toward Whiteness: How America's Immigrants Became White, The Strange Journey from Ellis Island to the Suburbs* (New York: Basic Books, 2005).

Roosevelt, Theodore, "The Value of Athletic Training," *Harper's Weekly* (December 23, 1893), 1236.

Ross, Edward Alsworth, *The Old World In the New: The Significance of Past and Present Immigration to the American People* (New York: The Century Co., 1914).

Ross, W. T., "Education in the Philippines," in Fred Eggan Papers, University of Chicago, Special Collections.

Runstedtler, Theresa E., *Jack Johnson. Rebel Sojourner: Boxing in the Shadow of the Global Color Line* (Berkeley: University Of California Press, 2012).

———, "The New Negro's Brown Brother: Black American and Filipino Boxers and the 'Rising Tide of Color,'" in Davarian L. Baldwin and Minkah Makalani, eds., *Escape from New York: The New Negro Renaissance Beyond Harlem* (Minneapolis: University of Minnesota Press, 2013), 105–26.

Ryan, Jr., W. Carson, "Education Exhibits at the Panama-Pacific International Exposition," Bulletin 1, Department of the Interior, Bureau of Education (Washington, DC: Government Printing Office, 1916), 92–93.

Salman, Michael, "'The Prison that Makes Men Free': The Iwahig Penal Colony and the Simulacra of the American State in the Philippines," in Alfred W. McCoy and Francisco A. Scarano, eds., *Colonial Crucible*, 117–28.

Salamanca, Bonifacio S., *The Filipino Reaction to American Rule, 1901–1913* (Norwich, CT: The Shoe String Press, 1968).

San Juan, E., Jr., *On Becoming Filipino: Selected Writings of Carlos Bulosan* (Philadelphia: Temple University Press, 1995).

Schirmer, Daniel, and Stephen Rosskamm Shalom, eds., *The Philippines Reader* (Boston: South End Press, 1987).

Schumacher, John N., "Father McKinnon: The First California's Chaplain: The Story of the Heroic Chaplain," *Philippine Studies*, 9:1 (1961), 194–97.

Second Conference of the Secretary of the Army-Navy Department of the YMCA, Manila, Philippine Islands, September 14–23, 1901, YMCA Archives, Philippines Box, 1901–1973.

Sexton, William T., *Soldiers In the Sun: An Adventure in Imperialism* (Freeport, NY: Books for Libraries, 1971 [1939]).

Shatkin, Gavin, "Colonial Capital, Modernist Capital, Global Capital: The Changing Political Symbolism of Urban Space in Metro Manila, the Philippines," *Pacific Affairs*, 78:4 (Winter 2005–2006), 577–600.

Shaw, Angel Velasco, and Luis H. Francia, eds., *Vestiges of War: The Philippine-American War and the Aftermath of an Imperial Dream, 1899–1999* (New York: New York University Press, 2002).

Silbey, David J., *A War of Frontier and Empire: The Philippine-American War, 1899–1902* (New York: Hill & Wang, 2007).

Simon, Tom, "Arlie Pond," sabr.org/bioproj/person/2d68aec2 (January 16, 2016).

Slotkin, Richard, "Buffalo Bill's Wild West and the Mythologization of the American Empire" in Kaplan and Pease, eds., *Cultures of United States Imperialism*, 164–81.

Soberano, Rawlein G., *The Politics of Independence: The American Colonial Experiment in the Philippines* (New Orleans: Alive Associates, 1983).

Stanley, Peter W., *A Nation in the Making: The Philippines and the United States, 1899–1921* (Cambridge, MA: Harvard University Press, 1974).

Stein, Michael, "Cult and Sport: The Case of Big Red," *Mid-American Review of Sociology*, 2:2 (1977), 29–42.

Sullivan, Rodney J., *Exemplar of Americanism: The Philippine Career of Dean C. Worcester* (Ann Arbor: University of Michigan Press, 1991).

Svinth, Joseph R., "The Origins of Filipino Boxing, 1899–1926," *Journal of Combative Sport* (July 2001), at ejmas.com/jcs/jcsart_svinth_0701.htm (July 8, 2011).

Taft, William H., *Civil Government in the Philippines* (New York: The Outlook Co., 1902).

Tooker, Elisabeth, "Lewis Henry Morgan: The Myth and the Man," *University of Rochester Library Bulletin*, 37 (1984), n.p.

Torres, Christina Evangelista, *The Americanization of Manila, 1898–1921* (Diliman, Quezon City: University of the Philippines Press, 2010).

Townsend, Kim, *Manhood at Harvard: William James and Others* (New York: W. W. Norton, 1996).

Tuason, Julie A., "The Ideology of Empire in National Geographic Magazine's Coverage of the Philippines, 1898–1908," *Geographical Review*, 89:1 (January 1999), 34–53.

Tucker, William H., *The Science and Politics of Racial Research* (Urbana: University of Illinois Press, 1994).

Walsh, Tom, "Baseball in the Philippines: A Capsule History," *Bulletin of the American Historical Collection*, 23:3 (July–September 1995), 106–9.

Walsh, Thomas P., *Tin Pan Alley and the Philippines: American Songs of War and Love, 1898–1946, A Resource Guide* (Lanham, MD: Scarecrow Press, 2013).

Webster, Yehudi O., *The Racialization of America* (New York: St. Martin's, 1992).

Welch, Richard E., Jr., *Imperialists vs. Anti-Imperialists: The Debate Over Expansionism in the 1890s* (Itasca, IL: F. E. Peacock, 1972).

———, "American Atrocities in the Philippines: The Indictment and the Response," *Pacific Historical Review*, 43:2 (May 1974), 233–53.

White, Lynn T. III, *Philippine Politics: Progress and Problems in a Localist Democracy* (New York: Routledge, 2014).

Wolff, Leon, *Little Brown Brother: How the United States Purchased and Pacified the Philippine Islands at the Century's Turn* (New York: Bookspan, 2006 [1960]).

Wood, Leonard, *Report of the Special Mission to the Philippines Islands to the Secretary of War* (Washington, DC: Government Printing Office, 1922).

Wooley, Monroe, "'Batter Up' in the Philippines," *Outdoor World and Recreation*, May 1913, 313–14.

Worcester, Dean C., "Field Sports Among the Wild Men of Luzon," *National Geographic*, 22:3 (March 1911), 215–67.

———, "The Non-Christian Peoples of the Philippine Islands: With an Account of What Has Been Done for Them under American Rule," *National Geographic*, 24:11 (November 1913).

———, *The Philippines Past and Present* (New York: Macmillan Co., 1914).

Zabriskie, Alexander C., *Bishop Brent: Crusader for Christian Unity* (Philadelphia: Westminster Press, 1948).

Zimmerman, Warren, *The First Great Triumph: How Five Americans Made Their Country a World Power* (New York: Farrar, Straus and Giroux, 2002).

Zialcita, Ferdinand N., "State Formation, Colonialism, and National Identity in Vietnam and the Philippines," *Philippine Quarterly of Culture and Society*, 33:2 (June 1995), 77–117.

Zinn, Howard, Mike Konopacki, and Paul Buhle, *A People's History of American Empire* (New York: Metropolitan Books, 2008).

INTERNET SOURCES

www.asianews.it/news-en/Saudi-Arabia,-70-of-Filipino-domestic-workers-suffer-physical-and-psychological-violence-24260.html (February 13, 2016).
asianhistory.about.com/od/philippines/p/Biography-of-Emilio-Aguinaldo.htm (September 1, 2015).
boxrec.com/boxer/12 (January 30, 2016).
boxrec.com/boxer/9601 (January 30, 2016).
boxrec.com/boxer/9907 (January 30, 2016).
boxrec.com/boxer/41793 (January 30, 2016).
boxrec.com/media/index.php?title=Human:9433 (January 30, 2016).
boxrec.com/media/index.php?title=Human:9601 (January 30, 2016).
boxrec.com/media/index.php?title=Human:88547 (August 1, 2015).
boxrec.com/media/index.php?title=Human:137869 (October 20, 2015).
coe.kstate.edu/annex/nlbemuseum/history/players/charleston.html (August 3, 2015).
countryeconomy.com/demography/life-expectancy/philippines (February 13, 2016).
cpu.edu.ph/about/history1.php (December 23, 2015).
kahimyang.info/kauswagan/articles/1449/today-in-philippine-history-february-1-1904-luke-e-wright-was-inaugurated-as-civil-governor-of-the-philippines (August 13, 2015).
kulturapilipinas.webs.com/about-magna-kultura (January 13, 2016).
library.la84.org/SportsLibrary/JOH/JOHv6n3/JOHv6n3f.pdf (August 15, 2015).
nationalhumanitiescenter.org/pds/gilded/empire/text1/turner.pdf (May 26, 2015).
opinion.inquirer.net/inquireropinion/columns/view/20080122-114113/Three-American-presidents-of-UP (September 7, 2015).
rlp.hds.harvard.edu/faq/protestant-christianity-philippines (February 7, 2016).
su.edu.ph/page/10-History (December 23, 2015).
uca.edu/politicalscience/dadm-project/asiapacific-region/philippinesmoro-national-liberation-front-1968-present/ (February 18, 2016).
www.philstar.com/sports/613932/wack-wacks-bill-shaw-and-social-responsibility (Januray 23, 2016).
www.asanet.org/about/presidents/Edward_Ross.cfm (July 22, 2015).
www.asj.upd.edu.ph/mediabox/archive/ASJ-09-02-1971/luna-general%20artemia%20ricarte%20y%20garcia%20filipino%20nationalist.pdf (August 13, 2015).
www.bibingka.com/phg/sakay/default.htm (August 13, 2015).
www.biography.com/people/elpidio-quirino-37511#profile (September 1, 2015).
www.biography.com/people/john-paul-ii-9355652#legacy (February 7, 2016).
www.britannica.com/biography/Benigno-Simeon-Aquino-Jr (September 1, 2015).

Bibliography

www.britannica.com/biography/Dwight-F-Davis (September 1, 2015).
www.britannica.com/biography/Diosdado-Macapagal (February 6, 2016).
www.britannica.com/biography/Elpidio-Quirino (February 6, 2016).
www.browsebiography.com/bio-carlos_p_garcia.html (February 6, 2016.)
www.gov.ph/1938/12/16/statement-president-quezon-on-the-murder-of-ex-governor-james-fugate-december-16-1938/ (September 1, 2015).
www.historylink.org/index.cfm?DisplayPage=output.cfm&file_id=5202 (July 24, 2015).
www.indiana.edu/~liblilly/digital/exhibitions/exhibits/show/crone/intro (January 26, 2016).
www.joserizal.ph/bg01.html (August 10, 2015).
www.marimari.com/content/philippines/best_of/games.html (January 13, 2016).
www.mvtimes.com/2012/07/25/prescott-jernegan-gold-from-seawater-swindle-11663/ (June 15, 2016).
www.nytimes.com/1985/11/13/world/falwell-on-visit-acclaims-marcos.html (February 7, 2016).
www.rsssf.com/tablesf/fareastgames17.html (September 24, 2015).
www.thefilipinomind.com/2012/09/the-friar-land-scandal-how-filipinos.html (October 17, 2015).
www.theodora.com/wfbcurrent/philippines_economy.html (November 7, 2015).
www.toqonline.com/blog/lothrop-stoddard-and-the-rising-tide-of-color/ (July 22, 2015).
books.google.com/books?id=1S1KAQAAMAAJ&q=Frank+R.+White,+Philippines+director+of+education&dq=Frank+R.+White,+Philippines+director+of+education&hl=en&sa=X&ved=0CFcQ6AEwCGoVChMI-cOavYLtyAIVzEcmCh0qkwAM (October 31, 2015).
books.google.com/books?id=8TLSAAAAMAAJ&pg=PA21&lpg=PA21&dq=Filipino+labor+strike+of+1903&source=bl&ots=j5Vd8lD-YD&sig=WezkBz0c_4Q9rJJk-mKgHDAjdso&hl=en&sa=X&ved=0CDsQ6AEwBWoVChMI8OzDi-S_yAIVTJMNCh1TKwDx#v=onepage&q=Filipino%20labor%20strike%20of%201903&f=false (October 13, 2015).
books.google.com/books?id=ZgjiAAAAMAAJ&dq=Paul+Freer%2C+Dean+Worcester%2C+Philippines&q=Paul+Freer%2C+Dean+Worcester%2C+Philippines#v=snippet&q=Paul%20Freer%2C%20Dean%20Worcester%2C%20Philippines&f=false (December 26. 2015).
philippinesfreepress.wordpress.com/tag/james-f-smith/ (August 13, 2015).
philippinesfreepress.wordpress.com/tag/moral-progress-league/ (September 27, 2015).
militaryhistorynow.com/2012/10/08/samoan-showdown-america-risks-war-with-germany-in-1880s/ (May 30, 2015).
slideshare.net/rovelynbasilad/historical-development-of-physical-education-in-the-philippines? (December 1, 2015)
http://www.heritage.org/index/country/philippines%20 (November 7, 2015).
www.odec.umd.edu/CD/RACE/CRT.PDF (July 7, 2015).

ARCHIVES

Amos Alonzo Stagg Papers, University of Chicago, Special Collections.
Baseball Hall of Fame, Cooperstown, New York.
Bishop Charles H. Brent Papers, Library of Congress.
Daniel Burnham Papers, Chicago Art Institute.
Dean C. Worcester Papers, in the Bentley Historical Library, University of Michigan.
Department of Physical Education and Athletics Papers, 1892–1974, University of Chicago, Special Collections.
Fred Eggan Papers, University of Chicago, Special Collections.

Frederic S. Marquardt Papers, University of Michigan, Bentley Library.
Frederick Starr Papers, University of Chicago, Special Collections.
Library of Congress.
Leonard Wood Papers, Library of Congress.
National Archives, Washington, DC.
Stephen Bonsal Papers, Library of Congress, "Philippines, Balangiga, 1901–1945" file.
University Presidents' Papers, 1889–1925, University of Chicago, Special Collections.
W. Cameron Forbes Papers, Harvard University.
YMCA Archives, University of Minnesota, St. Paul, MN.

DOCUMENTARY FILMS

"*The Modoc War*," PBS, WYCC, Chicago (July 9, 2015).
"*Forgotten Ellis Island*," PBS, WYCC, Chicago (July 11, 1915).

NEWSPAPERS

Chicago Sunday Tribune, July 7, 1912.
NCAA News, January 6, 1993.

Index

African Americans, 11, 20, 23, 31, 32, 33–34, 45, 53–54, 61n57, 65, 115, 117, 119, 148, 162
Aglipay, Gregorio, 88
Aguinaldo, Emilio, 7 8, 31, 46–47, 51, 54, 64, 65, 70, 74, 77, 78, 116
AIL. *See* Anti-Imperialist League
amateurism, 25, 72
American School, 136, 151
anthropology, 1–3, 21, 23, 27, 66, 140, 158, 173
Anthropology Days, 25–27
Anti-Imperialist League (AIL), 13–14
Aquino, Benigno, 79, 80
Aquino, Jr. Benigno, 170
Aquino III, Benigno, 79, 171
Aquino, Corazon, 58, 79, 171
Aquino, Francisco Reyes, 158
architecture, 23, 30–31
Army and Navy Club, 30, 57, 66, 149–150
assimilation, 5, 13, 19, 80, 128
Ateneo University, 134

badminton, 145, 150, 156
Baguio, 31, 57, 58, 73–74, 108–109
Barrows, David, 29, 52, 108, 128, 130
Bartlett, Murray, 87 88
baseball, 6, 11, 28, 32, 34, 43, 48–49, 54, 56, 57, 71–72, 74–75, 77, 80, 90, 92–93, 94, 96–97, 98, 99, 102n56, 112, 117–118, 119, 120, 128, 129, 131, 132, 133–134, 136, 137–139, 146, 147–148, 149, 150, 152–153, 154–155, 156–157, 162
basketball, 26, 43, 57, 72, 77, 79, 80, 95, 96, 97, 102n49, 132, 133, 137, 139, 141, 151, 153, 154, 155, 156, 157, 161, 162, 177, 178
Bataan Death March, 58

battles, 7, 48–49, 52, 55, 69; of Balangiga, 48–49, 52, 169; of Bayan, 55; of Bud Dajo, 55–56; of Manila, 7, 45, 46, 58, 147, 167; of Mukden, 31
Bean, Robert Bennett, 28, 35
Bell, Franklin, 48, 52, 66, 89
Bell Trade Act, 121, 174
Beveridge, Albert, 12, 50, 106–107
billiards, 57, 74, 90, 93, 116, 149
Bliss, Tasker, 69
Bonifacio, Andres, 7, 64
Bourns, Frank, 65, 67
Boxer Rebellion, 49
boxing, 6, 11, 33 34, 43, 45, 54, 57, 72, 93, 94, 118–119, 120, 133, 136, 145, 147, 148–149, 154, 158–161, 162, 178–179
bowling, 57, 72, 93, 148, 149, 150, 151, 154, 156, 178
Brent, Charles, 29, 74, 88, 90, 91, 92–93, 98, 111, 136
Brewer, David, 94
Britain (England, English), 4, 6, 9, 10–11, 32, 41, 86, 105, 106, 109, 117, 118, 148. *See also* English language
Brown, Elwood, 72, 73, 95, 98, 138, 154, 156, 157
bullfights, 7, 46, 146
Bulosan, Carlos, 36, 120
Burnham, Daniel, 23, 30–31, 108–110, 149

California, 35, 36, 51, 97, 158, 160. *See also* Los Angeles
capitalism, 3, 5, 6, 8, 9, 11, 55, 88, 99, 105–122, 137
Carnegie, Andrew, 13–14
Catholic Youth Organization, 95
Cebu, 90, 109, 116, 117, 128, 148, 149, 150, 155, 178

195

Charleston, Oscar, 54, 75
child labor, 5
China (Chinese), 10, 11, 12, 21, 31, 46, 49, 71, 72, 75, 88, 91, 97, 106, 112, 121, 122, 139, 154–156, 168, 175, 176
chieftains. *See datus*
Christianity, 3, 12–13, 31, 49, 55, 56, 80, 85–99, 105, 170, 172–173
Churchill, Frank, 118–119, 148, 158, 159, 160
civil service, 65, 67, 69, 70, 135
Clark Air Base, 58, 122, 148, 168, 175
Cleveland, Grover, 9, 13
climate, 20, 110–112, 140
cockfighting, 29, 46, 73, 88, 89–90, 95, 111, 113, 118, 129, 132, 137, 146, 158, 178
Cole, Harry, 21, 130, 131
Cole, Mary, 51, 130
Columbia Club, 93, 98, 149
commercialization, 8, 11, 12, 31, 69, 72, 80, 105–107, 129, 136
commonwealth status (Philippines), 77, 121, 152, 167, 174
communism, 76, 168–171, 172, 177
constabulary, 48, 56, 95, 114, 137, 138, 148, 179
corruption, 5, 46, 67, 70, 71, 79, 142n19, 168, 170, 171, 175, 176
coup, 79, 171
cricket, 74, 119, 133, 149
croquet, 43, 74, 119
Cuba, 7, 8, 11, 34, 45–46, 53, 55, 63, 85, 146
cycling, 32, 96, 154, 158

dancing, 66, 72, 73, 91, 98, 116, 120, 133, 137, 145, 146, 149, 151–152, 156, 158, 168, 178
Darwin, Charles, 3. *See also* Social Darwinism
datus (chieftains), 55, 63, 99
Davao, 91, 107, 112
Davis, Dwight, 77
democracy, 1, 4, 5, 11, 64, 65, 71, 80, 116, 131, 133, 135, 137, 141, 146, 169, 179
Dewey, George, 8, 11, 30, 42, 46, 147, 149

disease, 29, 45, 52, 55, 73, 91, 109, 111, 114, 140, 152; cholera, 29, 52, 55, 67, 109, 111, 112, 140; dysentery, 109, 111, 112, 139; malaria, 45, 112; smallpox, 29, 111, 114, 140
Dorsey, George, 27
Dunlap, George, 90, 148

economy, 1, 3, 5, 9, 77, 84n61, 105–107, 122, 141, 169, 171, 173–176
education, 5, 6, 13, 28, 36, 42, 46, 57, 63, 72, 80, 87–88, 96, 98, 107, 112, 116, 122, 127, 141, 146, 152, 153, 155, 173, 176–177, 179. *See also* industrial education
Elorde, Gabriel "Flash," 161
England. *See* Britain
English (language), 5, 25, 58, 65, 67, 68, 70, 71, 75, 80, 96, 109, 121, 127, 128, 129, 130, 131–132, 134, 135, 140, 141, 152, 177, 179
Estrada, Joseph, 79, 171, 172
ethnicity, 6, 178
ethnology, 2, 25, 140
eugenics, 2, 29, 35
Europe (Europeans), 2, 3, 4, 6, 10, 11, 23, 30, 32, 35, 46, 50, 91, 97, 107, 112, 120
evolution, 2, 3, 23

Far Eastern Games, 72, 96–98, 154–156
Fagen, David, 53, 54
Falwell, Jerry, 172
Federalist Party, 65, 69
Fee, Mary, 88, 130, 132
Filipinization, 70–71, 74, 76, 140–141, 156
Filipino Scouts, 48, 53–54, 114, 138, 148
fishing, 92, 111, 119, 122, 148, 150, 152, 168
football, 10, 11, 26, 32–33, 43, 44, 56, 71, 72, 92, 96, 131, 132, 145, 146, 156
Forbes, William Cameron, 30, 32, 71–72, 75, 93, 112, 115, 116, 119, 121, 129, 150, 154–155; as governor-general, 32, 71–74, 92, 93, 95–96, 107, 109, 136; as secretary of commerce, 71
Freer, Paul, 139, 140

France (French), 3, 6, 9, 10, 98
Fugate, James, 77
Funston, Frederick, 8, 54

Gall, Franz Joseph, 2
gambling, 29, 67, 73, 85, 89–90, 132, 137, 146, 158, 168, 178
games, 5, 23, 80, 95, 137, 138, 145–146, 158, 177
Gan, Benjamin (Small Montana), 160
Garcia, Carlos, 170
Garcia, Ceferino, 160–161
geography, 7, 177, 178
Germany, 6, 9, 10–11, 13, 46, 106
girls, 72, 96, 112, 127, 129, 132, 133, 136, 137, 139, 151, 154, 156, 164n50
Godkin, E. L., 13–14
golf, 43, 57, 66, 71, 72, 74, 92, 93, 119, 131, 148, 149, 151, 154, 178
Gompers, Samuel, 13–14
government, 7, 8, 11, 46, 47, 48, 55, 57, 63–80, 93, 121, 128, 131, 134, 138, 141, 158, 169, 177
Grant, Madison, 35
Guam, 48, 65
guerrilla warfare, 47–48, 54, 64, 132, 149, 168, 177, 178
Guilledo, Francisco (Pancho Villa), 119, 159–160
Gulick, Luther, 25–26, 137
gymnastics, 133, 156

Hall, G. Stanley, 5, 23, 26, 32
handball, 155, 156
Harrison, Francis Burton, 74, 76, 93, 98, 114, 152, 156, 173
Harty, Jeremiah, 86, 87, 90
Harvard University, 13, 32–33, 44, 46, 71, 127, 139
Hawaii, 9, 11, 26, 33, 42, 53, 79, 113, 148, 171
headhunting, 28, 29, 73, 146–147
hegemony, 23–36, 58, 80, 97, 121, 159, 179
higher education. *See* schools
hiking, 44, 45, 133
history, 1, 3, 4, 5, 6, 20, 35, 41, 46, 79, 96, 105, 107, 121, 129, 137

horseback riding, 44, 56, 64, 74, 93, 131, 149, 152
horseracing, 32, 90, 146, 152
hospitals, 88, 92, 111, 139
Hukbalahap (Huks) movement. *See* communism
hunting, 5, 11, 119, 152
hygiene, 46, 67, 73, 109, 110, 111, 113, 118, 129

Ide, Henry, 70–71
Igorots, 24, 25, 26, 27, 28, 29, 74, 112, 145
ilustrados, 64, 66, 67, 69–70, 74, 76, 78, 80, 132, 135, 136, 141, 146, 169
immigrants, 5–6, 19, 55, 107, 120, 122, 157, 158, 170, 175
immigration, 6, 11, 35, 55, 69, 76, 131, 160, 178
imperialism, 3, 4, 10–14, 41, 110, 117
independence, 58, 69, 75, 76, 77, 93, 110, 115, 140, 167, 170, 177
Indians (Native Americans), 2, 4, 5, 6, 19, 23, 25, 26, 33, 44, 47, 91, 112, 128
indoor baseball. *See* softball
industrial education, 5, 88, 107, 128, 129, 135, 136–137
industrialization, 9, 42, 80, 105
Insular Cases, 65, 66
intermarriage, 21, 30, 53
interscholastic athletics, 26, 95–97, 118, 133, 134, 137, 139, 148, 150, 153–154, 155, 177
Ireland, John, 86, 87
Islam, 85, 177. *See also* Muslims

jai alai, 46, 146
Japan, 6, 9, 10, 11, 25, 27, 31, 49, 58, 72, 75, 76, 78, 96, 97, 106, 113, 117, 122, 139, 147, 150, 154, 155, 161, 167, 168, 177
Johnson, Jack, 34, 159
Jolo, 93, 136, 150
journalism, 4, 8, 9, 20, 22, 50, 51, 55, 157, 159, 173, 176, 178

Katipunan, 7, 64
Kelley, Francis, 87
Kipling, Rudyard, 4

language, 7, 26, 80. *See also* English language
legacy, 14, 58, 80, 99, 122, 140–141, 161–162, 167–179
Leyte, 49, 133
literacy, 68, 127, 141, 144n56, 176
Lodge, Henry Cabot, 9, 11–12, 107
Los Angeles, 36, 120. *See also* California
Luzon, 8, 31, 47, 52, 53, 54, 65, 70, 73, 76, 91, 107, 108, 109, 113, 117, 128, 141, 145, 146, 150, 177

Mabini, Apolinario, 48
Macapagal, Diosdado, 122, 170
Macapagal-Arroyo, Gloria, 79, 122, 171
MacArthur, Arthur, 47, 48, 50, 65, 128, 167
MacArthur, Douglas, 78, 167
Magsaysay, Ramon, 78, 170
Mahan, Alfred Thayer, 6–7, 41–42, 43
Malcolm, George, 76, 131, 139
manifest destiny, 4, 41, 86
Manila, 7–8, 28–31, 34, 45–48, 51–54, 57–58, 64–65, 67, 69, 72, 74–75, 79, 85–87, 88, 91, 93–98, 106–110, 117, 119, 127, 129, 131, 132, 134, 138, 140, 146–153, 155, 157, 158, 160, 162, 167–169, 170, 174–175, 177
Manila Carnival, 67, 72, 77, 90, 95–97, 107, 120, 150, 153, 154–156, 158
Manila Hotel, 30, 57, 108, 149
Manila Times, 30, 67, 74, 108, 117, 135, 153
Marcos, Ferdinand, 78–79, 122, 170–171, 172, 177
Marcos, Imelda, 76, 170–171
Marquardt, Frederic, 133
Marquardt, Walter, 133
masculinity, 7, 8, 19, 28, 29, 32, 42–44, 48, 56, 57, 58, 64, 71, 73, 77, 97, 110, 112, 118–119, 128, 146
McGee, W J, 23–27, 28
McKinley, William, 7, 8, 9, 12, 13, 14, 21, 42, 54, 86
mestizos, 21, 63, 73, 74, 91, 121, 151, 169
Mideast, 14, 48, 50, 79, 167, 168, 175
militarism, 6–8, 11, 57–58
military, 1, 6, 14, 22, 41–58, 77, 78, 90–91, 114, 116, 117, 118, 119, 120, 121–122, 127–129, 133, 134, 137, 147–149, 150, 152, 153, 158, 162, 167–169, 170, 179
Mindanao, 8, 54, 55–56, 64, 69, 76, 93, 99, 107, 109, 112, 133, 134, 148, 150, 171, 172, 177
miscegenation, 53, 91, 120
missionaries, 3, 7, 11, 12, 21, 31, 80, 86, 87, 88, 89, 93, 99, 116, 134, 135, 137, 139, 146, 158, 172, 173, 179
Moro Exchange, 69
Moro War, 55–56
Moros, 25, 28, 46, 55–56, 69, 74, 93, 112, 115, 136
Moses, Bernard, 66
Moses, Edith, 66
Mott, John, 94
Murphy, Frank, 77
music, 128, 131, 150, 151, 158, 179
Muslims, 2, 55, 69, 80, 99, 170, 171, 172, 177. *See also* Islam

National Basketball Association (NBA), 79, 80, 162, 173
National Geographic, 28, 107
National Geographic Society, 23, 27–28, 68
Nationalist Party, 31, 69
Native Americans. *See* Indians
NBA. *See* National Basketball Association
Negritos, 19, 28, 91

oligarchy, 80, 121–122, 169, 170, 171, 174, 176
Olympic Games, 25, 33, 72, 96, 154, 157, 175
Osmena, Sergio, 70, 78, 121
Osmena, Jr., Sergio, 78
Otis, Elwell, 47, 50, 51, 64, 65, 91

PAAF. *See* Philippines Amateur Athletic Association
Pacquiao, Manny, 162, 178–179
Palawan, 72
Panay, 136, 137
Pancho Villa. *See* Guilledo, Francisco
Paxson, Frederic, 5
pensionados, 69, 76, 135

People Power, 79, 170, 172
Pershing, John, 55, 56, 69, 93, 99, 115
Philippines Amateur Athletic Association (PAAF), 72, 79, 93, 95, 98, 154, 156
Philippines Basketball Association, 79
Philippines Commission, 9, 21, 64–74, 66, 109, 134, 138; First (Schurman), 21, 64; Second (Taft), 9, 64–69; under Luke Wright, 70; under Henry Ide, 70; under James Smith, 71; under W. Cameron Forbes, 71–74
Philippines Medical School, 28, 139
Philippines Normal School, 135
Philippines Women's University, 139
phrenology, 2, 19–20, 29
physical education, 26, 129–130, 133–134, 137–139, 153–154, 177
Pinchot, Gifford, 107
playgrounds, 26, 95, 138, 157
plutocracy, 121–122
police, 48, 68, 138, 168
politics, 1, 2, 7, 11, 12, 14, 20, 21, 31, 45, 46, 49, 56, 58, 63–80, 118, 119, 127, 135, 155, 162, 169–171, 174, 176, 178–179
polo, 57, 66, 71, 72, 74, 92, 131, 148, 149, 150, 151, 154
Pond, Arlington, 147, 148, 149
popular culture, 14, 57, 116–119, 149–153
Posadas, Diosdado (Speedy Dado), 160, 161
poverty, 5, 36, 79, 162, 168, 173–179
priests, 7, 48, 51, 63, 72, 74, 85, 87, 92, 115, 127, 134, 140, 147
prisons, 46, 48, 71, 73, 113, 114, 146
Progressive Era, 5–9, 12, 15n14, 90, 95
prostitution, 67, 73, 74, 89, 90–91, 98, 116, 151–152, 168, 175
Puerto Rico, 7, 63, 77, 85

Quezon, Manuel, 57, 70, 76, 77, 98, 152, 173
Quirino, Elpidio, 78, 170

race, 2, 3, 6, 19–36, 42, 50, 66, 74, 76, 97, 99, 110–112, 113, 120, 131, 160, 179

racialization, 2, 3, 8, 14, 19–36, 27–29, 67, 68, 88, 91, 128, 159
Ramos, Fidel, 171
Rand, Philinda, 129, 131
recapitulation theory, 5
rebels, 7, 9, 31, 45, 46, 79, 178
religion, 1–2, 3, 7, 11, 12–14, 21, 22, 49, 56, 69, 80, 85–99, 127, 134, 136, 137, 157, 169, 172–173, 177, 179
residual culture, 158
Rizal, Jose, 64, 75, 80, 108, 133, 134
Roosevelt, Theodore, 3, 4, 7–12, 20, 30, 31, 32–33, 42, 43–45, 49, 75; as assistant secretary of the navy, 7, 8, 12, 42; as president, 7, 30, 31, 42, 52, 55, 69, 87, 92, 106
Roosevelt, Theodore, Jr., 77, 140
Root, Elihu, 22, 47, 52, 65, 67, 86
Ross, Edward Alsworth, 35
Rough Riders, 7, 44, 45
rowing, 72, 117, 147, 154
Roxas, Manuel, 78, 170
running, 25, 26, 72, 73, 98, 133, 137, 145, 146
Russia, 10, 11, 31, 49, 106, 117

sailing, 43, 150, 152
sanitation, 46, 109, 111, 113
schools, 5, 23, 26, 46, 55, 63, 65, 75, 87–88, 91, 92, 107, 118, 121, 127–141, 151, 153–154, 157, 170; higher education, 139–140; private, 135–136, 140
Schurman, Jacob Gould, 21, 64
Schurz, Carl, 13–14
science, 2, 19–36, 107, 110, 111, 140
segregation, 29–31, 57, 58, 66, 91, 92, 110, 112, 130, 131, 136, 140, 149, 150, 151, 169
shooting, 43, 56, 64, 74, 119, 133, 150, 152
Silliman Institute, 90, 135, 148, 173
Small Montana. *See* Gan, Benjamin
Smith, Jacob, 52
Smith, James F., 71, 87
soccer, 32, 72, 97, 147, 153, 154, 161, 175
social class, 11, 14, 20, 27, 45, 63, 66, 74, 80, 109, 128, 130, 140, 141, 150, 174–175, 176, 177

Social Darwinism, 6, 11, 19–36, 54, 72, 105, 118, 140, 156, 158
social media, 14, 178
sociology, 1, 19, 35, 173
softball (indoor baseball), 72, 98, 133, 137, 138, 151, 156, 164n50
Spain, 7, 10
Spalding, Albert, 117, 119, 147
Spanish, 3, 7–8, 12–13, 21, 46, 63, 64, 65, 68, 70, 80, 85, 88, 99, 109, 121, 127, 130, 132, 133, 134, 135, 140, 146, 169
Spanish-American War, 1, 4, 7, 8, 9, 14, 27, 41, 44, 85, 87, 106, 117, 147
Speedy Dado. *See* Posadas, Diosdado
sports, 1, 5–7, 14, 28, 43, 44, 56, 71–74, 75, 80, 89–90, 92–98, 116–121, 128–129, 132–135, 137–139, 141, 145–162, 173, 177, 178, 179; indigenous sports, 145–146, 156, 158; military sports, 147–149; Spanish sports, 146
statehood, 65
Strong, Josiah, 3
Subic Bay, 58, 122, 159, 168, 175
suffrage, 5, 42, 65
Sullivan, James E., 25–27
swimming, 25, 54, 57, 64, 72, 74, 93, 94, 98, 133, 138, 145, 148, 149, 150, 155, 156, 178

Taft, William Howard, 9, 21, 22, 64–69, 86, 107, 151; as governor general, 9, 21, 53, 64–69, 86, 92, 107, 113, 119
Tagalogs, 48, 134, 141, 177; language, 70
Tait, Bill, 118–119, 148
Tait, Eddie, 118–119, 148
taxes, 5, 55, 63, 65, 70, 78, 90, 93, 94, 109, 158, 170, 176, 177
teachers, 6, 21, 51, 87, 88, 107, 121, 127, 129–131, 132, 136, 139–140, 152, 153, 158, 177
technology, 3, 14, 23, 25, 31, 36, 112, 139–140
temperance, 5, 42, 45
tennis, 43, 44, 57, 72, 74, 77, 92, 93, 94, 96, 98, 118, 119, 129, 131, 133, 137, 148, 149, 150, 151, 154, 156, 178
tourism, 152–153

track and field, 54, 72, 133, 137, 154, 155, 156
tribes, 21, 22, 25, 28, 48, 91, 112, 114, 127, 131, 137, 145, 150, 153, 169, 177
Turner, Frederick Jackson, 4, 5, 106
Tydings-McDuffie Act, 35, 77, 121

University of Chicago, 76, 117, 152
University of Michigan, 21, 28, 139
University of the Philippines, 87, 139, 140, 156, 158
University of Santo Tomas, 87, 127, 134–135, 140

Vietnam, 14, 50, 56, 78, 167, 168, 170, 175
Villa, Pancho. *See* Guilledo, Francisco
Villamor, Ignacio, 140
Visayan Islands, 65, 116, 132, 133, 134, 135, 145, 148, 155, 174
volleyball, 34, 43, 73, 95, 96, 97, 102n49, 133, 137, 138–139, 145, 153, 154, 156, 161

WASPS. *See* White Anglo-Saxon Protestants
weight lifting, 26, 54, 133
West, Mae, 160, 161
White Anglo-Saxon Protestants (WASPS), 3, 5, 19, 21, 27–36, 50, 71, 91, 99
whiteness, 5, 15n11, 19–36
Wilson, Woodrow, 74, 97
women, 42–43, 44, 46, 48, 66, 74, 88, 98, 120, 129, 130, 131, 133, 135, 139, 150, 151–152, 154, 156, 159, 160, 171
women's rights, 5, 151, 169, 171
Wood, Leonard, 44–46, 49, 55–56, 68, 69, 75–76, 77, 91, 93, 121, 148; as governor general, 57, 68, 76, 91, 121, 156, 173
Worcester Dean, 21, 28, 64, 65, 67–68, 77, 107, 112, 114–116, 139, 140, 145, 146; as commissioner, 64, 67; as secretary of the interior, 29, 65, 91, 106, 115–116, 132
World's Fair, 4, 23–27, 30, 106, 108, 132
World War I, 57, 75, 98, 116, 120, 121, 148, 149, 151, 159, 167

World War II, 58, 76, 78, 97, 122, 141, 147, 151, 161, 162, 167, 169, 172, 173, 174
wrestling, 57, 133, 145, 146, 147, 154
Wright, Luke, 70

Yale University, 117, 139

Ylanon, Regino, 155
Young Men's Christian Association (YMCA), 3, 34, 54, 72, 77, 85, 89, 90, 93, 94–98, 115, 138–139, 151, 152, 156–157

Zamboanga, 56, 68, 69, 109, 150, 162

About the Author

Gerald R. Gems is a full professor in the Kinesiology Department at North Central College in Naperville, Illinois. He is a past president of the North American Society for Sport History and the current vice president of the International Society for the History of Physical Education and Sport. He was the recipient of the Fulbright Senior Scholar Award from the US government in 2011–2012. As an international scholar he has presented his work in more than two dozen countries, and he is the author or editor of more than two hundred publications, including eighteen books.